THE BOOK OF BEGINNINGS

A Practical Guide To Understand and Teach Genesis

VOLUME THREE:
THE PATRIARCHS, A PROMISED NATION,
AND THE DAWNING OF THE SECOND AGE

HENRY M. MORRIS III

INSTITUTE FOR CREATION RESEARCH

Dallas, Texas
www.icr.org

THE BOOK OF BEGINNINGS, VOLUME THREE
The Patriarchs, a Promised Nation, and the Dawning of the Second Age
by Henry M. Morris III, D.Min.

First printing: January 2014

All Scripture quotations are from the New King James Version.

ISBN: 978-1-935587-38-5
Library of Congress Catalog Number: 2013956308

Please visit our website for other books and resources: www.icr.org

Printed in the United States of America.

THE BOOK OF BEGINNINGS

A PRACTICAL GUIDE TO
UNDERSTAND AND TEACH GENESIS

VOLUME THREE:
THE PATRIARCHS, A PROMISED NATION,
AND THE DAWNING OF THE SECOND AGE

HENRY M. MORRIS III

TABLE OF CONTENTS

PREFACE

The first 11 chapters of Genesis provide insight into the first 2,000 years of Earth's history. Those few chapters leave the reader with many questions, some of which are answered as man begins to fulfill his role of steward, learning how to "subdue" and "have dominion" over the planet. Many more of those answers are provided by the Creator Himself as He continues to reveal His relationship with man, ultimately providing the Savior through the Lord Jesus Christ.

The First Age of history was characterized by such awful rebellion against the God of creation that God found it necessary to destroy all air-breathing, land-dwelling life with the horrific Flood that's recorded in great detail in chapters 6, 7, and 8. When Noah, his three sons, their wives, and the few thousand animals that God had selected to preserve life on the earth stepped off the Ark, they found a far different environment than they had known before. Even though purged from the wicked societies and evil leadership that dominated the previous age, the residual energies and altered surface of the planet would radically impact life for centuries to come.

God promised, however, not only to restrain Himself from ever again bringing total destruction by water as had just concluded, but to sustain the seasonal cycles of the earth so that "while the earth remains, Seedtime and harvest, Cold and heat, Winter and summer, And day and night Shall not cease" (Genesis 8:22). Both the apostles Paul and Peter reaffirmed that promise by noting that "all things consist" by the authority of the Lord Jesus (Colossians 1:17) and that the same authoritative Word who created all things in the beginning is now preserving everything "by the same word" (2 Peter 3:7). Our world, "the heavens and the earth which are now" (2 Peter 3:7), is being maintained by the omnipotent and omniscient Creator because

He is "longsuffering toward us, not willing that any should perish but that all should come to repentance" (2 Peter 3:9).

Simply put, after God's wrath was appeased with the judgment of the Flood, God began a relationship of endurance and forbearance with mankind for the sake of bringing about the salvation of those who would respond to His love. This Second Age, the age of redemption, began with the disembarking of Noah's family and the animal kinds from the Ark. It has continued for several millennia and will one day be terminated by the nuclear meltdown of the universe in the last judgment—often referred to as the Day of the Lord (2 Peter 3:10-12).

As was discussed in detail in volume two of this series, the growing population of post-Flood humanity that was centered around Babel under the leadership of Nimrod (Genesis 10) suffered God's second intervention in the confusion of their languages because of their proposed rebellion (Genesis 11) and began to quickly spread over the continents of Europe and Africa. Egypt became the major center of empire building and by the time of Abraham and Job (~2100 B.C.) was the foremost civilization of the day. According to the information implicit in John's book of Revelation, Egypt was the first empire controlled by the "great harlot" who was "sitting on [the] scarlet beast" pictured in the startling prophecies about the end of the age (Revelation 17:1-8).

This was the world into which Abram (later renamed Abraham) was born. Much of the relevant cultural and historical information concerning Ur of the Chaldees and the nations of Egypt, Babylon, and the various city states identified in the book of Job was outlined in the later chapters of volume two. That history will not be addressed specifically in this new volume other than to connect the reader to the cultural significance of various life decisions made by the patriarchs and the work of God as He began to establish the new nation of Israel.

There are four "chief fathers."

- **Abraham**—Called by God to be the "father of many nations" (Genesis 17:4-5). Abraham was given a covenant that applies to all who are saved by faith in the work of God through Jesus Christ and he becomes the example of salvation by faith (Romans 4:1-16; Galatians 3:9-24).

- **Isaac**—The "promised seed" from whom the nation Israel came. Isaac is used as the Old Testament example of the willing sacrifice (Hebrews 11:17-19) and is the genetic head of Israel—the first Jew (Romans 9:7).

- **Jacob**—The father of 12 sons who produced the tribes of Israel. Jacob is used as an example of God's sovereign right to choose those whom He wills to serve Him (Romans 9:10-13) and becomes known as "Israel" (Genesis 32:28; 35:22).

- **Joseph**—The prime minister of Egypt and the one responsible for preserving the budding nation. Joseph becomes an example of the steadfast, suffering, faithful ones who trust God to accomplish His "good" through them (Genesis 50:20; Acts 7:9-18).

All of this begins in Genesis 12 with the call of Abram out of Ur of the Chaldees. The focus of this book will concentrate on the lives of these four main patriarchs and their families. Several key events and eternal decisions are revealed to us in the remaining chapters of Genesis. Although many of these events are verified by contemporary historical writings, the reasons and future purposes of these events are only revealed to us in the pages of Scripture. It will be the central purpose of this book to discuss these key revelations and attempt to apply them (as does the rest of Scripture) to the edification of those who have been granted the privilege to be adopted into the eternal family of our gracious Creator and Lord.

CHAPTER ONE
THE NEW BEGINNING

As we saw in the earlier volumes of this series, the first 11 chapters of Genesis offer a sweeping overview of human history from creation to the dawning of a new age after God's global Flood judgment wiped out the wicked First Age world. Chapter 12, however, signals a change in God's dealings with His created humanity as He zeroes in on a single man—Abram—through whom He will work out His great plan of redemption.

> Now the Lord had said to Abram: "Get out of your country, From your family And from your father's house, To a land that I will show you. I will make you a great nation; I will bless you And make your name great; And you shall be a blessing. I will bless those who bless you, And I will curse him who curses you; And in you all the families of the earth shall be blessed." (Genesis 12:1-3)

This foundational promise given by God to Abram is so significant that it is cited by Peter on the day of Pentecost in the first New Testament sermon (Acts 3:25). And in Stephen's answer to the belligerent Jews who were disputing with him, he insisted that God's promise to Abram was the basis of his preaching on the glorious fulfillment of that promise in Jesus Christ (Acts 7:2-3). Paul identifies this promise to Abram as "the gospel" (Galatians 3:8) and certifies that all who believe in the work of Christ on Calvary are "blessed with believing Abraham" (Galatians 3:9). Later, the unknown writer of the book of Hebrews listed this event as a prime example of faith in the word of God (Hebrews 11:8).

We who are the later beneficiaries of this early calling and promise can begin to grasp something of the unilateral grace that God was extending to Abram. We have the benefit of nearly 4,000 years of history. Abram had *only* God's word. Perhaps that is why Abram's response to this message made him "the father" of all those who have found faith in Christ (Romans 4:16).

Abram

The use of the name Abram is worth exploring. It is composed of *ab* and a contraction of *ruwm*. All the Hebrew lexicons give it the basic compound meaning of "exalted father." The use appears to be more of a title than a proper name. When God Himself renamed Abram, he was given the name Abraham—"father of many nations" (Genesis 17:5). The three sons of Terah were Abram, Nahor, and Haran (Genesis 11:27). Although all of the names listed in Genesis 10 and 11 have derived meanings, none of them appear to be titles like Ab-Ram (or Ab-Ruwm).

It is at least possible that the inspired editor of Genesis (Moses), compiling the text several centuries after these events, gave the titular name because of the unique place in history of this man whom *Elohim* chose to father the nation of Israel. Surely the role of "exalted father" is most appropriate. It is also possible, although less likely, that Terah himself would have recognized the hand of God on his son and given him the titular name.

The Hebrew word *toledoth* appears at the end of 11 marked sections of Genesis and is translated with the phrase "these are the generations of" (or some similar phrase). It seems to identify the original records that Moses used to compile the entire book. If indeed that term is used as a "sign-off" to identify the original author of the records, then it would appear that either Ishmael (Genesis 25:13) or Isaac (Genesis 25:19) would have been the one to use the term Exalted Father (Abram) after their earthly father died and was entombed in the cave at Machpelah (Genesis 25:8-9).

Any of these scenarios would be plausible. The significance of these thoughts, however, is to emphasize the honor given to Abraham as the "father of many nations." It is by the latter title that Abraham is known throughout the Scriptures. Abram is used 61 times prior to his renaming by God. Abraham (his final and formal name) is used some 250 times through both the Old and New Testaments. The importance of the change is emphasized by its inclusion in later accounts of these events.

> "You are the LORD God, Who chose Abram, And brought him out of Ur of the Chaldeans, And gave him the name Abraham." (Nehemiah 9:7)

God's Call

It is not clear when God spoke to Abram. He and his family were still in Ur of the Chaldees when the family relocation to Haran was initiated by Terah, Abram's father (Genesis 11:27, 31). Later, when Abram left Haran with Sarai and the family of his nephew Lot, Abram was 75 years old (Genesis 12:4). Although the New Testament deacon Stephen cited the Jewish tradition that Abraham was still in Ur when God spoke to him (Acts 7:2), it is possible that the personal call to Abram was not given while he was living in Ur but after Terah died in Haran. It was then, at age 75, that Abram responded and began the trek to Canaan.

Ur of the Chaldees was documented by archaeologist Sir Leonard Woolley as a thriving city of some 200,000 that had been one of the major port cities of the Sumerian empire for a century or more at the time of Terah and his family. The decision to move to Haran, some 500 miles north and west of Ur, would have been a major commitment. It is likely that the death of Terah's son Haran precipitated the move (Genesis 11:28). It may well have been that Terah decided to relocate the family business to a new place on the east-west trade route that could take advantage of the growing international commerce and named the site in memory of his son.

Not much is confirmed about the initial location of Haran, although there is an archaeological site in southern Turkey that seems to date from that period. Haran is later called the "city of Nahor" (Genesis 24:10) and the place where Laban lived (Genesis 27:43). Nahor was one of the three named sons of Terah and apparently remained and prospered in the area. Laban was a direct descendant of Nahor (Genesis 29:5). Jacob later spent some 20 years there working for Laban (Genesis 31:41). All of the direct descendants of Terah remained in Haran after Terah died except Abram and Lot.

How long Abram was in Haran is unknown. Terah was 70 when his sons began to be born (Genesis 11:26) and was 205 when he died (Genesis 11:32). Abram was 75 when he left Haran to go toward Canaan after the death of his father (Genesis 12:4). Simple math would make Terah 130 years old when Abram was born (205 minus 75). Sarai, who was ten years younger than Abram (Genesis 17:17), was born to Terah by another wife (Genesis 20:12), making her Abram's half-sister.[1] According to Genesis 11:31, the move to Haran took place after Abram and Sarai were married.

Whenever may have been the actual time God appeared to Abram, the cultures of both Ur and Haran were under the influence of the pagan practices of the Babylonian pantheism of Nimrod. There is no indication in Scripture that either Terah or Abram were "believers" at that time in the *Elohim* of creation—other than perhaps a general acceptance of the influence of the family of Shem (Noah's son) from whom they were descended. No doubt they would have been aware of the great Flood and the events at Babel, since Shem was still alive well into the lifetime of Abram. Surely Terah, who was a direct descendant of Shem, would have shared the major histories of his family line with

---

1. As mentioned on page 112 of volume two of this series, *The Book of Beginnings: Noah, the Flood, and the New World*, there were no laws against such close marriages until the time of Moses because genetic mutations had not yet accumulated enough to warrant that kind of prohibition.

his sons—including the astounding events of God's protection in the Ark and the supernatural division of languages at Babel.

While Abram may not have been a practicing "believer" when God appeared to him, he would have been aware of these histories—enough to respond to the message and lead his family into a land occupied by the descendants of Noah's grandson Canaan.

God's Presence

We are not explicitly told how God gave His promise to Abram. The initial statement in Genesis 12:1 emphasized that God "spoke" to Abram in some way so that Abram could actually hear the commission. Stephen, during his inspired sermon just prior to his death, emphasized that God had "appeared" to Abraham (Acts 7:2). Other passages emphasize the "calling" of God and that He "gave" the promises to Abram. All of these records seem to support the likelihood that God manifested Himself to Abram in some visible and audible manner—probably as He later did when Abraham was told of the impending doom of Sodom and Gomorrah (Genesis 18:1).

After Abram's arrival in Canaan, Melchizedek received an offering from Abram after the slaughter of the armies of the five kings (Genesis 14:17). Mystery surrounds this "king of Salem...the priest of God Most High" (Genesis 14:18), who is later verified as the "'king of righteousness,' and then also king of Salem, meaning 'king of peace,' without father, without mother, without genealogy, having neither beginning of days nor end of life, but made like the Son of God, remains a priest continually" (Hebrews 7:2-3). Many would conclude that Melchizedek was none other than a pre-incarnate appearance of the Second Person of the Triune Godhead, the Word of God become visible in human form just as were the angels sent to destroy Sodom and Gomorrah.

Since "God is [a] Spirit" (John 4:24), Moses was told, "You cannot see My face; for no man shall see Me, and live" (Exodus 33:20). Much later, the apostle John concluded, "No one has seen God at any time" (1 John 4:12). That unalterable condition is clearly specified to young Timothy when Paul noted that God "alone has immortality, dwelling in unapproachable light, whom no man has seen or can see" (1 Timothy 6:16). However, the Lord Jesus told Philip, "He who has seen Me has seen the Father" (John 14:9). Since Jesus Christ incarnate is "one" with the father (John 10:30), the Holy Spirit insists through the writings of Paul to the Colossian church that in the Lord Jesus "dwells all the fullness of the Godhead bodily" (Colossians 2:9).

Clearly, the Second Person of the Godhead was active during the creation week (John 1:1-3; Colossians 1:16; Hebrews 1:2). The Creator was "walking" in the Garden of Eden during the time of fellowship with Adam and Eve (Genesis 3:8). This same "LORD spoke to Moses face to face, as a man speaks to his friend" (Exodus 33:11). Joshua met the "Commander of the army of the LORD" prior to the sacking of Jericho (Joshua 5:14). Isaiah, Ezekiel, and Daniel all saw the Lord in the form of a man. There can be no doubt that the *Elohim* and the *Yahweh* of the Old Testament personally appeared in corporeal form on specific occasions. One such occasion must have been the unique event of the commissioning of Abram to become the "exalted father" who would later be named the "father of many nations."

God's Promise

God's promise to Abram in Genesis 12 is one of the more obvious unilateral promises of God concerning man. There is no "if" clause. This was in the form of a command: "Get out of your country....I will make...." God had made plans for a nation that would bear His name and that nation would be initiated through Abram and Sarai. In one sense, this unilateral sovereignty applies to all human nations: "And He has made from one blood every nation of men to dwell on all the face of the earth, and has determined their preappointed times and the boundaries of their dwellings" (Acts 17:26). But uniquely, beginning with God's command to Pharaoh "Let My people go" (Exodus 5:1), Israel has been known as the chosen nation.

There are several parts to this initial unilateral pronouncement by God upon Abram.

- "I will make you a great nation" (v. 2).

- "I will bless you And make your name great; And you shall be a blessing" (v. 2).

- "I will bless those who bless you, And I will curse him who curses you" (v. 3).

- "And in you all the families of the earth shall be blessed" (v. 3).

The Great Nation

The scope of this promise goes well beyond the recorded history of the nation of Israel. Twice during the life of Abraham, God reiterated this portion of the promise with terms that have not yet been completed.

> "And I will make your descendants as the dust of the earth; so that if a man could number the dust of the earth, then your descendants also could be numbered." (Genesis 13:16)

> Then He brought him outside and said, "Look now toward heaven, and count the stars if you are able to number them." And He said to him, "So shall your descendants be." (Genesis 15:5)

Obviously, this uncountable number (the grains of dust, the stars of heaven) must include the eternal descendants of Abraham. Ultimately this will include every one of those who have been redeemed by the promised Messiah (Galatians 3:29). The scope of this promise seems to be eternal.

There is a historical aspect to this promise as well. Although the extended promise involved "many nations" (Genesis 17:4-5), the focus of God's plan would rest on the future nation of Israel. Those descendants would be established through Isaac (Genesis 17:19-21) and would occupy a defined geological territory during Earth's history.

On the same day the LORD made a covenant with Abram,

saying: "To your descendants I have given this land, from the river of Egypt to the great river, the River Euphrates." (Genesis 15:18)

And the LORD said to Abram, after Lot had separated from him: "Lift your eyes now and look from the place where you are—northward, southward, eastward, and westward; for all the land which you see I give to you and your descendants forever." (Genesis 13:14-15)

This may well have reached its historical zenith during the reign of Solomon over 1,000 years after Abraham lived (1 Kings 4:21), but there is yet to be a future fulfillment in which the nation of Israel will be made whole and dwell safely in the land that God promised so long ago to Abraham (Ezekiel 37:22-25).

The Personal Blessing

There really are two aspects of this portion of the promise. First is the personal promise to Abram himself: "I will bless you And make your name great; And you shall be a blessing" (Genesis 12:2). Surely this is easily seen. Not only does the Bible tell of Abram's personal wealth and significance, but history is full of the honor and influence of his life.

Not only was Abraham the father of Ishmael and Isaac, but after the death of Sarah he married Keturah and fathered another six sons (Genesis 25:1-4). Ishmael (the son through the bondwoman, Hagar) was the father of at least 12 sons (Genesis 25:13-15). Isaac was the father of Jacob and Esau. There are five sons listed for Esau (Genesis 36:1-5) and 12 for Jacob (Genesis 46:8-25). Thus, Abraham was the father of at least 35 sons and grandsons, all of whom became leaders and "fathers" of large tribes or other national identities.

Father of "many nations" indeed.

Abraham also became a man of wealth and stature during his life-time. After Abram moved the families of himself and Lot into Canaan, we are told that the two families became embroiled in a property dispute because "the land was not able to support them, that they might dwell together, for their possessions were so great that they could not dwell together" (Genesis 13:6). Evidently the personal wealth was very significant.

After Lot had become ensnared by the lure of Sodom and Gomorrah, Abraham was called on to rescue him and his household from capture by the allied armies of Chedorlaomer (Genesis 14). Abram armed 318 men of his own servants, defeated the armies, and delivered Lot and all the people (Genesis 14:14-16). It may be difficult for us to relate these statistics in terms of a modern business, but by any standards an enterprise that employs 318 people is much more than a "small business." Abram would have had an annual income of multiple millions, certainly, and the logistics of such a commercial operation would have required a support staff beyond the "trained servants" who were armed and deployed for battle.

Later, when Abraham purchased the property that included his final burial site at Machpelah from Ephron the Hittite, the negotiations took place publicly among the "sons of Heth." As Abraham presented his request (remember, he was still considered a stranger and had not yet claimed any property rights among the Canaanites), the tribal leaders said, "Hear us, my lord: You are a mighty prince among us; bury your dead in the choicest of our burial places. None of us will withhold from you his burial place, that you may bury your dead" (Genesis 23:5-6).

In terms of personal status, Abraham was "blessed" indeed.

The Universal Blessing

But more is involved.

> Now the LORD had said to Abram: "...I will bless those who bless you, And I will curse him who curses you; And in you all the families of the earth shall be blessed." (Genesis 12:1, 3)

As is often the case in the Scriptures, God establishes an eternal foundation by sovereign decree and then amplifies and clarifies the decree with subsequent information. The unilateral promise given to Abram at the beginning of his move to Canaan was given in broad statements that had only a single specific command (Go!) and a promise of future happiness.

At the time of the unveiling of the promise to Abram, there was little evidence that a "great nation" would ever be established, let alone a universal "blessing" to "all the families of the earth." Ensuing revelations by the Lord would help focus the promise through the "seed" that would come through Abram. The multiple nations and the expansion of the land would all depend on a physical heir.

The Hebrew text uses the word *zera'* to describe and define the hereditary issue that would come from Abram. The word is translated "seed" in the King James Version of the Bible but often translated "descendants" by other editions. The difficulty lies in the fact that of the 200-plus times the word appears in the Hebrew text, it always appears as a singular noun. Thus, the context of the passage would have to determine how to apply the word. Many times it is clear that the meaning is the physical nation of Israel, and on at least two other occasions the application is obviously extended to a sweeping historical extrapolation of all those whose genetic lineage came from Abram.

The Land

The initial promise to Abram contained the phrase "I will bless those who bless you, And I will curse him who curses you" (Genesis 12:3). Many would suggest that the blessing to the world involves interaction and participation with the nation of Israel. The application would suggest that those people groups who assisted and endorsed Israel would participate in the Abrahamic blessing.

Both the historical and biblical revelations would focus more specifically on that blessing coming through Jesus Christ. There is no question that the nation of Israel will be reconstituted and "blessed" during the Millennium (Isaiah 61:4-7), and evidently in the "new heavens and new earth" as well (Matthew 19:28; Revelation 21). Bible scholars differ on the timing and application of these issues, but it is clear that the nation Israel remains in the eternal plan of the sovereign Creator who set the process in motion.

The historical nation of Israel, however, has thus far not followed the instructions of Scripture, and in fact has rejected the very Messiah who presented Himself to them (Luke 13:34-35). Even a casual student of Scripture will recognize the cycles of rebellion and disobedience that characterized the nation throughout history. Even though it appears that God may be gathering the nation in a homeland now, it is still very much a secular nation. Those vestiges of religious fervor that surface in their politics are basically traditional and not biblical.

A specific land was promised to Abram's seed in Genesis 12:7. That land promise is repeated in Genesis 13:15-16 and 24:7, both of which use the same Hebrew word for seed (*zera*) as was used in Genesis 12:7. However, the part of the Abrahamic blessing that ultimately blesses the Gentiles (Genesis 12:3) is not a geographical territory promised to a group of people. Blessing the entire world, with its many dispersed Gentile nations, is not the same as blessing one nation with a single homeland to live in.

The Seed

The Holy Spirit caused the apostle Paul to focus on the singular seed as one person—the person of the Lord Jesus Christ.

> Now to Abraham and his Seed were the promises made.
> He does not say, "And to seeds," as of many, but as of one,
> "And to your Seed," who is Christ. (Galatians 3:16)

Paul is quoting from Genesis 22:18, where the Lord speaks to Abraham after his obedience in bringing his son Isaac to the altar of sacrifice on Mount Moriah. There is a series of reinforcements in Genesis to this definitive statement about Abraham's life purpose.

> And the LORD said, "Shall I hide from Abraham what I
> am doing, since Abraham shall surely become a great and
> mighty nation, and all the nations of the earth shall be

blessed in him?" (Genesis 18:17-18)

"In your seed all the nations of the earth shall be blessed; because Abraham obeyed My voice and kept My charge, My commandments, My statutes, and My laws." (Genesis 26:4-5)

"In you and in your seed all the families of the earth shall be blessed." (Genesis 28:14)

There can be no doubt that God had in His eternal plan a "seed" (first hinted at in Genesis 3:15) that would "bless" the entire world. Historically that played out through Abraham and the physical seed that would ultimately be brought about in the incarnation of the Lord Jesus.

In Galatians 3:14, which introduces the immediate context of Galatians 3:16, Paul refers to "the blessing of Abraham" as coming to the Gentiles "in Jesus Christ." But how does Paul know that the Abrahamic blessing of Genesis 22:18 is fulfilled in one person? Most of the Genesis passages seem to apply to the ultimate nation, Israel. Why does Paul specifically identify the incarnation as the universal blessing to the population of the earth and not a blessing in proportion to the treatment of the entire nation of Israel?

One major clue for understanding the teaching of Galatians 3:14-16 is to recognize that it applies to the last component of the multifaceted Abrahamic covenant first fully stated in Genesis 12:2-3. The last phrase contains the "big picture" that applies to all of humanity in which God blesses the entire world, not just the Jewish people: "And in you [Abram] all the families of the earth shall be blessed."

But how can all families of the earth be blessed through Abraham's seed?

As indicated previously, the Hebrew word *zera'* appears as a singular noun each time it is used in the Old Testament. It would be much easier if the Hebrew noun were plural when used collectively to refer to a group and singular only when used of one individual, but that is not how God chose to use the word. For example, the phrase "Abraham's seed" can refer collectively to all of the genetic descendants of Abraham combined as one (Genesis 13:15-16; 32:12)—a generic use of the term. It is absolutely correct to say that all of Abraham's biological offspring is his biogenetic seed.

The apostle Paul once used the phrase in this way when he claimed his own Jewish identity as part of the seed of Abraham: "Are they Hebrews? So am I. Are they Israelites? So am I. Are they the seed of Abraham? So am I" (2 Corinthians 11:22). Similarly, Paul told the Roman church, "For I also am an Israelite, of the seed of Abraham, of the tribe of Benjamin" (Romans 11:1). Paul considered himself part of "the seed of Abraham," referring to all of Abraham's descendants through Isaac.

Yet the phrase "seed of Abraham" can also refer to one human individual. That is the specific context of Galatians 3:14: "...that the blessing of Abraham might come upon the Gentiles in Christ Jesus, that we might receive the promise of the Spirit through faith." Paul obviously expects this blessing to the Gentiles to come through Jesus Christ, not through the genealogically related descendants who became the nation Israel. Blessing all nations is accomplished not through land but through a specific seed of Abraham—the incarnate Son of God, the Second Person of the Godhead, Jesus the Christ.

Furthermore, each biological descendant of Abraham will *not* receive all the promises God made to Abraham. Only those with Abraham's faith are the "children of God" and thus are the "children of promise" who are therefore blessed as God promised Abraham. These key passages in the New Testament speak directly to this vital application of God's unique promise to bless the entire earth through the seed of Abraham.

> For they are not all Israel who are of Israel, nor are they all children because they are the seed of Abraham; but, "In Isaac your seed shall be called." That is, those who are the children of the flesh, these are not the children of God;

but the children of the promise are counted as the seed. (Romans 9:6-8)

Therefore know that only those who are of faith are sons of Abraham. And the Scripture, foreseeing that God would justify the Gentiles by faith, preached the gospel to Abraham beforehand, saying, "In you all the nations shall be blessed." So then those who are of faith are blessed with believing Abraham. (Galatians 3:7-9)

...that the blessing of Abraham might come upon the Gentiles in Christ Jesus, that we might receive the promise of the Spirit through faith. Brethren, I speak in the manner of men: Though it is only a man's covenant, yet if it is confirmed, no one annuls or adds to it. Now to Abraham and his Seed were the promises made. He does not say, "And to seeds," as of many, but as of one, "And to your Seed," who is Christ. (Galatians 3:14-16)

For you are all sons of God through faith in Christ Jesus. For as many of you as were baptized into Christ have put on Christ. There is neither Jew nor Greek, there is neither slave nor free, there is neither male nor female; for you are all one in Christ Jesus. And if you are Christ's, then you are Abraham's seed, and heirs according to the promise. (Galatians 3:26-29)

Thus, by the inspiration of the Holy Spirit upon and through the apostle Paul, the intent and purpose of God is clearly defined.

- Being a genetic descendant of Abraham does not make anyone a child of God (Romans 9:6-8).

- Abraham's faith foreshadows "the gospel" that was preached to Abraham about the coming blessing through his seed (Galatians 3:7-9).

- The blessing was to come through "the seed"—which was uniquely and specifically the Christ, the incarnate God in flesh (Galatians 3:14-16).

- Faith in Jesus Christ (exampled by Abraham's belief in the promises of God) positions the believer "in Christ" (Galatians 3:27-28).

- Anyone who is "in Christ" is Abraham's seed and thus heir to the Abrahamic promise's legacy of blessing (Galatians 3:29).

Thus, faith in Christ as "the seed" through which the blessing became available to all the peoples of the earth is distinguished from the promise of a land that God made to Abraham and to his "seed."

And, just to make sure that all the readers of God's Word would understand the focus on the coming Messiah, Abraham was required to carry out a very personal demonstration. Abraham and Isaac were to display to the world what the ultimate sacrifice of God's own "beloved son" would be like.

> By faith Abraham, when he was tested, offered up Isaac, and he who had received the promises offered up his only begotten son, of whom it was said, "In Isaac your seed shall be called," concluding that God was able to raise him up, even from the dead, from which he also received him in a figurative sense. (Hebrews 11:17-19)

The focus of the promise went well beyond the national identity of the future nation of Israel. The promise contains the foundational platform upon which the identity of the coming Messiah would be based.

God's Man

> The book of the genealogy of Jesus Christ, the Son of David, the Son of Abraham... (Matthew 1:1)

Is it not interesting that the first book of the New Testament places such emphasis on the genealogical connection of Jesus Christ to Abraham? The records of human lineage are carefully preserved in

Scripture. Evidently, the Creator of humanity wanted us to know that He has had His hand on the "seed" from the very beginning. Surely the reader is familiar with the commentary recorded in Genesis 3 where God tells the Serpent, "I will put enmity Between you and the woman, And between your seed and her Seed; He shall bruise your head, And you shall bruise His heel" (Genesis 3:15).

Luke's genealogical record goes all the way back to Adam (Luke 3:23-38), verifying the details of the records in Genesis 10 and 11 as well as those summarized throughout the records of the Kings and Chronicles.

The book of Genesis contains 50 chapters. Abraham is the central figure in 12 of those chapters, Jacob in 17, and Joseph in 13. Isaac, interestingly, is just barely mentioned for his childhood and in the rather embarrassing situation with Esau and Jacob. The great chapter in Hebrews 11 that records several heroes of faith, however, gives six verses to the life of Abraham but only one each to the other four patriarchs. Abraham was unique and vitally important in God's sovereign plan.

- Abram is the honorific title Exalted Father.
- Abraham is the title Father of Many Nations (Genesis 17:5).
- Abraham is called "the friend of God" (James 2:23).
- Abraham is called "the father of all those who believe" (Romans 4:11).
- Abraham is called "the father of us all" (Romans 4:16).

Much more can and will be said about this great patriarch who, like the apostle Paul, was called out of an environment that would have led in an entirely different direction. Much can be learned from the history of Abraham's life as God worked out His will through this remarkable man.

CHAPTER TWO
STRANGERS IN THE LAND

By faith Abraham obeyed when he was called to go out to
the place which he would receive as an inheritance. And
he went out, not knowing where he was going. By faith
he dwelt in the land of promise as in a foreign country,
dwelling in tents with Isaac and Jacob, the heirs with him
of the same promise; for he waited for the city which has
foundations, whose builder and maker is God. (Hebrews
11:8-10)

As Abram and his entourage traveled from Haran toward Canaan,
God's promise of Genesis 12:2-3 may well have seemed a bit mixed.
Although there could have been no doubt that God was talking about
a long time, there would have been the natural tendency to expect
some sort of reasonably rapid success after the group arrived in the
new land. Abram and Lot were wealthy agricultural business barons
and would have anticipated both recognition and stability once they
found a good location and developed relationships with the tribal
leaders of Canaan.

No doubt tradesmen from Canaan would have held commerce
with the family of Terah in Haran as they passed to and from the
various centers of civilization that were rapidly developing after the
linguistic dispersion from Babel only a century or so prior. No doubt

the histories of Noah and his three sons were still clear in the minds of many—Shem, Ham, and Japheth all lived for several hundred years after the great Flood, and their sons and daughters would have kept the histories alive. Abram might have expected some honored treatment among the population in Canaan, given his direct lineage from Shem.

The Plain of Moreh

It had been many months, years possibly, since Abram had talked with the Lord and made plans to leave Haran for Canaan. It is likely that when Abram arrived with his family and herds, the country was sparsely settled. Although the "Canaanites were then in the land," the widespread grazing needs of his huge flocks would have required Abram to choose a route through open country. Genesis 12:6 mentions that Abram stopped in "the plain of Moreh" (KJV). Moses, as the inspired editor of Genesis, equates that location with Shechem.

Many of the translations render the Hebrew word 'allown (or 'elown) as "tree" rather than "plain" (as in a level, grassy area). The two words are only used 17 times collectively in the Old Testament and could be understood either way in most of the passages. Some translators have given a specialized name, "terebinth tree," for both terms. Others have used the simplified and familiar term "oak tree." There are at least two other similar Hebrew words used in passages in which they clearly mean "oak" or "tree." It is not clear that the structure of this initial reference in Genesis 12:6 to the plain of Moreh is to be understood as some sort of giant tree.

More likely, after traveling several weeks, Abram found a place roughly midway down into the land of Canaan that could permit forage for his large flocks and decided to encamp there for a while. The Hebrew word shechem is a word that describes a "shoulder." It is obvious from topographical maps of that region that the words would easily fit a mountain plain on the shoulder of the local mountains. The Hebrew mowreh is translated variously as "teacher" and "rain," depending on the context. All of these descriptive terms fit the basic needs of the large agricultural enterprise that Abram and Lot would have been driving down into the heartland of Canaan.

Reaffirmation

Now that he had arrived after a long journey, Abram stopped for a short time at Shechem, roughly halfway between the Sea of Galilee and the Dead Sea on the western side of the Jordan River. It was there that the Lord appeared to Abram again to reaffirm His promises that the land of Canaan would one day be the permanent possession of Abram's descendants (Genesis 12:7).

Once again, the text emphasizes that the Lord "appeared" to Abram. With no other information to counter the description, it is most likely that this is another bodily appearance of the Second Person of the Godhead, the Lord Jesus. It may be possible that this particular visit would have been as Melchizedek since the later accounts in Genesis and the commentary in the book of Hebrews indicate that Melchizedek was unique in all of history (Hebrews 7:3).

The account in Genesis 14 identifies Melchizedek as "king of Salem" and the "priest of God Most High." Abram, enriched with the plunder from the slaughter of Chedorlaomer and the recapture of the populations of Sodom and Gomorrah, gave Melchizedek "a tithe of all" (Genesis 14:20). The two titles of Melchizedek certainly fit the role of the Lord Jesus Christ. He is "king of peace" (Hebrews 7:2) and the great High Priest (Hebrews 4:14; 6:20).

Jewish tradition holds that Melchizedek resided in the city that later became known as Jerusalem. Biblical data indicate that Jerusalem was long occupied by the Jebusites, part of the Canaanite population (Genesis 15:21; Judges 1:21; 2 Samuel 5:6; 1 Chronicles 11:4). It is certainly plausible that a city-state had been established at Jebus by the time Abram and Lot arrived in Canaan. It is further plausible that Melchizedek traveled the 30 or so miles from Jerusalem to Shechem in the plain of Moreh to meet with Abram, whose long and arduous journey from Haran would have been well-known to the population of Canaan.

Identification

> Then the LORD appeared to Abram and said, "To your de-
> scendants I will give this land." And there he built an altar
> to the LORD, who had appeared to him. And he moved
> from there to the mountain east of Bethel, and he pitched
> his tent with Bethel on the west and Ai on the east; there
> he built an altar to the LORD and called on the name of
> the LORD. So Abram journeyed, going on still toward the
> South. (Genesis 12:7-9)

Twice the text mentions that Abram built an altar as commem-
oration of his arrival in Canaan and the confirmation of the Lord's
promise. With confidence renewed, Abram traveled farther south to
an area near Bethel, where he established a semi-permanent camp,
built an altar to *Yahweh*, and began a formal worship practice to call
"on the name of the LORD."

The sacrificial system that became formally codified under Moses
was not yet common practice. However, animal sacrifice had been
instituted by the Creator Himself in the Garden of Eden, and the
practice was certainly not unknown to the post-Flood civilizations.
Although the Bible text does not give a detailed description of that
initial sacrifice, the repetitive practice was certainly implied at the
time of Cain and Abel's formal sacrifice recorded in Genesis 4.[1] The
reader will also recall that Noah and his family built an altar and offered animal sacrifices immediately after disembarking from the Ark
on the side of the mountains of Ararat.[2]

Of note in the life of Abram is the phrase that he "called on the
name of the LORD" (Genesis 12:8). Here at Bethel, and again at Beersheba, Abram invoked a formal identification with the God who had

---

1. The implications of that event are discussed at some length in volume one of this series,
   The Book of Beginnings: Creation, Fall, and the First Age, pages 191-196.
2. Some additional detail and the obvious parallel between the two biblical events are
   discussed in volume two, *The Book of Beginnings: Noah, the Flood, and the New World*,
   pages 71-76.

given promise to him and his descendants (Genesis 13:4; 21:33). The other references using this phrase bear testimony to the association with some sort of recognized worship with a more formal identification than just personal prayer or meditation.

> And as for Seth, to him also a son was born; and he named him Enosh. Then men began to call on the name of the LORD. (Genesis 4:26)

> I will take the cup of salvation, and call upon the name of the LORD....I will offer to You the sacrifice of thanksgiving, and will call upon the name of the LORD. (Psalm 116:13, 17)

> For then I will restore to the peoples a pure language, That they all may call on the name of the LORD, To serve Him with one accord. (Zephaniah 3:9)

> For "whoever calls on the name of the LORD shall be saved." (Romans 10:13)

> To the church of God which is at Corinth, to those who are sanctified in Christ Jesus, called to be saints, with all who in every place call on the name of Jesus Christ our Lord, both theirs and ours. (1 Corinthians 1:2)

When the bold prophet Elijah faced the wicked prophets of Baal on Mount Carmel with the crowd of indifferent and backslidden Israelites watching, Elijah voiced the core of what is involved in "calling" on God's name:

> "Then you call on the name of your gods, and I will call on the name of the LORD; and the God who answers by fire, He is God." So all the people answered and said, "It is well spoken." (1 Kings 18:24)

Abram was making a public stand. He and his family and servants would identify with the *Elohim* of creation in this new land so dominated by pagan worship.

The Land of Egypt

> Now there was a famine in the land, and Abram went down to Egypt to dwell there, for the famine was severe in the land. (Genesis 12:10)

Egypt was a major political and economic power at the time Abram and Lot felt it necessary to escape the famine in Canaan. The prophetic insights in Revelation 17 and Daniel 2 identify Egypt as the first of the "heads" of the "seven-headed beast" roaming the centuries since the great Flood. The pharaonic dynasties were established by Abram's time, and the wealth and power of an enormous empire rested in the ruling personages of Egypt's throne room.[3]

Fear and Worry

Every one of us has felt the pressure of uncontrollable circumstances and the fear and worry that comes with an inability to "see" what to do. The famine that began in Canaan shortly after Abram arrived would have been a serious problem for an agricultural business like that of Abram and Lot. Large herds need lush grazing grounds and personnel need to be cared for. A drought-induced famine is not a sudden event, but can be both severe and long-lasting.

No doubt the decision to relocate south to Egypt was not made quickly. Not only would the logistics have been demanding, but the lives of all of his family and servants would be impacted—possibly in a negative way. Although Abram's personal wealth and business acumen would be some defense, coming under the political power of Egypt could well have been limiting to his livelihood and would have required new business relationships with unknown consequences. No doubt there were many long days of "business meetings" with his family and assistants, along with sleepless nights, tossing and turning the possibilities over in his mind.

But a decision had to be made. Either the entire business had to relocate to an area that could easily support their enterprise or they

---

3. The reader can get a quick summary of the conditions facing Abram and Lot in *The Book of Beginnings: Noah, the Flood, and the New World,* pages 194-200.

would need to stay in Canaan and suffer the physical consequences of the severe famine. The only supernatural instructions that had been given were a long-range promise to give the land of Canaan to Abram and his descendants. They had obeyed the command to move from Haran to Canaan, but they were still strangers to the inhabitants and were not much more than "free grazers" (as the early settlers in the Old West of the United States were known).

Surely "the Lord helps those who help themselves." (How often has that phrase popped up in conversations?) Whatever may have been going through Abram's mind and the conversations with Lot and the other members of his family, a decision was made to relocate to Egypt and attempt to preserve the wealth and possessions that had been gained in Haran. Preparations began to get underway, and the trek of some 200 miles ensued.

Imagined Problems

> And it came to pass, when he was close to entering Egypt, that he said to Sarai his wife, "Indeed I know that you are a woman of beautiful countenance. Therefore it will happen, when the Egyptians see you, that they will say, 'This is his wife'; and they will kill me, but they will let you live. Please say you are my sister, that it may be well with me for your sake, and that I may live because of you." (Genesis 12:11-13)

Imagination is a funny thing. It can be the source for magnificent inventions, strategic advances, and powerful developments. Yet it is more often the breeding ground for seeds of doubt and bad decisions that frequently lead to unintended self-fulfilling prophecies. After the long series of debates that led to the decision to relocate to Egypt, Abram had his mind full of the potential problems that might face him when he arrived.

Lurking in the background of his mind might well have been the concern that he was moving away from the area where God had promised to bless him—indeed, that appears to have been the case.

Perhaps you have heard the saying "If you feel far away from God, guess who moved?!" God is loving and merciful and will protect us in spite of bad choices, but during the implementing of those choices our self-doubt will grow exponentially. Abram was experiencing that very problem—and it all begins with a list of the conditions.

- My wife is a real beauty: True.

- The Egyptians are not known for their morality: True.

- Pharaoh has the power to kill me and take my wife for his harem: True.

- Therefore, I must do something to protect...me: Not true. Not necessary. Very self-centered!

- The only solution is for Sarai to tell a "white lie"...to protect me: Bad decision!

- Note: Solutions based on half-truths are *not* wise and may begin with initial success but almost always end in long-term disaster.

So, as sure as night follows day, he did, she did, and they did, and the whole situation became embroiled in a real mess! No sooner than they had settled down in the territory of Egypt, the agents of Pharaoh told the king of the raving beauty who had just entered the land, and Sarai was commanded to be ensconced in the palace. And since everyone was told that Sarai was "just" Abram's sister, then...well, no harm, no foul.

The real trouble was, however, that Abram had just placed one of the instruments of the Lord's promise into the hands of a wicked ruler. The seed that would "bless all the families of the earth" could now be either destroyed or denigrated. Apparently, Abram had not given any serious thought to *those* consequences! It may not have bothered him in that culture to have his wife bedded by another man, but Abram had certainly not considered the possibility that *Elohim* intended to fulfill the promises through Sarai as well! But God knew! The sovereign Lord cannot be thwarted by the bad decisions of human agents—

even one as worried as Abram or as arrogant as the pharaoh of Egypt.

> "Remember the former things of old, For I am God, and there is no other; I am God, and there is none like Me, Declaring the end from the beginning, And from ancient times things that are not yet done, Saying, 'My counsel shall stand, And I will do all My pleasure.'" (Isaiah 46:9-10)

Consequences

Neither history nor the biblical records give any specific information about the location of Pharaoh's court and the settlement of Abram's business interests. It is likely that the capital of the early Egyptian dynasty was at Memphis (west and somewhat south of modern Cairo). The farm and grazing land was north and east of Memphis, probably equivalent to what would later be called the "land of Goshen" at the time of Joseph.

Just like Abram had predicted, the agents of Pharaoh saw how beautiful Sarai was and commandeered her for the royal harem. And because Sarai obeyed her husband and told the half-truth that she was just his sister, Pharaoh "treated Abram well for her sake. He had sheep, oxen, male donkeys, male and female servants, female donkeys, and camels" (Genesis 12:16). The rather self-centered plan of Abram seemed to be working out well!

The list of domesticated animals given here provides us with a couple of key insights. First, these animals were well-integrated with the social use of humanity by Abram's time (2000 B.C.), indicating that these few short centuries after the great Flood (some 300–500 years) saw both a prolific rise in human population as well as rapid growth and adaptation of animal populations. Secondly, the listing of these particular animals may well indicate that Abram and Lot were involved with trade commerce as well as animal husbandry.

Then God stepped in.

But the LORD plagued Pharaoh and his house with great

> plagues because of Sarai, Abram's wife. And Pharaoh
> called Abram and said, "What is this you have done to
> me? Why did you not tell me that she was your wife?
> Why did you say, 'She is my sister'? I might have taken
> her as my wife. Now therefore, here is your wife; take her
> and go your way." So Pharaoh commanded his men con-
> cerning him; and they sent him away, with his wife and
> all that he had. (Genesis 12:17-20)

There is no specificity about the nature of the plagues that God
sent to the household of Pharaoh, but it is clear that the sickness (or
disaster, or failure) was "because of Sarai, Abram's wife." Whatever the
problems may have been, the entire royal household knew that Abram
had "done" something to Pharaoh and that the God of creation was
striking the royal household to make it clear that God did not want
the injustice to continue.

It is interesting to note that Pharaoh did not strike back at Abram.
(He had, rather, increased his wealth and did not confiscate it.) Apparently, the intervention of *Elohim* was so clear that Pharaoh was more
frightened than angry and merely commanded Abram to pick up his
belongings (and his wife!) and leave.

Return to Bethel

> Then Abram went up from Egypt, he and his wife and all
> that he had, and Lot with him, to the South. Abram was
> very rich in livestock, in silver, and in gold. And he went
> on his journey from the South as far as Bethel, to the
> place where his tent had been at the beginning, between
> Bethel and Ai, to the place of the altar which he had made
> there at first. And there Abram called on the name of the
> Lord. (Genesis 13:1-4)

Back to square one! Often, when a bad spiritual decision is made,
the result is a necessary return to initial commitment and resolution.
Sometimes we call such a moment "rededication." Abram returned to
Bethel, the altar, and "called on the name of the Lord."

Lot's Tragic Life

Over the next several chapters in Genesis, a real tragedy is played out in the life and family of Lot, Abram's nephew. Apparently, the worldly prosperity that increased while they were in Egypt overwhelmed the spiritual strength of Lot, and a downward spiral began upon their return to Canaan that ended in disaster from "the cares of this world and the deceitfulness of riches" (Matthew 13:22).

> Lot also, who went with Abram, had flocks and herds and tents. Now the land was not able to support them, that they might dwell together, for their possessions were so great that they could not dwell together. (Genesis 13:5-6)

Abram had been and was the "senior partner" in their successes, but the success was more than could be handled gracefully. The herdsmen of both parties began to squabble in the field—probably over territory or territorial rights—and fights ensued that threatened the relationship between the family members. (How often has that played out in other situations?)

By now, Abram had regained his trust in the Lord and offered to divide the territory in any way that would keep Lot happy. The choice and ultimate downfall of Lot set a classic pattern that is revealed many times in Scripture.

Eyes on the World

As Abram began to discuss solutions to their difficulties, he suggested that Lot take a long look at the available territory around them and pick the area he would like best. Whatever Lot desired Abram would agree to and take whatever remained.

> And Lot lifted his eyes and saw all the plain of Jordan, that it was well watered everywhere (before the Lord destroyed Sodom and Gomorrah) like the garden of the Lord, like the land of Egypt as you go toward Zoar. Then Lot chose for himself all the plain of Jordan, and Lot journeyed east. (Genesis 13:10-11)

Several implied concerns and background information may be helpful to recall. Their current "business headquarters" was located near Bethel in the mountain foothills of the central part of Canaan. The plain of Jordan would have been toward the east and somewhat south of their current location. Abram had returned to Bethel because it was there that the Lord had reconfirmed the promise and where Abram himself had recommitted his life to submit to God's oversight. The central part of the country would have been less settled—perhaps more suitable for grazing the large herds but less suitable for open commerce and interaction with the business trade.

Comments noted in the biblical record are very telling.

- "Lot...saw all the plain of Jordan, that it was well watered everywhere (before the LORD destroyed Sodom and Gomorrah) like the garden of the LORD, like the land of Egypt" (Genesis 13:10).

- "Lot dwelt in the cities of the plain and pitched his tent even as far as Sodom" (Genesis 13:12).

- "But the men of Sodom were exceedingly wicked and sinful against the LORD" (Genesis 13:12).

Apparently, Lot crossed a spiritual line here that set a direction for his life that would later end in disaster. From a purely physical and business point of view, this was a good decision. The land was very favorable for the business he was in. The location was close to the two biggest cities near a large body of water. The territory was well known along the trade routes. Everything made sense—except that the spiritual environment was awful!

Extended Consequences

Scripture notes that "righteous Lot" was "oppressed by the filthy conduct of the wicked" (2 Peter 2:7). Lot will join the twice-born in heaven in the ages ahead, but he made a self-centered choice that placed him under the dominion and influence of wicked people and destroyed his testimony, his influence, and ultimately his family and his descendants. The consequences of sinful choices are severe and will often impact the lives of many—even those yet unborn.

The progression of the worldly choice of Lot spanned many years and extended to his descendants. What might have been is answerable only by the sovereign God who declares "the end from the beginning" (Isaiah 46:10). History records the following:

- Lot and his family moved into the city of Sodom (Genesis 14:12).

- Lot and his family were captured by Chedorlaomer and treated harshly (Genesis 14:9-12).

- Lot escaped the fiery destruction of Sodom with his two daughters after the intercession of Abram and the protection of angels, then fled to a mountain cave with none of his vast possessions (Genesis 19:1-30).

- Lot fathered incestuous sons by his daughters who then fathered the nations of the Moabites and Ammonites (Genesis 19:31-38).

- Those nations were abandoned by God and became constant enemies and spiritual trouble for Israel (Ezra 9:1).

The consequences of sin are *not* abrogated in most circumstances. Sometimes God will override the ripples of a sinful choice to accomplish a greater impact (such as Abram's move to Egypt), but most often when there is ample example and information available for the right choice and a wrong choice is made knowingly, the choice sets in motion events and circumstances that will inexorably lead away from a godly lifestyle. Genuine repentance is always accepted by our loving Savior and restoration to His favor is promised in many passages, but memories and historical events are not erased from our lives—just forgiven (1 John 1:9; Luke 15:17-24).

Established in the Land

After the separation of Abram and his business from the daily relationship with Lot, Abram relocated to the plain of Mamre near Hebron and established another altar as the center of worship (Genesis 13:18). This area appears to be somewhat south and east of Bethel, some 20 miles south of modern Jerusalem in the mountainous region west of the Dead Sea. Obviously, the land's use and occupation have changed over the centuries, but the old names have survived and archaeological work has established fairly accurate pictures of that era.

Battle with the Kings

Just how long Abram and Lot were settled in their new locations is not identified in the biblical text. Lot has moved from a tent near Sodom to dwell in the city itself (Genesis 13:12; 14:12). Later, Sarai notes that they have been in the land ten years and she is still not pregnant (Genesis 16:2-3). It is likely that the battle recorded in Genesis 14 takes place several years after they left Haran to move to Canaan.

The identity of the allied kings is significant. It seems that Moses goes out of his way to establish the historicity of the events and open up the text for critical analysis by future generations. In spite of the names given, as well as the territorial identities, scholars love to write long tomes tweaking dates and comparing phonetic nuances, attempting to establish their theory of who these folks were and when they lived. Here are several points that may help in putting flesh to this event.

> And it came to pass in the days of Amraphel king of Shinar, Arioch king of Ellasar, Chedorlaomer king of Elam, and Tidal king of nations... (Genesis 14:1)

- Shinar is an area in the central Mesopotamian Valley. This is the place of the early post-Flood settlement under the leadership of Nimrod (Genesis 10:8-10; 11:2). Shinar covers the area of southern Iraq and the area around which the nation and city of Babylon were centered.

- Elam was a territory east of Shinar in the western portion of what is now Iran. Ellasar seems to be the area around the ancient city of Arioch and may well have been located near the city of Ur of the Chaldees near the southern portion of the Euphrates River.

- This four-king federation allied themselves under the leadership of Chedorlaomer in an attack against the five kings of southern Canaan who had been paying tribute to Chedorlaomer for some 12 years (Genesis 14:2-4).

Valley of Siddim

This location is cited in Genesis 14:10 as the place where the battle between the four-king alliance of Chedorlaomer and the five-king alliance of the cities of the plain took place. All researchers tend to agree that this area was near the southern end of where the Dead Sea is located today.

What is not clear is how far the Dead Sea extended down toward the south. The asphalt pits mentioned in Genesis 14:10 would indicate that the area may well have been struggling with the draining of the Jordan River Valley but was not yet flooded. Moses mentions that one of the main reasons that Lot chose to move toward Sodom and Gomorrah was that the area was "well watered everywhere (before the Lord destroyed Sodom and Gomorrah) like the garden of the Lord, like the land of Egypt as you go toward Zoar" (Genesis 13:10).

It is likely that the five-king federation of these southern Canaanite cities banded together to meet the armies of Chedorlaomer as he was coming south plundering the various Canaanite strongholds on his way to punish the rebellious city-states that had been under his tribute for 12 years. We are told that the five-king federation rebelled against Chedorlaomer in the thirteenth year and that it took a year for the four-king alliance under Chedorlaomer to make its way around the Fertile Crescent, down through Syria and into southern Canaan (Genesis 14:4-5).

The armies met in the Valley of Siddim, and the armies of the southern five-king federation fled in fear from the conflict, abandoning the cities of Sodom and Gomorrah specifically (Genesis 14:10-11). Lot and his family, along with the civilian population of those two cities, were taken captive and the two cities were looted (v. 12). The bedraggled prisoners and the victorious armies of Chedorlaomer then began their trek north, assuming they would have an easy march back to their homeland in the Mesopotamian Valley.

Abram's Rescue

Abram was informed by an escaped prisoner of the battle and the looting (Genesis 14:13). He then assembled and armed 318 of his own male servants and led them north, catching up with the armies of Chedorlaomer and the population of the looted cities dear Dan west of Damascus in Syria, some 150 miles north from Abram's headquarters in the mountains of Mamre (Genesis 14:15).

Dividing his small army, Abram attacked the enemies at night (apparently encircling the camp or attacking from several sides at once). The victory was sudden and a rout ensued that drove the enemies as far north as Hobah (Genesis 14:15). The language of the text indicates that Chedorlaomer himself and "the kings who were with him" were utterly defeated (Genesis 14:17). Despite the various debates on the historicity and timing of this event, the New Testament cites the victory tribute given Melchizedek when Abram came back from the battle with the army of the four kings (Hebrews 7:1-2).

Abram's Tithe

As indicated in chapter 1, Melchizedek seems to have been watching over Abram in a longer role as king of Salem from a city in Canaan—probably the early settlement of Jebus that later became the capital city of Judah, Jerusalem. Although there is disagreement among Bible scholars about the nature of this unusual king, it appears from the commentary in Hebrews 7 that Melchizedek was a temporary visitation of the Second Person of the Godhead, the Word of God, the Lord Jesus.

Abram certainly appears to recognize Melchizedek as more than a mere king on Earth. Returning as the rightful owner of all the plunder from Sodom and Gomorrah and the sacking of many central cities in Canaan, Abram refuses to keep any property for himself but does give one tenth of everything to Melchizedek (Genesis 14:20-24). In the commentary about Melchizedek recorded in the book of Hebrews, the writer cites this incident.

> Now consider how great this man was, to whom even the patriarch Abraham gave a tenth of the spoils. (Hebrews 7:4)

The tithe, officially instituted by the formal giving of the Law under Moses, has always been presented as a "tribute" (a tax) due to the Owner of all things—the Creator and God of the universe. The argument given in Hebrews notes that the act of tithing to Melchizedek and the giving and receiving of a blessing to Abram is proof that Melchizedek is much more than a mere earthly king of a small city-state in ancient Canaan.

> Now beyond all contradiction the lesser is blessed by the better. Here mortal men receive tithes, but there he receives them, of whom it is witnessed that he lives. Even Levi, who receives tithes, paid tithes through Abraham, so to speak, for he was still in the loins of his father when Melchizedek met him. (Hebrews 7:7-10)

Abram's Belief

Sometime after the blessing from Melchizedek, the Lord appears to Abram again as Abram's "shield, your exceedingly great reward" (Genesis 15:1). Abram gives vent to the burning problem that must have been festering in his heart ever since the family moved to Canaan: "You have given me no offspring; indeed one born in my house is my heir!" (Genesis 15:3). Abram's agonizing cry implies: "How can a promise of 'many nations' ever come to pass if I don't have any children? In fact, if *another* (implied) is born in my house, that one becomes the heir!"

The Lord's answer to Abram is the most complete given thus far.

> And behold, the word of the LORD came to him, say-
> ing, "This one shall not be your heir, but one who will
> come from your own body shall be your heir." Then He
> brought him outside and said, "Look now toward heaven,
> and count the stars if you are able to number them." And
> He said to him, "So shall your descendants be." (Genesis
> 15:4-5)

Well, that was enough for Abram. It was on the basis of that renewed promise and the very personal application to Abram that he
"believed in the LORD, and He accounted it to him for righteousness"
(Genesis 15:6). It is that statement that is picked up by the apostles
Paul and James when they discussed the event of transformation from
an unsaved sinner to a twice-born child of God.

> For what does the Scripture say? "Abraham believed God,
> and it was accounted to him for righteousness." (Romans
> 4:3)

> Just as Abraham "believed God, and it was accounted to
> him for righteousness." (Galatians 3:6)

> And the Scripture was fulfilled which says, "Abraham be-
> lieved God, and it was accounted to him for righteous-
> ness." And he was called the friend of God. (James 2:23)

Genesis 15 records the extensive information that God gave to
Abram. It is a remarkable revelation. Not only does God reaffirm the
promise given initially to Abram, He also takes the time to involve
Himself in a very personal and striking oath ceremony using Abram
in such a way that he could have no doubt that God was making
a promise that would be carried out. Furthermore, God reveals to
Abram that this promise would be fulfilled over centuries, citing the
coming enslavement of the budding nation by Egypt. (This would
have been all the more poignant to Abram, having spent some time
there.)

After the ceremony was complete, the coming physical fulfillment of the promise was reiterated, even listing the names of the current nations that would be conquered and subsumed by the future descendants of Abram. There now could be no doubt. The purpose and mission for which Abram was born was clarified. The job remaining was in the hands of the Creator of the universe. All Abram had to do was obey!

CHAPTER THREE
THE SON OF THE BONDWOMAN

But, as he who was born according to the flesh then persecuted him who was born according to the Spirit, even so it is now. Nevertheless what does the Scripture say? "Cast out the bondwoman and her son, for the son of the bondwoman shall not be heir with the son of the freewoman." (Galatians 4:29-30)

God had chosen Abram to be the federal head of many nations, and after the very personal confirmation of the covenant between God and Abram described in Genesis 15, Abram finally "believed in the LORD." That astounding affirmation from God included a reiteration of the national boundaries that this new nation would occupy and the prophetic insight that several centuries would elapse before the promise would begin to be fulfilled.

Abram is simply required to trust God's promise and expect God to bring about the specific physical events that will execute the promises in history. Much time has elapsed as we enter chapter 16, however, and the promise is not yet realized.

Abram was 75 years old when he left for Canaan (Genesis 12:4) and ten years had passed (Genesis 16:3). Earlier, when he had come back from the rather astounding victory over the armies of Chedorlaomer and the interchange with Melchizedek, Abram had previously asked for the possibility of Eliezer, his chief servant, to substitute as "the heir" (Genesis 15:2-3). The Lord rejected that request and re-iterated that "the seed" that would fulfill the promises would come through Abram (v. 4-5).

Sarai's Request

But the ten years of waiting was too much for Sarai.

> Now Sarai, Abram's wife, had borne him no children. And she had an Egyptian maidservant whose name was Hagar. So Sarai said to Abram, "See now, the LORD has restrained me from bearing children. Please, go in to my maid; perhaps I shall obtain children by her." And Abram heeded the voice of Sarai. (Genesis 16:1-2)

Sarai's request was socially and legally acceptable back then. Hagar (the maid acquired while the family was in Egypt) was Sarai's "property." The "primary" wife could provide an heir by proxy. Should the first wife later bear a son, he would rank over a son born to the second wife. Less than a century after this, Jacob fathered several of the heads of the tribes of Israel through the handmaids Bilhah and Zilpah, who belonged to his wives Rachel and Leah.

A library of tablets dating from 1600 to 1350 B.C. was found at Nuzi, an ancient trade center in Assyria. The major find was more than 5,000 family and administrative archives spanning six generations, uncovered by American teams from 1925 to 1933. The site possibly had been settled since the time of ancient Babel and was first called Gasur. Among the more interesting discoveries in the tablets were some of the social and religious practices of the periods recorded in the deeds, wills, marriage agreements, and adoption proceedings. They shed light on many of the customs documented in the Scriptures that may appear unusual to us.

In the case of a childless couple, the wife could locate another wife for the husband.

If Gilimninu (the wife) will not bear children, Gilimninu shall take a woman of Lulluland as a wife for Shennma (the husband).[4]

"OK" Is Not Always Right

There would be no social stigma placed on Abram and Sarai for this action. They both were well within the acceptable standards of their society—but it is very likely that Abram at least would have known that this was not what God intended in a marriage, either at creation or for him and Sarai. It is likely that both of them discussed the issue at length and their reasoning may well have gone something like this:

- Abram is getting old (he is 85) and may well not be able to father children much longer. If it doesn't happen soon, "we will miss out on the blessing."

- Sarai is barren. There has been plenty of time and proof of her inability to produce children. They had been trying for a long time. Nothing!

- God has been silent (at least to Sarai) for several years and the promise is ten years old with no hint that it will be fulfilled through Sarai.

- "Everybody" does it and it's perfectly "normal."

- Sarai (and maybe Hagar) is willing to sacrifice for "the good" of all concerned.

There are many polygamous marriages recorded in Scripture, but none meet the standard set by God at creation. None are happy marriages. There are many out-of-wedlock affairs and pregnancies recorded in the Bible. Not one works out well. God may, in mercy, use the people involved to accomplish His plans, but the circumstances are

---

4. Basem El-Sharkaway, ed., 2010, *The Horizon: Studies in Egyptology in Honour of M. A. Nur El-Din*, Cairo: American University in Cairo Press, 14.

always more difficult than they might have been had the choice been to trust God and to stick with His standards.

God's design for those who bear His image is always good. Whenever those standards are violated—even when the social milieu in which we may find ourselves looks with disdain on those standards—those who through rationalization, indifference, or open rebellion break out of God's design will discover that serious consequences are the result. Adam "heeded the voice" of his wife (Genesis 3:17) and the result impacted all of mankind (Romans 5:12). Abram's action has impacted many nations (Arabs, Jews—and those who side with either of them) for nearly four millennia.

Several biblical principles should be recalled whenever "big" choices are considered.

> Behold, to obey is better than sacrifice, And to heed than the fat of rams. (1 Samuel 15:22)

> And let us not grow weary while doing good, for in due season we shall reap if we do not lose heart. (Galatians 6:9)

> Therefore, my beloved brethren, be steadfast, immovable, always abounding in the work of the Lord, knowing that your labor is not in vain in the Lord. (1 Corinthians 15:58)

> And we desire that each one of you show the same diligence to the full assurance of hope until the end, that you do not become sluggish, but imitate those who through faith and patience inherit the promises. (Hebrews 6:11-12)

> Therefore do not cast away your confidence, which has great reward. For you have need of endurance, so that after you have done the will of God, you may receive the promise. (Hebrews 10: 35-36)

God may test our patience as He works out His will through each of us, but God is never late or forgetful. Our time and our perspective are contained within the few years around our own existence and whatever knowledge we may have gained about history—but we are not omniscient and we do not "see" the plans of eternity as God does.

Yes, God has revealed much through His Word. We are instructed to "let the word of Christ dwell in [us] richly" (Colossians 3:16) and to do our best "to present [ourselves] approved to God, a worker who does not need to be ashamed, rightly dividing the word of truth" (2 Timothy 2:15).

The Inevitable Reaction

> So he went in to Hagar, and she conceived. And when she saw that she had conceived, her mistress became despised in her eyes. Then Sarai said to Abram, "My wrong be upon you! I gave my maid into your embrace; and when she saw that she had conceived, I became despised in her eyes. The LORD judge between you and me." So Abram said to Sarai, "Indeed your maid is in your hand; do to her as you please." And when Sarai dealt harshly with her, she fled from her presence. (Genesis 16:4-6)

Sarai's early shame at being barren turns to anger at both Hagar and Abram. Hagar's willing submission turns to rebellion against both Sarai and Abram. Abram throws up his hands at the problem and allows Sarai to compound the broken relationship with Hagar.

What an interesting (and inevitable) series of outcomes. Hagar rather quickly becomes pregnant and "despises" Sarai. That is, given the value placed on childbearing, Sarai becomes something of "less value" than Hagar. That snobby reaction on Hagar's part brought about harsh treatment from Sarai, which in turn made life intolerable for everybody!

Naturally, Sarai blames Abram. *He* was the one who got Hagar pregnant. Sarai had nothing to do with it! (Sounds somewhat foolish, doesn't it?) Abram delegates "justice" back to Sarai, abrogating his role as head of the family. Please remember what Abram had recently gone through. He had just participated in the stunning (and very memorable) covenant with the Creator. He had been given a detailed outline of the land that would eventually become the territory of his heir and had been told that centuries would be involved with the fulfillment of those promises. There was no excuse for this blunder. But bungle he did!

Sarai plunges into a "scorned woman" self-pity. The household must have been cringing every time duties brought them near the three main players. "But God, who is rich in mercy, because of His great love with which He loved us..." (Ephesians 2:4)—that little phrase "but God" appears over 50 times in Scripture, reminding us of the frequent display of God's longsuffering with us. In spite of their behavior, God still forgave and used them.

God's Grace to Hagar

Whatever may have been the emotionally clouded thinking that caused Sarai to mistreat Hagar, the end result was that Hagar fled the security of the home headquarters and ran into the uninhabited countryside. Apparently, this was early in the pregnancy. Abram was still at Hebron (south of Jerusalem and west of the Dead Sea). Hagar was found "on the way to Shur" (Genesis 16:7), somewhere back along the southwestern trek toward Egypt. The distance traveled is significant, perhaps as much as 75 miles; it would have taken Hagar several days to arrive at the spring where she was met by "the Angel of the LORD."

> Now the Angel of the LORD found her by a spring of water in the wilderness, by the spring on the way to Shur. And He said, "Hagar, Sarai's maid, where have you come from, and where are you going?" She said, "I am fleeing from the presence of my mistress Sarai." The Angel of the LORD said to her, "Return to your mistress, and submit yourself under her hand." (Genesis 16:7-9)

The use of the definite article in this passage ("*the* Angel of the

LORD") seems to imply that this personage may well have been the same pre-incarnate appearance of the Second Person of the Godhead. Obviously, He has been very active in the life of Abram and will continue to be directly involved for some time. The direction and encouragement that He gave to Hagar secured the legacy of Ishmael and extended the nations that came from Abram.

> Then the Angel of the LORD said to her, "I will multiply your descendants exceedingly, so that they shall not be counted for multitude." And the Angel of the LORD said to her: "Behold, you are with child, And you shall bear a son. You shall call his name Ishmael, Because the LORD has heard your affliction. He shall be a wild man; His hand shall be against every man, And every man's hand against him. And he shall dwell in the presence of all his brethren." (Genesis 16:10-12)

It is intriguing how this prophecy has been carried out over the centuries. All Islamic nations count their lineage from Ishmael and are the sworn enemy of Israel, and are also constantly at war within and among themselves. These many nations have prospered and faltered in cycles like no other ethnic group. But "God hears" (that's what Ishmael means) and has promised to bring all of these nations back to Him and the worship of the true Creator in the ages to come (Isaiah 19:25).

Hagar named the well Beer Lahai Roi: "The Well of Him Who Sees and Lives." That area became something of a northern border of the territory where she and Ishmael ultimately settled after their later banishment from the presence of Abraham.

New Names

The Bible narrative skips over 13 years as Genesis 17 begins. Abram is 86 when Ishmael is born (Genesis 16:16) and is 99 years old when the Lord appears personally to him for the fourth time since the initial commission to leave Ur of the Chaldees.

El Shaddai

> When Abram was ninety-nine years old, the LORD ap-
> peared to Abram and said to him, "I am Almighty God;
> walk before Me and be blameless. And I will make My
> covenant between Me and you, and will multiply you ex-
> ceedingly." (Genesis 17:1-2)

Genesis 17:1 is the first time the name *El Shaddai* appears in Scripture. This title is used some 48 times in the Old Testament, including
31 times in the book of Job. The term is composed of *el* (mighty one)
and *shadday* (almighty). Of the 48 times *shadday* appears, only seven
connect it directly to *El*, thus "God Almighty." In all but the passage
in Ezekiel 10:5, the compound title is used in connection with this
specific covenant with Abram and the promises to the descendants of
Israel—"those who have power with God."

Surely the reader is aware that God is first known as *Elohim* (the
plural form of *el* used in Genesis 1:1). *El* is used of angels, strong
men, and judges, and appears well over 200 times throughout the
Old Testament. *El Shaddai* compounds the two terms, with a focus on
"supply." The word *shadday* has two possible roots, according to several lexicons—*shad*, the Hebrew term for the "breasts" of females, or
shadad, the "spoils" or "plunder" of war. From those terms, the deriva-
tive *shadday* (and *shaddai*) is coupled with *el* to render "the strong one
who provides plunder." Hence comes the translation the "Almighty
God" or "God Almighty."

Abraham

> Then Abram fell on his face, and God talked with him,
> saying: "As for Me, behold, My covenant is with you, and
> you shall be a father of many nations. No longer shall
> your name be called Abram, but your name shall be
> Abraham; for I have made you a father of many nations."
> (Genesis 17:3-5)

The Hebrew word *ab* is used almost 1,200 times in the Old Testament and is the term for the "head," "chief," or "father" of everything from a family unit to the head of state. As discussed in chapter 1, Abram is probably a title rather than a proper name and has the general meaning of "exalted father." In this instance, *El Shaddai* ("the Powerful Plunderer"—"Almighty God") certifies that He has made Abram the *Ab-raham*, "father of multitudes."

The word choices of the Holy Spirit recorded in Scripture are never incidental. In this case, the source of this term is probably the Hebrew *rob*, or possibly *rabah*. Both express the concept of uncountable numbers. And to insure that His meaning was perfectly clear, *El Shaddai* translates the new title as *ab hamôn gôyim*—father of a multitude of nations.

Furthermore, God continues to clarify:

> "I will make you exceedingly fruitful; and I will make nations of you, and kings shall come from you. And I will establish My covenant between Me and you and your descendants after you in their generations, for an everlasting covenant, to be God to you and your descendants after you. Also I give to you and your descendants after you the land in which you are a stranger, all the land of Canaan, as an everlasting possession; and I will be their God." (Genesis 17:6-8)

Once again, the Great One who "plunders" (*El Shaddai*) emphasizes to this human father of many nations that the land of Canaan is to be an "everlasting possession" for the special seed that will come through Abraham. Recall the setting. Abram has now been in the territory of the Canaanites for nearly 24 years. He is still a stranger and does not officially own a single plot of ground. He is 99 years old and "as good as dead" (Hebrews 11:12) as far as the human potential to produce children.

Sarah

Then God said to Abraham, "As for Sarai your wife, you

shall not call her name Sarai, but Sarah shall be her name. And I will bless her and also give you a son by her; then I will bless her, and she shall be a mother of nations; kings of peoples shall be from her." Then Abraham fell on his face and laughed, and said in his heart, "Shall a child be born to a man who is one hundred years old? And shall Sarah, who is ninety years old, bear a child?" (Genesis 17:15-17)

After introducing the sign of circumcision (more on this to follow), the Originator of the covenant with Abram now commissions his wife the "queen." Not merely a princess, but a queen (noble lady) from whom will come future kings.

Abraham understands that this is humanly impossible and begins to roll in laughter. He understands that the time for childbearing is long gone for the two of them and cannot bring himself to grasp the miracle that God is promising. If Sarah were to become pregnant that very day, Abram would be 100 years old and Sarah 90 when such a promise could be fulfilled. Impossible!

Circumcision

God had just finished introducing the concept of physical circumcision, and no doubt Abraham found the whole idea unusual.

And God said to Abraham: "As for you, you shall keep My covenant, you and your descendants after you throughout their generations. This is My covenant which you shall keep, between Me and you and your descendants after you: Every male child among you shall be circumcised; and you shall be circumcised in the flesh of your foreskins, and it shall be a sign of the covenant between Me and you." (Genesis 17:9-11)

There is some evidence that circumcision was practiced in Egypt prior to the introduction of this rite to Abraham. Some inscriptions on temple walls and rituals mentioned in the Egyptian Book of the

Dead allude to the formal circumcision of young boys among the nobility of Egypt. However, the dating of these inscriptions and the various tomb analyses are by no means certain. Some scholars date the same references as far apart as 1,000 years. It is more likely that the Egyptian and Near Eastern practices stem from the event described in Genesis 17—just prior to the birth of Isaac and the circumcision of Abraham and Ishmael.

It is also obvious that while the physical surgery probably had positive medical consequences, the main reason that the Covenant God introduced this practice was to initiate a memorable sign that would signify the genetic descendants as belonging to the line of the promised Blessing who would come through Isaac.

> "He who is eight days old among you shall be circumcised, every male child in your generations, he who is born in your house or bought with money from any foreigner who is not your descendant. He who is born in your house and he who is bought with your money must be circumcised, and My covenant shall be in your flesh for an everlasting covenant. And the uncircumcised male child, who is not circumcised in the flesh of his foreskin, that person shall be cut off from his people; he has broken My covenant." (Genesis 17:12-14)

Although copied by many of the Abrahamic ethnic groups that would arise over the centuries and widely practiced by many of the Western nations of today's world, God intended this to be a private and physical, masculine and national reminder that a special line of descendants would be recognized in a unique covenant between the *El Shaddai* of creation and the promised heir.

From this point onward, every male child born into the household of the descendants of Isaac (who was not yet conceived) would be "marked" with the sign of this relationship. Although the instructions appear to be focused on the future male descendants, Abraham required that all of the male personnel of his entire household be circumcised—apparently that very day. The practice was continued through the families of Jacob and under the protection of Joseph and Pharaoh in Egypt, but it was discontinued after Joseph died and did not resume until Moses led the nation out of Egypt centuries later.

Circumcision does have several parallels to New Testament baptism (Colossians 2:11-12). Baptism is to be administered only once, as was circumcision. The New Testament ordinance is designed to identify the people of God, as was circumcision, and conveys a picture of covenant with God, as did circumcision. Baptism also requires the one baptized to be wholly passive (receives what another performs), as did circumcision. However, the New Testament picture shifts the analogy from the purely physical and genealogical lineage to the spiritual birth that embraces all who are the "heirs according to the promise" (Galatians 3:29). Therefore, the baptism of a twice-born child of God is now administered upon all redeemed individuals rather than just on males (Galatians 3:28).

Ishmael Remembered

> And Abraham said to God, "Oh, that Ishmael might live before You!" Then God said: "No, Sarah your wife shall bear you a son, and you shall call his name Isaac; I will establish My covenant with him for an everlasting covenant, and with his descendants after him. And as for Ishmael, I have heard you. Behold, I have blessed him, and will make him fruitful, and will multiply him exceedingly. He shall beget twelve princes, and I will make him a great nation." (Genesis 17:18-20)

Abraham genuinely loved Ishmael and was torn internally because of the conflict between his sons. Isaac later had much the same conflict between Jacob and Esau. Both sets of sons were demonstrations of the irresolvable gap because of the spiritual differences between "the son of the bondwoman" and "the son of the freewoman" (Galatians 4:30). Yet God does recognize the human pathos of a father's love for a son, and as the events of history are beginning to come to fruition with the conception of Isaac, God declares that He will bless Ishmael because God has heard Abraham's plea for him.

Ishmael is 13 years old when God brings this tight focus on Abraham and Sarah (Genesis 17:25). Another several years will pass before Ishmael and Hagar are finally banished from the household. Isaac is born and is weaned prior to their being cast out (Genesis 21:8). That would imply that Ishmael was probably in his late teens when God confirmed to Abraham that Ishmael and Hagar needed to go. Although submissive to God's orders regarding Ishmael, Abraham was seriously burdened and grieved by the necessity.

Ishmael Banished

> And Sarah saw the son of Hagar the Egyptian, whom she had borne to Abraham, scoffing. Therefore she said to Abraham, "Cast out this bondwoman and her son; for the son of this bondwoman shall not be heir with my son, namely with Isaac." And the matter was very displeasing in Abraham's sight because of his son.
>
> But God said to Abraham, "Do not let it be displeasing in your sight because of the lad or because of your bondwoman. Whatever Sarah has said to you, listen to her voice; for in Isaac your seed shall be called. Yet I will also make a nation of the son of the bondwoman, because he is your seed." (Genesis 21:9-13)

Abraham obeyed (as all of us should—no matter how harsh the circumstances may seem). Hagar and Ishmael were sent out from the family headquarters (located then at Gerar near the ocean), provisioned with minimal supplies, and began the trek in the Wilderness of Beersheba (Genesis 21:14). Hagar was probably trying to find her way back to the well where God had met her when she ran away while she was pregnant with Ishmael. That well, Beer Lahai Roi, would have been to the south and east of Gerar.

Somewhere along the way while they were wandering, the water and food ran out, and Hagar left Ishmael a "bowshot" away from her in the wilderness so that she would not have to watch him die (Genesis 21:15-16). Both Hagar and Ishmael began to cry out in their sorrow and desperation, thinking that their end had come. Please recall that both Hagar and Ishmael had heard the promises of God for life and blessing, but the awful plight of their banishment and the desolate countryside had driven all thoughts of rescue out of their minds.

Ishmael Blessed

God, of course, hears their cry and responds directly to Hagar, reiterating the promise that He made to her and to Abraham that Ishmael would live and become a great nation.

> And God heard the voice of the lad. Then the angel of God called to Hagar out of heaven, and said to her, "What ails you, Hagar? Fear not, for God has heard the voice of the lad where he is. Arise, lift up the lad and hold him with your hand, for I will make him a great nation." Then God opened her eyes, and she saw a well of water. And she went and filled the skin with water, and gave the lad a drink. (Genesis 21:17-19)

Ishmael lives another 115 years or more and is 137 years old when he dies (Genesis 25:17). Hagar finds a wife for Ishmael out of Egypt, and they all settle in the Wilderness of Paran (Genesis 21:21) in the Sinai Peninsula. Ishmael has 12 sons who become leaders of major tribes among the nations of the east (Genesis 25:13-16). Although the descendants of Ishmael figure prominently in the history of Israel throughout Scripture, they are always presented as nations to be avoided, if not actual enemies actively seeking the destruction of Israel.

Setting the Stage

Prior to Sarah becoming pregnant and the birth of Isaac, a period of nearly two years passes from the events recorded in Genesis 17. Abraham was 99 and Ishmael was 13 when they were circumcised

(Genesis 17:24-25). During the angelic visitation regarding the destruction of Sodom, Sarah was told that she would conceive (Genesis 18:11-14). The birth of Isaac took place after Abraham was 100 years old (Genesis 21:5), after they had moved their encampment to Gerar, had reprised the foolish "wife as sister" incident of Egypt with Abimelech, and had settled down in Beersheba (Genesis 21:33-34).

Right after the fourth appearance of the Lord to Abraham recorded in Genesis 17, while Abraham is still operating out of the plain of Mamre, three men suddenly appear in the camp. Abraham recognizes them as personages of power and authority (Genesis 18:1-2), and it is later revealed to Abraham that one of the three is none other than the Lord with whom he has had several sessions (Genesis 18:13-19). The other two were powerful angelic messengers sent to destroy Sodom and Gomorrah (Genesis 19:1)

Abraham hastens to invite the visitors to remain as his guests and issues orders to prepare a fine meal worthy of the status of these "men" (Genesis 18:3-8). After the meal was completed, these guests asked to see Sarah. Their use of the more formal "Sarah your wife" (v. 9) may well have been intentionally stated to drive home the tight focus of God's plant to produce "the heir" through Sarah and not Hagar. Enough trouble had already come from Abram's losing confidence in God's promise—and would still create tension in the years to come.

Sarah Laughs

> Then they said to him, "Where is Sarah your wife?" So he said, "Here, in the tent." And He said, "I will certainly return to you according to the time of life, and behold, Sarah your wife shall have a son."
>
> (Sarah was listening in the tent door which was behind him.) Now Abraham and Sarah were old, well advanced in age; and Sarah had passed the age of childbearing. Therefore Sarah laughed within herself, saying, "After I have grown old, shall I have pleasure, my lord being old also?"

And the Lord said to Abraham, "Why did Sarah laugh, saying, 'Shall I surely bear a child, since I am old?' Is anything too hard for the Lord? At the appointed time I will return to you, according to the time of life, and Sarah shall have a son."

But Sarah denied it, saying, "I did not laugh," for she was afraid. And He said, "No, but you did laugh!" (Genesis 18:9-15)

The confrontation with Sarah is filled with tension. By this time it is quite likely that Sarah is very familiar with the promise that God made to her husband and may well sense that these "men" whom Abraham is now entertaining are much more than mere strangers. Not only does Sarah know the repeated promise of an heir, but surely she is specifically aware of the recent detailed prophecy that she, Sarah herself, would become pregnant and be the mother of the promised heir (Genesis 17:15-21).

As the conversation develops during the meal, the Lord is aware that Sarah is listening behind the tent curtain. Whether Sarah's laughter is audible or not, the Lord specifically notes that she disdains His promise. He asks the rhetorical question "Is anything too hard for the Lord?" and immediately states His sovereign authority to all within earshot: "At the appointed time I will return to you, according to the time of life, and Sarah shall have a son."

Earlier, when Abraham had heard this miraculous promise, he had laughed at the thought that he and Sarah (who both knew they were unable to have children) would in some way be renewed or revived physically so that intimacy and conception would be made possible. The use of the Hebrew term *tsachaq* for Abraham stresses the involuntary bubble of pleasure at the thought. But in Sarah's case, the same term is used in a way that stresses some sort of "mocking" or "deriding" laughter. Notice how the translators convey that side of the word in other passages.

So Lot went out and spoke to his sons-in-law, who had

married his daughters, and said, "Get up, get out of this place; for the LORD will destroy this city!" But to his sons-in-law he seemed to be *joking*. (Genesis 19:14)

And Sarah saw the son of Hagar the Egyptian, whom she had borne to Abraham, *scoffing*. (Genesis 21:9)

Then she spoke to him with words like these, saying, "The Hebrew servant whom you brought to us came in to me to *mock* me." (Genesis 39:17)

That "mocking" inference seems to be borne out by the way the Lord responds to Sarah's laugh when He challenges her (Genesis 18:13-14). Sarah had reacted to the personalized announcement about her forthcoming pregnancy by essentially denying the ability of the Lord to perform the miracle—so she "mocked" (laughed at the thought). There is some possibility that this might even have involved some "acting out" among the ladies present. The text notes that she "laughed within herself." That is the translation of two Hebrew words, *tsachaq* and *qereb*. That latter word is often translated "among" (others).

Remember, Sarah is the "queen" among the large household of Abraham. She is listening from behind the tent wall that separated the men from the women. Sarah's station in the formal part of the "business" tent would have been very similar to a noble lady sitting amid her handmaids. There would have been other women present, listening as well to the conversation that was taking place out of sight but well within their hearing.

Whatever may have been the actual case at the time of the announcement by the Lord to Abraham, when Sarah was confronted by the Lord she strongly denied that she had "mocked," and was then rebuked by the Lord's clear and authoritative statement: "No, but you did laugh!" (Genesis 18:15). God does not lightly react to any who presume that He is not omnipotent.

Ah, Lord GOD! Behold, You have made the heavens and the earth by Your great power and outstretched arm.

There is nothing too hard for You. (Jeremiah 32:17)

God Informs

After the meal is completed and the interchange between God and Sarah is over, the men all get up to leave for their mission at Sodom. Abraham "went with them to send them on the way."

> And the LORD said, "Shall I hide from Abraham what I am doing, since Abraham shall surely become a great and mighty nation, and all the nations of the earth shall be blessed in him? For I have known him, in order that he may command his children and his household after him, that they keep the way of the LORD, to do righteousness and justice, that the LORD may bring to Abraham what He has spoken to him." (Genesis 18:17-19)

God's commentary on Abraham in this passage tells us much about the character of this great patriarch. Obviously, God has decided that Abraham will become a "great and mighty nation," but the insight into the sovereign choice is very important. God's foreknowledge is clear since God has "known him" (past, completed action). Peter alludes to this feature when he discusses how God "elects" those who will obey (1 Peter 1:2), even as Paul stresses the "predestination" God determines so that we will be "conformed to the image of His Son" (Romans 8:29).

The chain of God's reasoning is interesting. God selected Abraham—so that Abraham would teach his children to keep the commandments of God—so that they would do justice and righteousness—so that God could do for Abraham what He intended to do! And since that was so, God is now going to tell Abraham His immediate plans for the coming judgment on Sodom and Gomorrah.

> And the LORD said, "Because the outcry against Sodom and Gomorrah is great, and because their sin is very grave, I will go down now and see whether they have done altogether according to the outcry against it that has come to

Me; and if not, I will know." Then the men turned away from there and went toward Sodom, but Abraham still stood before the LORD. (Genesis 18:20-22)

Abraham Intercedes

This intercessory interchange between God and Abraham has been the classic passage from which further intercessory prayer has often been modeled.

> And Abraham came near and said, "Would You also destroy the righteous with the wicked? Suppose there were fifty righteous within the city; would You also destroy the place and not spare it for the fifty righteous that were in it? Far be it from You to do such a thing as this, to slay the righteous with the wicked, so that the righteous should be as the wicked; far be it from You! Shall not the Judge of all the earth do right?" (Genesis 18:23-25)

Please notice that Abraham approaches God with a sincere question that focuses on the integrity and reputation of God's name. Abraham is absolutely sure that God's judgment is sure and just, but he is concerned that the "fallout" from the event might well be misunderstood by the Canaanites in the area—and perhaps by the generations to come (the promised descendants). The motive on Abraham's part is not to *prevent* the judgment but to have it done in such a way that no possible misunderstanding can be attributed to God's character.

The city of Sodom and its sister city Gomorrah would have had a combined population of at least several hundred, if not thousands. For Abraham to ask for "fifty righteous" was a very small percentage of the numbers involved. Abraham was well aware that men of Sodom were "exceedingly wicked and sinful against the LORD" (Genesis 13:13).

> So the LORD said, "If I find in Sodom fifty righteous within the city, then I will spare all the place for their sakes." (Genesis 18:26)

Encouraged by the positive response from the Lord, Abraham continues to request greater depths of mercy, all the while maintaining a conscious bold humility toward his Creator. There is no hint in all that follows that Abraham is trying to "wheedle" the Lord away from His intended judgment or that Abraham is fearful of the slaughter. What seems to be implied in the drumbeat of sequential requests is a fear for Lot's family and for the awful consequences of the pending catastrophe.

> Then Abraham answered and said, "Indeed now, I who am but dust and ashes have taken it upon myself to speak to the Lord: Suppose there were five less than the fifty righteous; would You destroy all of the city for lack of five?"
>
> So He said, "If I find there forty-five, I will not destroy it." And he spoke to Him yet again and said, "Suppose there should be forty found there?" So He said, "I will not do it for the sake of forty." Then he said, "Let not the Lord be angry, and I will speak: Suppose thirty should be found there?" So He said, "I will not do it if I find thirty there."
>
> And he said, "Indeed now, I have taken it upon myself to speak to the Lord: Suppose twenty should be found there?" So He said, "I will not destroy it for the sake of twenty." Then he said, "Let not the Lord be angry, and I will speak but once more: Suppose ten should be found there?" And He said, "I will not destroy it for the sake of ten."
>
> So the LORD went His way as soon as He had finished speaking with Abraham; and Abraham returned to his place. (Genesis 18:27-33)

Sodom Disappears

Genesis 19 provides a detailed record of the terrible wickedness of Sodom, the desperate and pathetic picture of Lot's family, and the awful destruction of "all the plain, all the inhabitants of the cities, and what grew on the ground" (Genesis 19:25).

The location of Sodom and Gomorrah is still unknown. Several archaeological and geological efforts have been made to identify them, but the topography has changed enough—and the destruction by God was so thorough—that the specific location remains a mystery.

Much work was done in the 1970s and 1980s by biblical archaeologist Dr. Bryant Wood of Associates for Biblical Research and later by Dr. Steven Austin that corroborates the likely locations on the eastern side of the Dead Sea near the southern end. Much of that work depends on the location of the biblical city of Zoar (to which Lot and his daughters fled). The "five cities of the plain" mentioned in Genesis all seem to have left little trace—except the site of Zoar.[1]

Lot Loses

The tragic end of Lot and his family is truly a study in human pathos. Wealthy by any standards, Lot leads his family into Sodom and grows further and further away from Abraham, as well as deeper and deeper into a worldly environment that ultimately brings about the demise of several of his daughters and his wife. Slowly, over some 25 years, Lot chooses to enrich himself and ally his business with the cities of the plain. As his family grows, they become enmeshed in the lifestyle of Sodom particularly, so much so that when the angels come to rescue them the sons-in-law refuse to listen (Genesis 19:12-14).

Even after the disgusting episode with the homosexual men of Sodom at the door of his home—Lot was so far scarred by the godlessness of the city that he was willing to offer his unmarried daughters to the raucous and insatiable crowd (Genesis 19:4-11)—Lot still

---

1. Drs. Wood, Austin, and John Morris have all written extensively on this subject. More detail can be found in the following articles available on the Internet: Bryant Wood, 1999, The Discovery of the Sin Cities of Sodom and Gomorrah, *Bible and Spade,* 12 (3): 67-80; Steven Austin, 2010, Greatest Earthquakes of the Bible, *Acts & Facts,* 39 (10): 12-15; and John Morris, 2013, Have Sodom and Gomorrah Been Discovered?, *Acts & Facts,* 42 (4): 15.

begged the angels to let him stay in the area (that "little" city near Zoar) instead of following the instructions of God's messengers and fleeing away. Sad.

Lot's wife "looked back" rather than follow her husband out of the city (Genesis 19:26). That term, by the way, is a colloquial phrase that simply means that she turned around and went back toward Sodom—evidently unwilling to leave. She died in the conflagration that the Lord sent in judgment on that horrible city.

Their personal story ends with Lot's incest with his two daughters and the starting of two enemy nations, the Ammonites and Moabites (Genesis 19:30-38). Sinful choices have consequences—sometimes the ripples of those consequences bounce up against shores that could not be imagined by the choosers. Lot's choices negatively impacted thousands and lasted centuries.

Satan's Persistence

The Archenemy never rests. With Sodom and Gomorrah destroyed and Lot and his daughters driven away and disgraced, Abraham decides to move from Hebron to the city of Gerar, the capital city of the Philistines. Modern excavations at Gerar (today's Gaza) document a prosperous city that was probably the central trade route and business center on the road from Damascus to Egypt.

The Philistines were descendants of Ham's son Mizraim, who was the common "father" of both the Egyptians and Philistines (Genesis 10:6-14). The social structure of Gerar and the Philistines was very similar to that of Egypt—similar enough for Abraham to lapse into old fears. Abraham and Sarah are now "renewed" by God to bear Isaac. Sarah is 90 and Abraham 100. Sarah is beautiful—probably because of the miracle of her restoration to bear children. Abraham, who was "dead" physically, was able to father six more sons after Sarah's death—35 years later (Genesis 25:1-2)! God's miraculous healing is instantaneous and long-lasting!

The situation is essentially a duplicate of the incident in Egypt

25 years earlier (compare Genesis 12:10-20 and Genesis 20:1-18). Both Pharaoh and Abimelech are told the same half-truth. Abraham uses the same reasoning in Gerar as he did in Egypt (Genesis 12:10-13; 20:11). They repeat their sin even after the stinging rebuke from Egypt. Abraham did deeds that "ought not to be done" (Genesis 12:18-19; 20:9). Both Pharaoh and Abimelech take Sarah into their harems. Sarah could well have become pregnant by a pagan king. Abraham, by his fear, endangered (humanly speaking) the great promise of God to bless the whole earth. This was a terrible lapse of faith.

God sent Pharaoh plagues (Genesis 12:17) and Abimelech a terrifying dream (Genesis 20:3-7) to protect Sarah. Both Pharaoh and Abimelech are given instructions by God to return Sarah to Abraham. Pharaoh's public rebuke and public banishment should never have been forgotten (Genesis 12:18-20), and Abimelech's rebuke and warning were a humiliating shame (Genesis 20:9)

God's Sovereignty

God intervenes in both instances and prevents the human tragedy. Neither Pharaoh nor Abimelech were blamed by God, and both were used by Him to enrich and enable Abraham and Sarah for the future. God's sovereign will is always "in charge" of human affairs.

After having spent time in the details of Abraham's life thus far, it may be helpful to review the broader perspective of the eternal Creator as expressed by Paul and Barnabus to an unruly crowd in Lystra many centuries later.

> "We also are men with the same nature as you, and preach to you that you should turn from these useless things to the living God, who made the heaven, the earth, the sea, and all things that are in them, who in bygone generations allowed all nations to walk in their own ways. Nevertheless He did not leave Himself without witness, in that He did good, gave us rain from heaven and fruitful seasons, filling our hearts with food and gladness." (Acts 14:15-17)

Sometimes we get enmeshed in the stress of the moment and blinded by the swirling dust of the circumstances. When such pressures come (and they will and do), we tend to forget that we are told not to "fret because of evildoers, Nor be envious of the workers of iniquity (Psalm 37:1). Although one who is caught up in wickedness may well be "in great power" and spread himself out "like a native green tree, Yet he passed away, and behold, he was no more; Indeed I sought him, but he could not be found (Psalm 37:35-36).

God's mercy goes way beyond what we may expect. The "Lord is good to all, And His tender mercies are over all His works" (Psalm 145:9). Jesus said, "He makes His sun rise on the evil and on the good, and sends rain on the just and on the unjust" (Matthew 5:45). Abraham fought with the challenge of those two very different issues. On the one hand, he (like us) had been promised an eternal blessing, but he (like us) saw the apparent success of the wicked and attempted to solve the problem himself.

Perhaps the simplest lesson that we can learn from the biblical narrative as given to us thus far is "let us not grow weary while doing good, for in due season we shall reap if we do not lose heart" (Galatians 6:9).

CHAPTER FOUR
THE SON OF PROMISE

After the rebuke from Abimelech and the obvious intervention of God to protect Sarah during the time she was in the harem of the Philistine king, both she and Abraham returned to their headquarters near Gerar. Their flocks and herds had been relocated earlier from the foothills and valleys of the Hebron area to the fertile plains of the Mediterranean coastline somewhat south and east of Hebron.

It is not clear how long Sarah was taken from Abraham by Abimelech, but it was long enough for him and his household to recognize that "the LORD had closed up all the wombs of the house...because of Sarah" (Genesis 20:18). That would have been several months at least, enough time for Abraham and Sarah to realize the awful mistake they had made—again—and to begin to understand something of the absolute sovereign authority of the Creator God who had singled them out to accomplish a blessing for all the families of the earth.

Miracle Baby

And the LORD visited Sarah as He had said, and the LORD did for Sarah as He had spoken. For Sarah conceived and bore Abraham a son in his old age, at the set time of which God had spoken to him. And Abraham called the name of his son who was born to him—whom Sarah bore to him—Isaac. (Genesis 21:1-3)

The two little phrases "as He had said" and "as He had spoken" are the understated "I told you so's" of God for all the record. Thus far in the narrative, God has provided five distinct occasions wherein He delivered, reiterated, and amplified His promise to Abraham.

1. Genesis 12:1-3 was given as a general overview of the blessing.

2. Genesis 13:14-17 stressed ownership and expansion. Abraham was told to "look" and "see" the land—it is yours forever—and that his "seed" would be like the "dust of the earth," impossible to number.

3. Genesis 15:4-21 offered much more detail: The "heir" will come specifically from Abram's seed (v. 4); the "seed" will outnumber the stars (v. 5) and will be strangers in a strange land for 400 years (v. 13). Even in that forced exile, the nation that will enslave them will give them great riches (v. 14), and ultimately Abram's descendants will occupy a vast land (vv. 18-21)

4. Genesis 17:1-21 stressed the specificity of the blessing. Again, Abraham was told that he would father "many nations" (vv. 4-6) because God was establishing an "everlasting covenant" with him (vv. 7, 13). Then God specially insisted that Abraham and Sarah would bear Isaac (v. 21).

5. Genesis 18:10-14 provided the famous rhetorical question "Is anything too hard for the LORD?" and focused on the timing of the birth of Isaac.

If anything, one should wonder why God would have put up with the many years of doubt and wandering. There is no excuse. Abraham and Sarah know full well that God has been faithful, patient, and forgiving. The heir is born and the new line has begun.

Laughter

> Then Abraham circumcised his son Isaac when he was eight days old, as God had commanded him. Now Abraham was one hundred years old when his son Isaac was born to him. And Sarah said, "God has made me laugh, and all who hear will laugh with me." She also said, "Who would have said to Abraham that Sarah would nurse children? For I have borne him a son in his old age." (Genesis 21:4-7)

Abraham is 100 (Genesis 21:5) and Sarah is 90 (Genesis 17:17). Clearly, Abraham is carefully following the Lord's earlier instructions about circumcision (Genesis 17:10-12). The reader will recall that Abraham had previously circumcised his entire male household on one day not too many months past. Now, after the promised heir has been finally conceived and born, Abraham is vigilant to obey this most important of covenantal signs. This may have been especially poignant for him, having just gone through the episode with Abimelech. Isaac is the one promised over 25 years before when God first revealed to Abram that his seed would fulfill the promise. The promise is now in flesh, time, and real history. The fulfillment can begin.

But Sarah recalls the laugh they gave at the announcement. This passage is an interesting play on words and an important point of understanding for both Abraham and Sarah. Please recall that Abraham laughed when the Lord told him that he would have a son by Sarah in his old age (Genesis 17:17), and Sarah laughed when she heard the promise from the Lord to Abraham while she was behind the curtain in the tent (Genesis 18:12).

The Hebrew word translated "laugh" is *tsachaq* in the verb form. There is an earlier discussion of these events in the previous chapter of this book. The noun form is used twice, once here in Genesis 21:6 where Sarah references her laugh at the time of God's visit with Abraham just prior to the destruction of Sodom. The other reference is in Ezekiel 23:32, in which God uses a parable to describe the judgment that will come on Samaria (Israel) and Jerusalem (Judah) because of their wickedness: "Thus says the Lord GOD...You shall be laughed to *scorn* And held in derision."

The other 13 times the verb appears, the emphasis is much the same. Sarah "mocked" (Genesis 18:12) when she first heard that she would conceive and bear a child in her old age. Lot was "mocked" when he told his children about the coming destruction of Sodom (Genesis 19:14). Ishmael "mocked" Isaac (Genesis 21:9), and Isaac "played with" Rebecca (Genesis 26:8). Potiphar's wife accused Joseph of "mocking" her (Genesis 39:14, 17); Israel's people "played" around the golden calf (Exodus 32:6); Samson was "played with" before his death (Judges 16:25).

Isaac

The name given to this promised son was "he laughs" or "laughter." Sarah cites her laughter and her own surprise at bearing a child in her old age (Genesis 21:6-7). The play on words is very interesting. The Hebrew word is *yits-chaq*—appending the "jot" to *tsachaq*. The *yod* is the tenth letter of the Hebrew alphabet, the smallest letter and the "jot" mentioned by the Lord Jesus in Matthew 5:18. "Isaac" is the only translation for the 108 times that *Yitschaq* (the proper name) appears in the Scriptures. It might well be translated "he mocks me!" Or maybe "the joke is on us!"

Sarah, at least, attempts to use the name in a positive way. "God has made me laugh, and all who hear will laugh with me" (Genesis 21:6). But God was the one who named the promised heir Isaac (Genesis 17:19). Neither Abraham nor Sarah invented the name. The main purpose of the name seems to be that Abraham and Sarah are chastised for having "mocked" at the Lord when He promised them something impossible. Isaac will always remind them of their disbelief at the Lord's great promise and of God's absolute faithfulness and fulfillment.

Casting Out the Bondwoman

> So the child grew and was weaned. And Abraham made a great feast on the same day that Isaac was weaned. (Genesis 21:8)

Some years pass after the birth and circumcision of Isaac. The weaning of a child in the early days of history was much different from the modern Western practice. Modern families try to wean a child from the breast or the bottle as quickly as possible. There may be some sort of celebration (at least by the mother), but most Western ethnic groups do not throw a "great feast" as Abraham did.

However, the personal care by the mother or a wet nurse appears to have lasted much longer in the millennia prior to the Industrial Revolution in Europe. There is a passage in the apocryphal book of 2 Maccabees that sheds some light on the process: "My son, have pity upon me that carried thee nine months in my womb, and gave thee suck three years, and nourished and brought thee up unto this age" (2 Maccabees 7:27). Hannah, the mother of Samuel, kept her son with her until he was weaned before she brought him to Eli for service in the tabernacle (1 Samuel 1:23). Samuel was at least old enough to fend for himself and to follow the instructions of Eli when he was placed in the priest's care.

There is some indication in ancient Egyptian literature that children were kept (and nursed) by their mothers for the first three to five years. This seems to have been especially true for children of royalty or the upper nobility. Abraham, as well as many of the early ethnic groups of the Canaanites, may have copied the practices seen in Egypt, since the Egyptians were the epitome of civilization and were established as the greatest empire of that time. More than likely, a weaned child during that era would have been between two to four years old.

Hagar and Ishmael

Ishmael was 13 years old when he was circumcised (Genesis 17:25). Abraham was 86 when Ishmael was born (Genesis 16:16) and in his 100th year when Isaac was born (Genesis 21:5). That data would make Ishmael 14 years old at the birth of Isaac, and if the feast at Isaac's weaning was some three years after his birth then Ishmael would have been at least 17 or 18 years old when he and Hagar were banished from the family household at Gerar.

There is no record of how old Hagar may have been. She was acquired when Abraham and Sarah were in Egypt and may well have been much younger than Sarah (who was ten years younger than Abraham—Genesis 17:17). They had all been in Canaan for ten years when Hagar was given to Abraham as a "substitute" wife (Genesis 16:3). If Hagar had been in her mid-teens when she was given as a handmaid to Sarah, then Hagar would have been in her early 40s when she and her son were banished.

For example, perhaps Hagar was 15 when she left Egypt. Add ten years to when she was given to Abraham, plus 13 more years up to the time Ishmael was circumcised, another year or so before Isaac was born, then probably three years more until Isaac was weaned. 15 + 10 + 13 + 1 + 3 would make Hagar at least 42 years old. And she may well have been in her 50s or 60s since Sarah was much older than she.

As already mentioned, Sarah was ten years younger than Abraham. Therefore, she would have been 65 years old when they left Haran for Canaan (Genesis 12:4). The travel time from Haran to Canaan might have taken a year, and they moved from place to place in Canaan before they went to Egypt because of the famine. Although Sarah would have been seen as a princess in Egypt as the wife of a very wealthy and notable man, being gifted with a young handmaid some 50 years her junior might have been unusual. It is at least probable that Hagar was well into her 50s at the time she left.

Banishment

> And Sarah saw the son of Hagar the Egyptian, whom she had borne to Abraham, scoffing. Therefore she said to Abraham, "Cast out this bondwoman and her son; for the son of this bondwoman shall not be heir with my

son, namely with Isaac." And the matter was very displeasing in Abraham's sight because of his son. But God said to Abraham, "Do not let it be displeasing in your sight because of the lad or because of your bondwoman. Whatever Sarah has said to you, listen to her voice; for in Isaac your seed shall be called. Yet I will also make a nation of the son of the bondwoman, because he is your seed." (Genesis 21:9-12)

As indicated, Ishmael was a strapping teenager when this took place. For all of his life before Isaac's birth, he had been the prince among Abraham's people. Hagar, although technically a servant, was the "second wife" and would have been treated with respect and dignity. Yes, Sarah had tried to banish her many years earlier, but God had intervened and brought Hagar and Ishmael back with the promise that Ishmael would become a great man (Genesis 16:9-10).

For over a decade, Hagar and Ishmael had lived as luxurious a life as could be had in the developing world, with food and clothing provided without any forethought and domestic help available. Hagar would have enjoyed the personal attention of Abraham as the mother of his only son up to that point and would have no doubt been protected somewhat from the jealousy of Sarah. Ishmael had the attention and pleasure of Abraham (if not Sarah) and would have been used to the pampered treatment of the potential heir. Surely both of them would have known of the prophecy about the "promise," but their favored status had continued for so long that no doubt they would have expected things to continue as they had always been.

Until Isaac was born.

Then everything changed. Sarai was now Sarah. Abram was now Abraham. The miracle baby was beautiful, strong, and healthy. Hagar no longer had the favored position. Ishmael had fallen from his anticipated role as heir and was nothing more than a handmaid's son. Servants no longer responded instantly to their beck and call. Sarah became aloof and unresponsive. Abraham remained courteous and gracious, but was obviously focused on Sarah and Isaac.

Perhaps it was during the great feast of the weaning of Isaac that Ishmael could no longer hold his tongue and "mocked" Sarah and Isaac (Genesis 21:9). It is not clear, of course, just what Ishmael said or did, but the context would indicate that it was both public and rude. You may recall that God had told Hagar earlier that Ishmael would be a "wild man," using the term for a wild donkey (Genesis 16:12). The implication was that Ishmael would be both independent and impulsive, and even though slated to become the leader of a great nation, he would be hard to control.

Whatever wild character had been bottled up in Ishmael until then burst out in a torrent of foolish rage and disdain. Everyone either saw the tantrum or knew about it, and Sarah reacted swiftly. "Cast out this bondwoman and her son," she orders, "for the son of this bondwoman shall not be heir with my son." This was not a request as it was when Hagar first became pregnant (Genesis 16:5). Sarah was exercising her ownership over Hagar and demanding that this "bondwoman" and "her son" be banished (notice there are no names used, just terms—objects to be disposed of).

Judgment Rendered

Abraham is grieved by this. He did care for Ishmael and no doubt felt pity for Hagar, but God gives His approval of the judgment and insists that the banishment be carried out. It is interesting to note that the Scripture uses the name *Elohim* rather than *Yahweh* or *El Shaddai* when God renders approval of the judgment.

Elohim, of course, is the plural noun used to identify the Creator in the opening verse of Scripture. In a good portion of the 2,600-plus times that this term appears in the Bible, it is used both as a general description of the triune Godhead and as a term of judgment and authority over the affairs of men. *Yahweh*, on the other hand, so often translated by the capitalized term Lord in the Old Testament, seems to connect most directly to the sovereign focus of God on the behalf of His plans for eternity. *El Shaddai* seems to be used to identify the action that God takes to execute those plans. God told Moses:

> "I appeared to Abraham, to Isaac, and to Jacob, as God Almighty, but by My name Lord I was not known to them." (Exodus 6:3)

Sarah speaks the sentence of banishment, and although humanly harsh, God approves. Hagar and Ishmael then become the physical and historical "type" of the distinction between the "flesh" and the "heir" for all future generations of God's people to grasp. God will exercise His mercy on all humanity (He is the Creator, after all), but only those who are the "heirs" will reap His eternal blessings.

Paran

Hagar and Ishmael are sent away with only meager supplies of some food and a bottle of water. As Hagar and her son wander in the Wilderness of Beersheba (Genesis 21:14), she and the boy soon run out of supplies and give in to the overwhelming grief and fear of being abandoned in the middle of an uninhabited land.

> And the water in the skin was used up, and she placed the boy under one of the shrubs. Then she went and sat down across from him at a distance of about a bowshot; for she said to herself, "Let me not see the death of the boy." So she sat opposite him, and lifted her voice and wept. (Genesis 21:15-16)

But God is watching over them and responds to their plea, assisting Hagar to locate the well of water nearby (probably the same well of Beer Lahai Roi she had found years earlier—Genesis 16:14). They survive, and Ishmael matures and is given a wife from Egypt (Genesis 21:20-21).

Even though the banishment was permanent and neither Hagar nor Ishmael ever regained a relationship with the people through whom God would develop His great promised deliverance, God's mercy is extended to all humanity: "For He makes His sun rise on the evil and on the good, and sends rain on the just and on the unjust" (Matthew 5:45). And in this particular case, God grants a special blessing on Ishmael because he is Abraham's son (Genesis 21:13).

That blessing will produce a great nation, according to the promise in Genesis 21:18, and after Hagar and Ishmael settled in the Wilderness of Paran, Ishmael's descendants developed into 12 nations (Genesis 25:12-18) that are included in the Arabic nations today.

Biblical Emphasis

The New Testament makes a significant application of the historical events documented in the lives of Abraham, Sarah, Isaac, Hagar, and Ishmael. Obviously, Abraham has been identified as the father of the new nation of Israel, as well as the prototype of a believer. Isaac is the "son of promise" and will be used in the most poignant way possible to demonstrate the sacrifice of the coming Lord Jesus.

Hagar and Ishmael become the clear illustration of the distinction between those who belong to the God of heaven and those who do not. Their human lives and experiences are a historical drama played out in real time that identifies the irreversible separation that takes place when one is cast out from the family of God and banished into the "wilderness" for the remainder of their existence.

Focus on "the" Seed

As was identified earlier in chapter 1, the promises of God to Abraham were focused very specifically *through* Abraham *toward* a blessing that would impact "all the families of the earth." Yes, there would be an immediate fulfillment in an heir and "many nations" would develop from Abraham's descendants, but the emphasis is clearly focused on one particular "seed."

> Now to Abraham and his Seed were the promises made.
> He does not say, "And to seeds," as of many, but as of one,
> "And to your Seed," who is Christ. (Galatians 3:16)

The sequence of applications that the apostle Paul uses in Galatians 3:16-29 is very clear and inescapable.

- The promise is made to Abraham but is intended to apply to the Messiah (v. 16).

- The legal system instituted at Mount Sinai did not replace that promise or annul it (v. 17).

- The inheritance came because of the promise, not because of the law (v. 18).

- The law only serves as a mediator until "the seed" arrives in history (vv. 19-20).

- The law cannot remove sin; it only "teaches" the need for the promise (vv. 21-23).

- The arrival of the promise—and faith in that promise—removes the need for the "tutor" (vv. 24-25).

- The "promise" (the Seed) produces the true familial relationship with Christ (vv. 26-27).

- The relationship with Christ relates us to Abraham as "heirs" of the promise (vv. 28-29).

Focus on the Inheritance

Becoming a "seed of Abraham" brings us into a relationship with "the Seed," which produces a guarantee of an inheritance with the Seed who is the Heir. That relationship and subsequent right to share in the inheritance are part of the promise.

> The Spirit Himself bears witness with our spirit that we are children of God, and if children, then heirs—heirs of God and joint heirs with Christ, if indeed we suffer with Him, that we may also be glorified together. (Romans 8:16-17)

When God reiterated the promise to Abraham, you may recall God performed a rather striking covenantal ceremony to seal both His oath and His promise for the ages to come (Genesis 15:7-18). Abraham then endured years of hope until the promised heir came in the person of his son Isaac. We who now believe the promise that was ultimately revealed and fulfilled in the Lord Jesus Christ have that same hope as an "anchor of the soul, both sure and steadfast" (Hebrews 6:19) that is "incorruptible" and "reserved" for us in heaven—all the while kept by the same sovereign power that protected and preserved Abraham (1 Peter 1:3-5).

Focus on the Bondwoman and Her Son

The distinction between the heir and the son of the bondwoman is an important concept in Scripture. Its application is succinct and eternal. All mankind receives something of the grace of the Creator. But only those who are *not* of the bondwoman receive the inheritance. Once again, the apostle Paul's tight reasoning clarifies this in Galatians 4:22-31.

- The two sons of Abraham are symbolic. The son of the bondwoman is produced by the flesh. The son of the free-woman is by promise (vv. 22-23).

- The son of the bondwoman equates to the law of Mount Sinai and earthly Jerusalem (vv. 24-25).

- The son of promise equates to heavenly Jerusalem and is free (v. 26).

- The twice-born are like Isaac, children of the promise (v. 28).

- The twice-born will be persecuted by those of the flesh (v. 29).

- Those of the flesh will not participate in the inheritance (vv. 30-31).

All of history continues to verify these conditions that were developed during the life of Abraham. All of eternity will adhere to the symbolic relationship demonstrated by the distinctions exhibited in the lives of Isaac and Ishmael.

Life Among the Philistines

After Hagar and Ishmael are sent away, Abraham enters into a covenant with the rulers of the Philistine peoples on the Mediterranean coastline of Canaan. The Philistines were descendants of Pathrusim and Casluhim, who were descendants of Noah's son Ham. Their older "relatives" would have included Nimrod, who was the leader of the revolt at Babel, and Mizraim, from whom the Egyptians were descended.

Moses mentions that the just-released people of the exodus from Egypt initially considered traveling a route along the seacoast known as "the way of the land of the Philistines" (Exodus 13:17). God instructed the Israelites to turn south away from that route because the Philistines were warlike and might attack the new nation. Later, the Philistines became the long-term enemies of the growing nation of Israel during the conquest of Canaan and the time of the Judges, a situation that lingered well into the time of Kings Saul and David. They occupied five major cities during the era of the conquest of Canaan under Joshua: Gaza, Ashkelon, Ashdod, Gath, and Ekron.

Not much is known of the Philistines at the time of Abraham. They were apparently sufficiently settled to have a king (Abimelech) and a war captain (Phichol). Some historians suggest that the earliest descendants of Pathrusim and Casluhim had settled on the island of Crete after their disbursement from Babel. If so, that would give credence to the warlike and seafaring reputation of the later Philistines who became the incessant enemies of Israel. Artifacts from the area bear out the biblical reference that the Philistines had mastered the use of iron for their weapons and farming tools (1 Samuel 13:19-21).

The Oath of Beersheba

Abraham has made a semi-permanent camp near Gerar, one of the largest cities in southern Canaan, covering some 40 acres inland from the coast and near to where modern Gaza is located. No doubt there has been some commerce between Abraham and the Philistine people, so Abraham negotiates an "oath" with Abimelech and Phichol that serves as a model for peaceful association between the disparate cultures.

> And it came to pass at that time that Abimelech and Phichol, the commander of his army, spoke to Abraham, saying, "God is with you in all that you do. Now therefore, swear to me by God that you will not deal falsely with me, with my offspring, or with my posterity; but that according to the kindness that I have done to you, you will do to me and to the land in which you have dwelt." And Abraham said, "I will swear." (Genesis 21:22-24)

This is a promise to live faithfully among the pagans and for each group to treat each other kindly. It may well be the first recorded instance of the so-called Golden Rule (Luke 6:31).

Genesis 21:28-34 records a more formal second "oath" that is executed regarding Abraham's residence. A dispute had arisen between the herdsmen of Abraham and those of the Philistines over a well that had been dug by Abraham's men. Rather than leave that dispute in doubt, Abraham did what should be done by anyone seeking a peaceful co-existence—he brought up the matter with the Philistine leadership and a settlement was made that secured the water rights for Abraham. That formal agreement led Abraham to call the place "Beersheba"—the "well of the sevens."

Obviously, the name Beersheba appears in the text prior to this event. When Moses is compiling the book of Genesis, he uses the name that has been in use for several hundred years, referring to the geographical location that had been a center of activity for several decades before it was formally named at the event of the oath by Abraham and Abimelech. This is where Abraham and Isaac dwell in the land of the Philistines for decades (Genesis 21:34).

The Sacrifice of the Beloved

The Bible cites this incident as a clear picture of what the Lord

Jesus would be required to do when He came later as the Messiah who would take away the sins of the world (Hebrews 11:17-19). Obviously, in the allegory played out in real time by the lives of Abraham and Isaac, Abraham represents the heavenly Father and Isaac the "beloved Son," the Lord Jesus.

The age of Isaac at the time of this event is difficult to determine. Abraham is 100 (Genesis 21:5) and Sarah 90 (Genesis 17:17) at the birth of Isaac. The next specific date recorded is the death of Sarah when she is 127 years old (Genesis 23:1). That would make Isaac at least 35 years old at his mother's death. The "many days" that Abraham and Isaac live at Beersheba are indeterminate (Genesis 21:34), as is the "after these things" referenced as the narrative begins in Genesis 22. Both citations would indicate that a considerable time has elapsed between the birth of Isaac and the incident at Mount Moriah.

Isaac is called a "lad" in Genesis 22:5, but the Hebrew word is the same for the young men (vv. 3, 5) who went with them. Isaac is big enough to carry the wood (v. 6) and intelligent enough to question the event (v. 7). Surely Isaac would have been a young man in his late teens or early twenties—and there is nothing in the biblical record that would prevent us understanding Isaac to be near the age of the Lord Jesus when He was crucified. Isaac was not married until after the death of his mother (Genesis 24), when he was 35 or more. Given the use of this incident as a biblical figure to help underscore the pathos of the sacrifice of our Lord Jesus, it is certainly possible that Isaac was into his thirties when this event occurred.

Isaac's Obedience

Isaac's obedience foreshadows a picture of Christ. Often the work of the Lord Jesus is couched in terms that would seem to indicate that Jesus was sacrificing Himself. Actually, it is God the Father who is sacrificing the Lord Jesus. Jesus submits Himself, as did Isaac, but the execution—the actual act of sacrifice—was done by God the Father on His beloved Son (Isaiah 53:10). Yes, the Lord Jesus willingly laid down His life for us, but the judgment was both required and executed by the Father on His son (John 3:16-17).

Please notice the language of *Elohim's* direct order to Abraham.

> Now it came to pass after these things that God tested
> Abraham, and said to him, "Abraham!" And he said,
> "Here I am." Then He said, "Take now your son, your
> only son Isaac, whom you love, and go to the land of
> Moriah, and offer him there as a burnt offering on one of
> the mountains of which I shall tell you." (Genesis 22:1-2)

Isaac is the "only" son, the "beloved" son. The words are precise
and repetitive, penetrating deeply into the heart of Abraham. It should
be obvious to any observer that the God of creation has issued an order that seems to contradict all of the promises and hopes that have
motivated Abraham for several decades. In the same way, the Bible
makes it absolutely clear that Jesus of Nazareth is the "beloved Son,"
the "only begotten of the Father," the "promised" one who would
bless "all the families of the earth."

The biblical parallel is sharp and clear. It gives us some insight into
the infinite, wrenching pain that must have seared the heart of the triune Godhead when the Second Person of the Trinity was "slain from
the foundation of the world" (Revelation 13:8). Our human hearts
can empathize with Abraham—and with Isaac—but we will never
know what the eternal Godhead endured for us and on our behalf.

> All we like sheep have gone astray; We have turned, every
> one, to his own way; And the LORD has laid on Him the
> iniquity of us all. He was oppressed and He was afflicted,
> Yet He opened not His mouth; He was led as a lamb to
> the slaughter, And as a sheep before its shearers is silent,
> So He opened not His mouth. (Isaiah 53:6-7)

Just so, even though Isaac became fully cognizant of what was
happening, he did not resist or refuse to obey. Isaac may not have been
aware of the precise command from *Elohim* to Abraham, but he surely
knew what was going to happen by the time that Abraham bound
him and placed him on the altar. Isaac was fully grown and certainly

capable of physically overpowering his aging father. Yet in all of that, "he opened not" his mouth to utter one word of protest.

Isaac is silent in his obedience, just as was the Lord Jesus, and voluntarily lays down his life. The transactions are eerily similar. Abraham laying his beloved son on the altar as he passively submits. God the heavenly Father, watching His beloved Son fulfilling all that He had been commissioned to do—even though the Lord Jesus had the power to prevent the awful action from taking place. In both cases, the father must execute. In both cases, the son must submit. In both cases, the purpose for the sacrifice was hidden from those who watched—and for whom the sacrifice was being made.

> Then they came to the place of which God had told him. And Abraham built an altar there and placed the wood in order; and he bound Isaac his son and laid him on the altar, upon the wood. (Genesis 22:9)

> "Therefore My Father loves Me, because I lay down My life that I may take it again. No one takes it from Me, but I lay it down of Myself. I have power to lay it down, and I have power to take it again. This command I have received from My Father." (John 10:17-18)

The Lord Provides the Sacrifice

The human pathos of this incident is so poignant that every little word seems chosen for maximum impact. Isaac and his aging father have traveled three days with some servants to the very foot of Mount Moriah. It is not clear in this brief section how important Mount Moriah will become, but centuries later it would be the site of the great temple of Solomon (2 Chronicles 3:1). Evidently, in the sovereign foreknowledge of God, this place of the initial sacrifice of Isaac would become the place where the ongoing sacrifices of the nation of Israel would be offered in a foreshadowing of the ultimate Lamb of God who would fulfill all of the promises couched in God's words to Abraham—and even to Adam and Eve long ago.

They had arrived. Abraham asks the servants to remain on the plain and wait for their return. Isaac accepts the "wood for the sacrifice" on his back. (Remember, Jesus carried His cross.) And the two of them, alone, walked the last miles to the foot of the mountain and up the side of the hill to a small plateau where Abraham would build an altar to sacrifice his son. On the way, Isaac asked the most obvious question: "Where is the sacrificial lamb?"

> But Isaac spoke to Abraham his father and said, "My father!" And he said, "Here I am, my son." Then he said, "Look, the fire and the wood, but where is the lamb for a burnt offering?" And Abraham said, "My son, God will provide for Himself the lamb for a burnt offering." So the two of them went together. (Genesis 22:7-8)

Flash forward to the dark hours in the garden of Gethsemane. Jesus is fully aware of the task before Him, but in those final moments before the deeds are perpetrated, He groans out the question: "O My Father, if it is possible, let this cup pass from Me; nevertheless, not as I will, but as You will" (Matthew 26:39). The ignorance of Isaac, slowly washing away like some mist before his eyes as he walks up the side of Mount Moriah, is nothing like the conscious agony of the Lord Jesus as He prays in the garden. Isaac was willingly obedient (as was the Lord Jesus) but was still somewhat mystified by the unknown. Our Messiah, the Lamb of God, was fully aware of the coming awful physical death and spiritual separation from the holiness of the "glory which [He] had with You before the world was" (John 17:5).

Isaac would have known about the sacrifice of lambs to *Elohim* the Creator. He could expect a quick and somewhat painless death as his jugular was cut and his life blood gushed out. Yes, Isaac was willing to die. Yes, he was gentle and obedient. Yes, this was an immensely selfless act that bears honor for eternity. Yet the sacrifice was connected with a worship of the Creator and had a connection to the very act of the Creator on the behalf of Adam and Eve. In some ways, the sacrifice that Isaac was submitting himself to would have been a noble act.

But Jesus knew what crucifixion meant. That death was as horrible a torture as could be publicly devised. It was the death of the most awful criminals and social deviants. It had no honor connected with it. It was not religious in any sense—crucifixion was reserved for the most evil of society. He would most likely not die quickly; most crucified criminals lingered for several days in awful pain and agony. It was designed as a spectacle of horror that would act as a deterrent for others. There was nothing noble about crucifixion!

Yet that horrible death was not what brought agony to the soul of our holy Lord Jesus. He was the sinless Son of God. He had no guilt. What He was facing was some form of judgment that compensated for the entire guilt of the whole world, past, present, and future. He knew, as no other being could possibly know, what separation from the triune Godhead meant. He knew what judgment awaited those who embraced sin and rebelled against the Creator. He knew what will take place

> ...when the Lord Jesus is revealed from heaven with His mighty angels, in flaming fire taking vengeance on those who do not know God, and on those who do not obey the gospel of our Lord Jesus Christ. These shall be punished with everlasting destruction from the presence of the Lord and from the glory of His power. (2 Thessalonians 1:7-9)

No wonder in His prayer of agony in the garden of Gethsemane that "His sweat became like great drops of blood falling down to the ground" (Luke 22:44). No wonder He cried out on the cross, "My God, My God, why have You forsaken Me?" (Matthew 27:46). The sacrifice of the Lord Jesus for your sin and for mine was far more than the allegorical event that Isaac and Abraham willingly endured for a few moments so long ago. They helped paint a picture that would instruct many of what was yet to be. Jesus accomplished what only God could do on behalf of His creation. "He Himself is the propitiation for our sins, and not for ours only but also for the whole world" (1 John 2:2).

The Promise Confirmed

Back on the mountain, Abraham has built the altar, laid the wood that Isaac had carried, bound Isaac and placed him on top of the wood, set the fire pot down by the side of the altar, and raised the sacrificial knife to make the mortal cut. Both Isaac and Abraham are as physically and mentally committed as they can be prior to the actual swipe of the knife.

> But the Angel of the LORD called to him from heaven and said, "Abraham, Abraham!" So he said, "Here I am." And He said, "Do not lay your hand on the lad, or do anything to him; for now I know that you fear God, since you have not withheld your son, your only son, from Me." Then Abraham lifted his eyes and looked, and there behind him was a ram caught in a thicket by its horns. So Abraham went and took the ram, and offered it up for a burnt offering instead of his son. And Abraham called the name of the place, The-LORD-Will-Provide; as it is said to this day, "In the Mount of the LORD it shall be provided." (Genesis 22:11-14)

Jehovahjireh—The LORD Will Provide. This is the only place in the Bible where this compound Hebrew term is used as a form of *Jah* or *Yahweh* and the Hebrew word *ra'ah*. That word is used most often to convey the act of "seeing" something. *Ra'ah* is used twice in the above verses: "Then Abraham lifted his eyes and *looked*....as it is said to this day, 'In the Mount of The LORD it shall be *provided*.'"

As in all of the previous testing, the Lord not only provides a way out of the perceived problem, but strengthens Abraham for the remaining years. And as had always been the case, the Lord also reiterates and amplifies the great promise of blessing and prosperity.

> Then the Angel of the LORD called to Abraham a second time out of heaven, and said: "By Myself I have sworn, says the LORD, because you have done this thing, and have not withheld your son, your only son—blessing I

will bless you, and multiplying I will multiply your descendants as the stars of the heaven and as the sand which is on the seashore; and your descendants shall possess the gate of their enemies. In your seed all the nations of the earth shall be blessed, because you have obeyed My voice." (Genesis 22:15-18)

The Cave at Machpelah

Abraham returns to his permanent headquarters established at Beersheba, the well of the seven oaths. Sarah is living in Hebron some distance to the southeast when she dies at age 127 (Genesis 23:1-2). After Abraham and Isaac have mourned for Sarah, Abraham enters into negotiations for a piece of property that can be a permanent place of memory for his family to inter their honored dead.

> Then Abraham stood up from before his dead, and spoke to the sons of Heth, saying, "I am a foreigner and a visitor among you. Give me property for a burial place among you, that I may bury my dead out of my sight." (Genesis 23:3-4)

Heth is a descendant of Ham through Ham's son Canaan. The sons of Heth were the cousins listed in the lineage of Canaan recorded in Genesis 10:

> ...the Jebusite, the Amorite, and the Girgashite; the Hivite, the Arkite, and the Sinite; the Arvadite, the Zemarite, and the Hamathite. (Genesis 10:16-18)

Negotiations with Ephron the Hittite

One of the rising families was the Hittites. Ephron was apparently a major business person among the Hittites and would have had commerce with Abraham during the decades he had lived in the area. Following the social protocol of the culture, Abraham addresses the greater heads of the family, the sons of Heth, and acknowledges that he is a foreigner living by their leave in their territory.

The Hittites became a major nation in history and would ulti-mately become a part of the inheritance for Abraham's descendants (Genesis 15:20). Many Hittites are mentioned in Scripture over the course of Israel's dealings with them. Esau married Hittites (Genesis 26:34; 36:2), much to the dismay of Isaac and Rebekah. God insisted that the Hittites were to be destroyed by Israel when they took their territory under the leadership of Joshua (Deuteronomy 20:17).

Unfortunately, Israel did not complete that task, and the Hittites intermarried with Israel to the extent that Uriah the Hittite became one of David's "mighty men" (2 Samuel 23:39). You will recall that Bathsheba was Uriah's wife and so tempted King David that he had Uriah murdered to cover up his adultery with her. Solomon, David and Bathsheba's son, did not learn the lesson and was led into idolatry by his Hittite wives (1 Kings 11:1).

The Hittites were not the friends of Israel. They did, however, agree to sell Abraham a burial place for Sarah and subsequent family members. After the customary back and forth of business pleasantries, Ephron the Hittite agreed to sell Abraham the cave at Machpelah and the surrounding property for "four hundred shekels of silver" (Genesis 22:15).

The purchase included the field, the cave, the trees in the field, and the trees on the borders. Most archaeologists agree that an ancient silver shekel would have contained approximately 180 grains of silver. There are 480 grains of silver in one troy ounce. Thus, 400 shekels would have had approximately 72,000 grains of silver, or about 150 troy ounces. The worth of silver fluctuates a good bit in today's mar-ket, but in late 2012 it was around $23 per ounce. If we can extrapo-late that back to a similar value in Abraham's day, he would have paid about $3,450 for the property.

Where Are We?

This might be a good time to figure out where we are in the dating of the narrative. Most archaeologists and biblical scholars agree that Abraham was born around 2165 B.C. Genesis 11:10-26 gives the precise dates for how we may calculate the time of the birth of Abraham.

Shem (Noah's son) gave birth to Arphaxad two years after the Flood. Arphaxad had his son Salah 35 years after that. Salah had his son Eber after 30 more years, and Peleg was born to Eber when Eber was 34. Peleg was 30 when his son Reu was born, and Reu's son Serug was born 32 years later. Serug begot his son Nahor when Serug was 30 years old, and Nahor fathered Terah when he was 29. Terah had Abram when he was 70.

Add them up and you get 292 years after the Flood when Abraham was born.

Abraham was 100 when Isaac was born; Sarah died 35 years later—that means 427 years elapsed from the time of the Flood until the death of Sarah.

If we apply the same addition to the recorded dates of the key births from Adam to Noah, we arrive at 1,656 years that elapsed from Adam to the beginning of the Flood. Add 427 years to 1,656 years and the death of Sarah takes place 2,083 years after creation.

Using the widely accepted secular date of 2165 B.C. as the date for the birth of Abraham, we can place the death of Sarah at ~2030 B.C. (2165 B.C. minus 100 for Abraham at the birth of Isaac and minus 35 more for the death of Sarah = 2030 B.C.)

Now if we use those dates—which are the only dates that have specific records to them—and the agreed-upon date of the birth of Abraham, the creation event would have taken place not much more than 6,000 years ago. Sarah died 2,083 years after creation—which was roughly 2030 B.C., according to our calendar. Therefore, add 2,083 and 2,030 to 2014 A.D. and the sum is 6,127.

Not that long ago! Certainly not millions or billions of years.

CHAPTER FIVE
FINDING REBEKAH

Genesis 24 opens with "Abraham was old, well advanced in age." Sarah has died and was buried in the cave at Machpelah. Isaac is nearing 40 years old (Genesis 25:20), and although Abraham will live for some time yet, he is concerned that the heir of his household is not yet married.

> So Abraham said to the oldest servant of his house, who ruled over all that he had, "Please, put your hand under my thigh, and I will make you swear by the LORD, the God of heaven and the God of the earth, that you will not take a wife for my son from the daughters of the Canaanites, among whom I dwell; but you shall go to my country and to my family, and take a wife for my son Isaac." (Genesis 24:2-4)

Abraham commissions his chief servant to go to Mesopotamia and locate a suitable wife for the heir to the great responsibilities that God has appointed Abraham to initiate. There is little to guide us about the unusual vow that Abraham requires of his servant, but there is no doubt that all involved understood the matter to be of the utmost importance.

This wife must not be someone from the long lines of Canaanite royalty. (There were many of those among whom Abraham lived.) It is likely that Abraham was aware of God's rebuke of Lot's family at Sodom, and he certainly would have been aware of the history of God's protection of Noah (from the family of Adam's son Seth). And no doubt Abraham would have been mindful of his own lineage as a direct descendant of Noah's son Shem. The way God used to impress Abraham of the necessity of a pure genetic connection is not given, but it is surely implied in the many times that "the promise" was emphasized during the nearly 65 years since Abraham entered the land.

The chief of the household referred to is probably Eliezer (identified in Genesis 15:2). If so, Eliezer would have been elderly like his master and therefore would have been thoroughly familiar with the spiritual significance of his assignment. Even if this servant is a successor to Eliezer, his position as one "who ruled over all that [Abraham] had" would insure his full agreement with the mission and purpose of God's plan for "all the families of the earth."

The ceremony of the vow that Abraham required of his trusted servant would have sealed the most solemn commitment on the part of any person. The phrase that Abraham uses, "place your hand under my thigh," is only used in two events in Scripture—here in Genesis 24:2 and 9, and again in Genesis 47:29 when Jacob asked Joseph to promise him that he would not be finally buried in Egypt but would be carried back into Canaan where the ultimate land of Israel was to be established. In both cases, the physical gesture is that the one making the promise is to place his hand under the other's genitals, thus symbolically embracing the entire family line in his promise.

The Ideal Steward

Having taken the vow to seek a suitable wife for Abraham's son, the servant wastes no time in idle speculation or debate. He knows his master's thoughts perhaps even better than Abraham himself. He no doubt has a better understanding of the business and capabilities of the household enterprise. So, with total access and freedom to do with the family's wealth as he pleases, he prepares for the success of his mission.

Herein lies the model for the ideal servant—and as such, a model for all of God's servants. He is fully aware that the wealth is not his own and that he is only a manager of the owner's estate. Just so, in the broadest sense, all humanity has the "steward's" role that was commissioned on Day Six of creation (Genesis 1:27-28). But more so, those who have been twice-born into the family of God are the "servants of Christ and stewards of the mysteries of God" (1 Corinthians 4:1).

Clarifying the Objective

> And the servant said to him, "Perhaps the woman will not be willing to follow me to this land. Must I take your son back to the land from which you came?" But Abraham said to him, "Beware that you do not take my son back there. The LORD God of heaven, who took me from my father's house and from the land of my family, and who spoke to me and swore to me, saying, 'To your descendants I give this land,' He will send His angel before you, and you shall take a wife for my son from there. And if the woman is not willing to follow you, then you will be released from this oath; only do not take my son back there." (Genesis 24:5-8)

One of the more common mistakes made by the servants of our Lord's Kingdom is an immediate leap into (or onto) a half-understood plan, program, or passion. Abraham's servant exemplifies the careful attention of the New Testament Christians in Berea who, after hearing the powerful preaching of the apostle Paul, "searched the Scriptures daily to find out whether these things were so" (Acts 17:11). Responsible servants, especially those who have leadership or positions of influence as did Abraham's faithful steward, cannot—and must not—begin executing a particular responsibility without first checking to see exactly what God is requiring them to do.

Surely the warning to "count the cost" (Luke 14:28) and the potential of embarrassing failure are understood by any who would embrace a major task. Those who are given the ability to teach are warned that they "shall receive a stricter judgment" (James 3:1). Those responsible for ordaining pastoral authority in the churches are cautioned to evaluate everything in the candidate's life from household authority to knowledge of the Scripture, since a "novice" can "fall into the same condemnation as the devil" (1 Timothy 3:6).

> Make me understand the way of Your precepts; So shall I meditate on Your wondrous works. (Psalm 119:27)

> My son, if you receive my words, And treasure my commands within you, So that you incline your ear to wisdom, And apply your heart to understanding; Yes, if you cry out for discernment, And lift up your voice for understanding, If you seek her as silver, And search for her as for hidden treasures; Then you will understand the fear of the LORD, And find the knowledge of God. (Proverbs 2:1-5)

Mature servants of the Lord are careful to seek His perfect will—as far as a sinful human can know it—by spending time in learning God's Word and seeking His face in personal prayer. Eliezer is not a random choice. He has served Abraham for many years and proven both his faithfulness and his discernment. Just so, delegation of authority is just as important as the responsibility and authority to delegate. A hastily chosen leader sometimes proves either untrustworthy or incapable of the assignment. Hence the emphasis on this episode.

Preparation for the Task

> Then the servant took ten of his master's camels and departed, for all his master's goods were in his hand. And he arose and went to Mesopotamia, to the city of Nahor. And he made his camels kneel down outside the city by a well of water at evening time, the time when women go out to draw water. (Genesis 24:10-11)

Although the biblical description is scant, the task described in these two verses is really big. Twice in Genesis 24 we are told that this servant was the chief of Abraham's household and had access to all of the wealth of its business enterprise. After having lived in Canaan for nearly 65 years, returning to a "foreign" land would have been as challenging for Eliezer as if you and I were suddenly expected to leave our home of many years and conduct a major business deal in, say, Japan or China...or in this case, Iraq.

Perhaps there had been commerce between the region of Haran and Abraham's agribusiness over the years, and surely there would have been information available about the "city of Nahor." But getting ready for the trip would not have been done without researching what would be expected by another culture—especially since the charge was to bring back a "princess" from another ruling family to begin a dynasty that would, ultimately, compete with the family descendants of Nahor.

After Eliezer meets Rebekah, he brings out of the provisions brought from Canaan a "golden nose ring weighing half a shekel and two bracelets for her wrists weighing ten shekels of gold," and later "jewelry of silver, jewelry of gold, and clothing, and gave them to Rebekah. He also gave precious things to her brother and to her mother" (Genesis 24:22, 53). All of this was anticipated and prepared in advance. A wise servant makes preparation and carefully anticipates what may be faced during the effort to accomplish the task that has been assigned.

Prequalifying Success

> Then he said, "O Lord God of my master Abraham, please give me success this day, and show kindness to my master Abraham. Behold, here I stand by the well of water, and the daughters of the men of the city are coming out to draw water. Now let it be that the young woman to whom I say, 'Please let down your pitcher that I may drink,' and she says, 'Drink, and I will also give your camels a drink'—let her be the one You have appointed for Your servant Isaac. And by this I will know that You have

shown kindness to my master." (Genesis 24:12-14)

This may seem somewhat presumptuous to expect God to give a special sign in recognition of the right decision. But that is precisely what we must always do when attempting to carry out God's will in and for our lives. Yes, of course, we must be sure that we are not violating anything in the written Word of God, but much of what we must deal with in our active lives is not specifically covered in writing!

Perhaps the reader will recall that we are to "work out" the salvation that the Lord has graciously given us "with fear and trembling" (Philippians 2:12). The reason that we are to be very careful how we work out our salvation is because "it is God who works in you both to will and to do for His good pleasure" (Philippians 2:13). We are held responsible to "do" the work and will of God, always understanding that it is God who is working in us to accomplish His sovereign will in the world.

In the two New Testament parables that speak of using the "talents" and "pounds (or minas)" that are given to us by God, both indicate that we are to "occupy," or do business, until He returns to claim His own. We have the responsibility to invest what God has given to us. Whether it is the gift of salvation (Luke 19) or the individually denominated gifts "each according to his own ability" (Matthew 25:15), all are expected to do something with the gifts. Furthermore, in both of those illustrations, the servant who did nothing with what he was given was rebuked as a "lazy" and "wicked" servant and suffered the judgment of his lord rather than his commendation.

Most assuredly, Eliezer's prayer is not presumptuous. He knows the assignment and is just asking for guidance on how to "see" the character of the wife who would meet the criteria of Abraham's promised heir. Implicit in the entire dialog that follows, as well in the prayer itself, is the expectation that this lady would be strong and healthy. (She would need to be to both bear the future children and maintain the rigors of managing a large household.) She must also be industrious with no delusions of a life of ease, and have the internal character of graciousness, sensitivity, and compassion.

These parameters would have been considered as Eliezer undertook to start the journey and no doubt would have been finalized in his mind and heart during the many weeks of travel to the city of Nahor. As with any good plan, the execution requires verification and feedback.

Focusing on the Mission

Eliezer goes straight to his destination. There is no wasted time en route. Time was taken beforehand to prepare, plan, and focus, but once underway the mission had his entire attention. It is so easy to get distracted. Many, many "good" things can come up along the way of accomplishing a mission. But like Nehemiah, this chief servant would not be detained from his responsibility. Eliezer would stay focused on the task, just as Nehemiah would build the walls of Jerusalem no matter how many "problems" or "requests" came along to deter him from the mission.

> "Blessed be the LORD God of my master Abraham, who has not forsaken His mercy and His truth toward my master. As for me, being on the way, the LORD led me to the house of my master's brethren." (Genesis 24:27)

This short prayer of thanksgiving offered by Eliezer after he encounters Rebekah gives keen insight into the servant's heart. He is "on the way" and acknowledges that the "LORD led" him to the place that he had been looking for since receiving orders to find a wife for Isaac. God leads us with clear directions when—and only when—we are "on the way" to fulfilling what He has in mind for us.

Several biblical passages promise God's personal help when we are seeking to find and follow His will.

> The steps of a good man are ordered by the LORD, And He delights in his way. (Psalm 37:23)

> Trust in the LORD with all your heart, And lean not on your own understanding; In all your ways acknowledge

Him, And He shall direct your paths. (Proverbs 3:5-6)

Commit your works to the LORD, And your thoughts will be established. (Proverbs 16:3)

I will instruct you and teach you in the way you should go; I will guide you with My eye. (Psalm 32:8)

If any of you lacks wisdom, let him ask of God, who gives to all liberally and without reproach, and it will be given to him. (James 1:5)

Evaluating the Circumstances

Once the Lord has given the insight and focus for a specific responsibility, the necessary feedback loop is an evaluation of the circumstances as the process unfolds. Sometimes the Lord will impress a lifetime "calling" on a person (i.e., a desire for full-time service in the Kingdom), and there is a sense in which all twice-born children of God should see themselves as "full time" in the service of the Creator. However, more often than not the sense of mission or particular assignment has a shorter focus.

In the case of the servant of Abraham, the responsibility to find a wife for Isaac had a physical dimension to the job as well as a major spiritual impact for the future. He certainly had some idea of the "ideal" candidates, but he needed some immediate feedback in order to make an adequate judgment on how to proceed.

Noteworthy here is the amount of biblical text given to this episode. Genesis 24 is entirely given over to the selection of Rebekah and the details of Eliezer's efforts to secure her on behalf of Abraham for his son Isaac. It is the longest chapter in the book of Genesis (67 verses, 1,771 words) and contains what might ordinarily be considered a rather mundane account.

Eliezer prayed for specific circumstances to help him verify that he had found the right person. His particular task involved some unique responsibilities and the added dimension of the age-long impact of the decision, but it is often the case that our jobs or responsibilities require identification of the "right" person for a particular role. Pastoral search committees would be a prime example. Board responsibilities often require evaluation of potential leadership. Every business executive knows how important the right person is for a particular job. Eliezer has prepared himself for the "job interview" as carefully as he can.

The first thing he is looking for is evidence of a servant's heart and evidence that she is "genuine"—i.e., that she fits the qualifications required for the job (in this case, being of the proper family and lineage).

> "Now let it be that the young woman to whom I say, 'Please let down your pitcher that I may drink,' and she says, 'Drink, and I will also give your camels a drink'— let her be the one You have appointed for Your servant Isaac." (Genesis 24:14)

Obviously, since it is impossible for us to see into a person's heart, what needs evidential verification is the initial reaction to a carefully presented request. In the context of the culture of that day, all women were expected to show respect and deference to authority (as should any godly person). Eliezer was certainly right to expect the future wife of Isaac and the future mother of the chosen nation to demonstrate a gracious character—perhaps even in spite of the wealth and position of her family.

And that is precisely what Rebekah demonstrated.

> And the servant ran to meet her and said, "Please let me drink a little water from your pitcher." So she said, "Drink, my lord." Then she quickly let her pitcher down to her hand, and gave him a drink. And when she had finished giving him a drink, she said, "I will draw water for your camels also, until they have finished drinking." Then she quickly emptied her pitcher into the trough, ran back to the well to draw water, and drew for all his camels. (Genesis 24:17-20)

Surely this was a "God thing" in that our Lord was behind the selection of Rebekah, but it is not without significance that Eliezer was looking for the first response to his "interview" question. Any intelligent person can figure out what someone wants to hear given enough time. But "out of the abundance of the heart his mouth speaks" (Luke 6:45). Often the best clues to a person's character are what is said "right out of the gate." Eliezer and Rebekah had never met. The reaction to the initial request was, therefore, of major importance. Surely Rebekah would have been within her rights to stand back from this stranger and order her handmaids (Genesis 24:61) to perform this menial task.

And, since actions do speak louder than words, Rebekah immediately offered the drink to Eliezer and his men, and then "ran" (Genesis 24:28) back and forth to the well until the camels were finished drinking. This lady was full of energy and committed to serving the needs of others! A rare find.

But the *bona fides* were not yet verified.

> And the man, wondering at her, remained silent so as to know whether the LORD had made his journey prosperous or not. So it was, when the camels had finished drinking, that the man...said, "Whose daughter are you? Tell me, please, is there room in your father's house for us to lodge?" So she said to him, "I am the daughter of Bethuel, Milcah's son, whom she bore to Nahor." Moreover she said to him, "We have both straw and feed enough, and room to lodge." (Genesis 24:21-25)

Yes! This lady met the qualifications—at least, it appeared to be so. Eliezer was a wise man and later verified Rebekah's statements in person as he spent time with the family. This biblical notation is not a minor point. How many times have you heard of someone falsely representing themselves, their education, background, or experience? When it falls to us to evaluate the character and capabilities of someone else for responsibilities, it is absolutely important that our initial observations (as important as they are) be verified by whatever means are available to us.

Completing the Task

Once the "field interview" was completed and the qualifications of the candidate verified, Eliezer set about gaining the appropriate permissions and release from the current authorities (in this case, her family) for Rebekah to be completely free to give herself over to the new responsibilities that she would assume.

Again, this is no minor point. Not only is it important to follow protocols in assuming a new role, but it is very important that the one accepting the new responsibilities has been released from any former obligations so that the new job can be entered into with no reservations. The Lord Jesus did not lightly insist that "no one can serve two masters" (Matthew 6:24). That immediate focus was to the apostles, who would soon assume His delegated authority to preach the gospel and "make disciples" out of every nation on Earth (Matthew 28:19). No small responsibility.

Just so, loyalty to a Kingdom responsibility is vitally important. Yes, there are sometimes apparently overlapping conflicts in responsibilities (job, church, family, community), but all of these can and should be manageable by mature adults—especially those who are the twice-born. The Scriptures insist that God has provided "all things that pertain to life and godliness" and that we can be guided by the wisdom provided in God's revelation to us in all the decisions that must be made in life (2 Peter 1:3). Part of that freedom requires clear release from former obligations.

> Then the man came to the house. And he unloaded the camels, and provided straw and feed for the camels, and water to wash his feet and the feet of the men who were with him. Food was set before him to eat, but he said, "I will not eat until I have told about my errand." (Genesis 24:32-33)

Part of insuring freedom from former obligations is making sure that those in the former relationships are fully aware of the new role. This would especially be true if the new responsibilities involve Kingdom work. Difficult as this may be (particularly if the recruitment is to be done privately), the best release possible is for those involved in the former relationship and the former authority to have knowledge of the importance of the new role and give their blessing for the change.

And that is precisely what Eliezer did. He recounted his own commission and the personal experiences of what God had done in bringing him before the family. That testimony set the stage for a positive response. Nothing is as convincing as clear evidence of God's provision and guidance through the challenges of finding the right person for a new role. In many business relationships, the former employer has no feel for the spiritual side of the equation, but nonetheless it is important to make clear to those who had former authority that the new role is a clear fit and a convincing opportunity. If this is not done, often subsequent "deals" will surface or conflicting loyalties will materialize that will disturb the new work unnecessarily.

Finally, a clear and public acceptance of the new "job" is absolutely necessary.

> But her brother and her mother said, "Let the young woman stay with us a few days, at least ten; after that she may go." And he said to them, "Do not hinder me, since the LORD has prospered my way; send me away so that I may go to my master." So they said, "We will call the young woman and ask her personally." Then they called Rebekah and said to her, "Will you go with this man?" And she said, "I will go." (Genesis 24:55-58)

There is always a tendency to delay the start of something new—especially a change that will bring about the separation of long associations and relationships. Do not give in to such a temptation. When God has made something clear by His direction, circumstantial verification, inner conviction of the Holy Spirit, and conscious positive response by the people affected by the decision, act on it as quickly as possible. All too often, second guessing has stirred doubt or raised obstacles that are nothing more than hindrances to God's blessing.

Professional test evaluators will verify that the first impression is most often the correct answer to a test question, with reflective worry almost always ending in a wrong selection. Just so, the response of a godly person, after all of the preliminaries are completed, is most often a reflection of the internal witness of the Holy Spirit.

Lessons Learned

Perhaps it might be helpful at this juncture to review the main characteristics of a faithful servant. Eliezer's execution of the important task that Abraham entrusted to him is given serious coverage in this great book of beginnings. Surely it is well for us to emulate the lessons illustrated by this faithful man in those tasks that God will entrust to us.

- *Personal Commitment.* All important tasks require a strong personal commitment to complete the task. Without an awareness of the importance of a task and a clear dedication to its success, the likelihood of failure is increased. Opposition is sure to come—especially if the task is Kingdom-related. Only those who are dedicated and motivated will realize "good success" (Joshua 1:8).

- *Personal Qualification.* Someone has observed that responsibility without authority is frustrating. It should be further noted that authority without resources is futile. Before accepting a job (a position, a role, an obligation), be as sure as you can that you have the personal qualifications to complete the task and the authority and resources to carry it out (Proverbs 20:6).

- *Clarify the Objective.* Make sure of the definitions of success. It has been observed that if you aim at nothing, you are sure to hit it. Wandering off on a quixotic adventure is not the way to find or fulfill the will of God in your life. Emotive reactions are seldom indicators of God-ordered responsibilities. "Without counsel, plans go awry, But in the multitude of counselors they are established" (Proverbs 15:22).

- *Prepare for Success.* Personal qualifications are surely part of this important aspect of any mission, but the key element here is a careful study (analysis, inquiry, research) of the job to be done. "Do your homework" is an oft-repeated cliché. Another well-used phrase is "an ounce of prevention is worth a pound of cure." The Bible puts it this way: "Ponder the path of your feet, And let all your ways be established" (Proverbs 4:26).

- *Focus on the Mission.* Distraction produces diversion. Ancillary issues collapse ambition. Nebulous plans obliterate initiative. When the apostle James discussed the need to pray for God's wisdom, he insisted that our prayer should be without any doubt, since "a double-minded man" will always be "unstable in all his ways" (James 1:8). Never take your mind off the goal. Whenever that happens, failure is sure to follow.

- *Evaluate the Circumstances.* Some tasks are quickly achieved. Others (many times, the more important ones) take years or decades to complete—some missions are generations long. Rare is the task that can be completed by a single decision. Once we are sure that the biblical requirements are met, then the observable circumstances become the tool through which God will verify His will as the process unfolds (Proverbs 16:9).

- *Complete the Task.* Bringing a task to fruition must include a final follow-through that involves clear liberty and release from all former obligations. Eliezer maintained control of the process from the initial vow to Abraham until he watched Isaac take Rebekah into his tent. Oftentimes the job is not complete until the goal is well underway. "No one, having put his hand to the plow, and looking back, is fit for the kingdom of God" (Luke 9:62).

Rebekah

Although this chapter in Genesis deals mainly with the actions and processes exemplified by Abraham's faithful steward, there are a number of key revelations about Rebekah's character that are significant.

Early considerations by Eliezer would have determined that the wife of Abraham's heir must be strong and healthy, industrious with no delusions of a life of ease, and gracious, sensitive, and compassionate, as befitting the wife of a major patriarch. It would have been without question that she would have been a virgin without any moral taint—even though such matters were viewed differently in the social and cultural mores of that time. Eliezer assumed this would be so before he even saw the young lady.

> "And this day I came to the well and said, 'O LORD God of my master Abraham, if You will now prosper the way in which I go, behold, I stand by the well of water; and it shall come to pass that when the virgin comes out to draw water...'" (Genesis 24:42-43)

Having seen the trauma of the events involving Hagar and Ishmael, it is likely that Eliezer would have been most cautious about the family background and the need for guarantees that the wife of his master's heir would have a clear lineage tying back to the line of Shem. And no doubt it would have been important that this lady come from a family whose cultural and social status would be compatible with those of the wealthy Abraham. Such things may be looked at with some skepticism in the eclectic and egalitarian views of modern romance, but the Bible places a premium on godly authority and moral purity.

Godly Fathers

It is not without reason that most societies place the decisions about weddings under the authority and wisdom of the father rather than the impulsive and emotional criteria of youth. Western societies appear to encourage emotional attachment rather than careful consideration of one of life's most important commitments—and the price is a divorce rate of 50 percent! Not a good track record. The Bible makes it very clear that the most important qualification is spiritual compatibility, not erotic stimulation. Godly fathers want their sons and daughters to rest in the pleasure and fidelity of faithful marriages and usually are keenly aware of the temperaments and needs of their children—as well as the pitfalls of hasty decisions.

There is not much in these records about Rebekah's father, Nahor's son Bethuel. What little we do see of the family's response to the information about Abraham and Eliezer is that they quickly recognize the hand of the Lord in the circumstances.

> Bethuel answered and said, "The thing comes from the LORD; we cannot speak to you either bad or good. Here is Rebekah before you; take her and go, and let her be your master's son's wife, as the LORD has spoken." (Genesis 24:50-51)

No doubt Nahor, Abraham's brother, would have told his family about the unique call of *Elohim* to Abraham. Perhaps, with the long lives of their common ancestors, they would have either met or known of Noah and Shem. Surely they would have known of the terrible judgment of the Flood and the dispersion of nations from the tower at Babel. All of that would have been "family history" to them. Rebekah and her brother Laban, it seems, had become the most spiritually affected of the immediate family. Apparently, both her grandfather and her father had impacted them with the importance of the godly line.

While the specific instance of securing a proper wife for Isaac may be bound by the special circumstances of God's requirements for originating the new nation of Israel, the timeless requirements instituted at creation are still by far and away the best criteria for marriage. Those rules are not many and not complex. There is to be one man for one woman for life. They are to leave their childhood homes and establish a home for themselves and for their children. They are to have children and to raise them under God's oversight and for His glory. By implication at creation, and by example throughout Scriptures, they are to recognize God's approval on their union.

Although there are many examples of polygamous marriages in the Bible, there is not one that is happy. Although there are many examples of unruly children of godly parents in the Scriptures, none of them bring about a good end. God's design has always been that one man should embrace one woman as a life partner and raise their children together to "bring them up in the training and admonition of the Lord" (Ephesians 6:4). That union is to be led by the husband/father (Ephesians 5:21-31), loving his wife with the same unilateral and self-sacrificing love exemplified by the Lord Jesus. Children of that union are to surrender their behavior to their parents while they are under their care (Ephesians 6:1-3), understanding that this arrangement "is well pleasing to the Lord" (Colossians 3:20).

The biblical arrangement may not be popular, but it is God's plan and it will produce lasting happiness and maximum correlation with God's sovereign will for the individuals and for His eternal kingdom.

Godly Mothers

What we will later see from Rebekah is a willingness to sacrifice just about everything to keep the Kingdom mission alive. Isaac has started out well but winds up a very worldly and sensual person. The twins who are born to their marriage are vastly different. Isaac "loves" Esau, but Jacob is the one whom God has chosen. Were it not for the steadfast commitment of Rebekah, a terrible tragedy would have occurred that (apart from the sovereign intervention of God) could well have derailed the lives of millions yet unborn.

A godly mother, who has been a godly wife, is as Proverbs 31:30 tells us: "Charm is deceitful and beauty is passing, But a woman who fears the LORD, she shall be praised."

CHAPTER SIX
TROUBLE BREWING

One of the more subtle surprises about the lives of these great men of the past is the contrast in the life of Isaac. His young life is an obvious answer to long prayer and the fulfillment of the promise of God to begin a new "seed" through him. Isaac's reaction to Abraham's request from God to sacrifice his son provides both insight into Isaac's personal character and a scriptural example of what our Lord Jesus did for us.

However, as Isaac married and matured, his life drifted radically toward a love for a wicked and wild son (Esau) and a rejection of the son (Jacob) that God Himself had prophesied to Rebekah would be the continuation of the promised seed. Isaac was very similar to Solomon, whose younger life was filled with spiritual wisdom and promise but whose later life was "turned aside" from God as Solomon began to wrap himself in the pagan life of his many wives. Fortunately, both Isaac and Solomon came to their senses before they totally ruined the opportunities that God had given them, but their indecision initiated events that caused much damage for centuries.

Abraham's Final Years

Abraham again took a wife, and her name was Keturah. And she bore him Zimran, Jokshan, Medan, Midian, Ishbak, and Shuah. Jokshan begot Sheba and Dedan. And the sons of Dedan were Asshurim, Letushim, and Leummim. And the sons of Midian were Ephah, Epher, Hanoch, Abidah, and Eldaah. All these were the children of Keturah. (Genesis 25:1-4)

After Sarah died and was interred in the burial cave at Machpelah (Genesis 23:19), Abraham married Keturah, whose nationality and background are obscure. The children of that union were called "sons of the concubines" (including Ishmael from Hagar). A later reference calls Keturah a "concubine" (1 Chronicles 1:32), indicating that she may have been part of the family entourage for some time before Sarah died.

Abraham was 137 years old when Sarah died (her 127 years listed in Genesis 23:1 plus the ten-year age difference between Abraham and Sarah indicated in Genesis 17:17). Abraham was 100 when Isaac was born (Genesis 21:5). Isaac was 40 when he met and married Rebekah (Genesis 25:20). Abraham was 175 when he died (Genesis 25:7). It appears likely that Abraham took Keturah to wife after Isaac was finally married and then fathered the six named sons by Keturah in addition to Ishmael by Hagar some 70 years earlier.

> And Abraham gave all that he had to Isaac. But Abraham gave gifts to the sons of the concubines which Abraham had; and while he was still living he sent them eastward, away from Isaac his son, to the country of the east. (Genesis 25:5-6)

All of the other sons of Abraham were acknowledged with monetary and substantive gifts from their earthly father but were sent to establish their livelihoods and their destinies in "the country of the east"—"away from Isaac his son." The names of these other sons and their descendants are mentioned from time to time in biblical history but in each instance are identified only as "neighbors" or in many cases as military or cultural enemies of the "promised son."

Abraham lived another 35-plus years after Isaac was married to

Rebekah and lived to see the birth of Jacob and Esau. The biblical record notes that Isaac had been married to Rebekah 20 years before Jacob and Esau were born (Genesis 25:26). Thus, Abraham would have had about 15 years to get to know his grandsons and gain some firsthand knowledge of the growing disparity of their personalities.

> This is the sum of the years of Abraham's life which he lived: one hundred and seventy-five years. Then Abraham breathed his last and died in a good old age, an old man and full of years, and was gathered to his people. And his sons Isaac and Ishmael buried him in the cave of Machpelah, which is before Mamre, in the field of Ephron the son of Zohar the Hittite, the field which Abraham purchased from the sons of Heth. There Abraham was buried, and Sarah his wife. (Genesis 25:7-10)

Many Nations

Ishmael and Isaac had become reunited in some way by the time their father died. Ishmael would have been 90 years old when Abraham died, and his 12 sons (Genesis 25:12-16) would have been grown men with budding "nations" of their own. Isaac (apparently) added the notation in verse 18 that "they dwelt from Havilah as far as Shur, which is east of Egypt as you go toward Assyria." Ishmael died at age 137 some 58 years before Isaac's death, and although the specific territories of Ishmael's descendants cannot be precisely identified, it is clear that they settled in northern Arabia.

Keturah's six named sons, more than likely born early in the 35 years after Sarah died, were sent "away from Isaac." The only name that has come down through the centuries as a significant "nation" is Midian. The Midianites are mentioned several times in the Old Testament, most notably as the merchant tribe that sold young Joseph into slavery in Egypt (Genesis 37:36). They appear in the book of Numbers as significant enemies of the new nation of Israel just out of Egypt under the leadership of Moses, and again as the army attacking Israel at the time of Gideon (Judges 6–8).

Sheba and Dedan (Genesis 25:2), two of the grandsons of Abraham by Keturah, were probably named after descendants of Noah's son Cush. Sheba (either Keturah's grandson or the son from the line of Cush) is likely the founder of the nation of Sheba from which came the queen of Sheba who is noted for her visit to Solomon (1 Kings 10). The rest of these descendants appear to have settled in southwest Arabia near what is modern Yemen.

As will become clear shortly, Esau becomes the head of the nation of Edom. Truly, Abraham was the "father of many nations."

The Two Nations

> Isaac was forty years old when he took Rebekah as wife, the daughter of Bethuel the Syrian of Padan Aram, the sister of Laban the Syrian. Now Isaac pleaded with the LORD for his wife, because she was barren; and the LORD granted his plea, and Rebekah his wife conceived. But the children struggled together within her; and she said, "If all is well, why am I like this?" So she went to inquire of the LORD. And the LORD said to her: "Two nations are in your womb, Two peoples shall be separated from your body; One people shall be stronger than the other, And the older shall serve the younger." (Genesis 25:20-23)

Obviously, something big is about to happen. It is not clear if Rebekah had some kind of personal interview with the Lord, as had so obviously been the case with Abraham. The text just simply tells us that she "went to inquire." The Hebrew word choices are very interesting. The word translated "went to" is *yalak*, almost always describing a physical journey (e.g., Genesis 12:4; 13:3; 18:22; etc.). "Inquire" is the translators' choice for the Hebrew word *darash*, with an emphasis on "careful" or "intense" seeking (e.g., Leviticus 10:16; Deuteronomy 4:29; etc.). Rebekah was not merely "praying" to ask something from God, she (apparently) went on a journey to find an answer to her very troubling problem!

Some have suggested that Rebekah went to Melchizedek to get an answer. That is not specified by the text, but neither is the possibility eliminated. Melchizedek was a real person, as was discussed in chapter 2—and was most probably a pre-incarnate presence of the Son of God. Abraham and Melchizedek were closely involved together, and it is likely that Rebekah knew of Melchizedek since Abraham was still alive and active with the family during Rebekah's pregnancy. If Melchizedek was still "king of Salem" (Genesis 14:18), as was definitely the case less than 50 years previously, then Salem (Jerusalem) and the area near Beer Lahai Roi where Isaac had his business headquarters were not that far apart (Genesis 25:11).

However Rebekah "went to inquire," and whether or not she physically traveled any distance as is implied by the word choices, she definitely was able to determine precisely what was said to her about the "two peoples" that struggled within her womb. Again, the word choices are precise. "The LORD said" is a translation of *Yahovah 'amar*, a frequently used format and always meaning an audible and verbal engagement. Rebekah spoke with the Lord and *He* answered back. What was said about her twins was stunning!

From the twins in Rebekah's womb would come two competing nations. The struggle that she sensed already happening between the two infants inside her would develop into a tension and competition for dominance that would have an impact for thousands of years to come. One line would be more "courageous" than the other, and one line would wind up "working for" the other. And most importantly, the descendants of the younger twin would rule the descendants of the elder. This declaration by the Lord was intended to be understood as a pronouncement of events to come—and therefore also understood as the sovereign will of *Elohim*, the Creator of the universe.

> So when her days were fulfilled for her to give birth, indeed there were twins in her womb. And the first came out red. He was like a hairy garment all over; so they called his name Esau. Afterward his brother came out, and his hand took hold of Esau's heel; so his name was

called Jacob. Isaac was sixty years old when she bore them. (Genesis 25:24-26)

Modern science is just beginning to give us some insight into the feelings and activities of babies who are still in the womb. What is beginning to become very clear, however, is that they are not mere lumps of biological "stuff" that do not have a human nature prior to "viability" outside of the womb. The more that we learn about neo-natal processes, the more clear it becomes that the child is the one responsible for the internal development and that the mother's role is that of a majestic incubator, "responding to signals emanating from the baby—even at times to her own detriment."[1]

So, just as was prophetically pronounced earlier, "there were twins in her womb," and the children who had engaged in a personal struggle even during their gestation time together began to emerge. As promised in Genesis 25:23, the son who would one day serve his brother was indeed born first. He was absolutely covered with the most unusual red hair and was immediately named Esau. Obviously, that term means "hairy." (The Hebrew word for "hairy" is *se'ar*, so naming this child *'Esav* was a quick and easy choice.)

Apparently, while Esau was still attached to the umbilical cord, the second child began to emerge—and he reached out and grabbed the heel of his elder brother! Because of that very extraordinary sight, they immediately named him *Ya'aqob,* or Jacob. The Hebrew word for "heel" is *'aqeb,* and the Hebrew word for "take hold" or "possess" is *'achaz.* Thus, we have now named the young "heel grabber." These two boys would become the initial offspring of the "promised seed" spoken of so long ago to Abraham. Esau becomes a feared and hated enemy. Jacob becomes the nation of Israel.

Spiritual Evaluation

So the boys grew. And Esau was a skillful hunter, a man of the field; but Jacob was a mild man, dwelling in tents. (Genesis 25:27)

---

1. Randy J. Guliuzza, 2009, *Made in His Image: Examining the complexities of the human body,* Dallas, TX: Institute for Creation Research, 31.

This small biblical passage is often either overlooked or badly misunderstood. Apparently, God intends for us to grasp something about these two young men that He knew before their birth. Later, the Lord would inspire Paul to amplify the citation of Malachi 1:2-3, where God notes: "Yet Jacob I have loved; But Esau I have hated." Obviously, much more is behind the statements, and the apostle Paul observed:

> When Rebecca also had conceived by one man, even by our father Isaac (for the children not yet being born, nor having done any good or evil, that the purpose of God according to election might stand, not of works but of Him who calls), it was said to her, "The older shall serve the younger." As it is written, "Jacob I have loved, but Esau I have hated." (Romans 9:10-13)

What is there in this initial comment in Genesis that is so important for us to note? On the surface, it doesn't seem like much. Esau is a "skillful hunter." Well, that's good, but what about that would cause God to focus His hatred on him? Jacob is said to be a "mild" man (or as the King James translates, a "plain" man). Esau was a "man of the field," but Jacob was one who was "dwelling in tents." Very different, one can notice, but why the "love" and the "hate" for such apparently indifferent physical or cultural traits?

Perhaps one could conclude that God favors men who do not give undue attention to physical pursuits. Esau was noted for his hunting activity, and young Timothy was later told that "bodily exercise profits a little, but godliness is profitable for all things" (1 Timothy 4:8). Yet that doesn't allow for all the praise that God gave to King David and his "mighty men" or the use of such warriors as Gideon, Samson, and Barak—and the very strange physical existence of John the Baptist, who lived a hermit's life in the desert. No, the focus is not just on the activities of these two young men (even though there are some clues in their behavior), the key is in the character that produces their lifestyles.

Esau

The life of Esau was the life of a total pagan. There was certainly no need for Esau to develop skill as a hunter. The family was quite wealthy and in the food business! The household or business staff would have been sufficient to provide protection. (In fact, it is clear later on that they did exactly that.) The only purpose in this "skillful hunter" seems to be to show off athletic prowess.

Furthermore, Esau is known as a "man of the field"—not of work. As any business executive quickly learns, especially if the business is a family business, the need for capable management is paramount if the enterprise is to succeed. Esau shows no interest in the business side of the family's life; rather, in fact, he "despised his birthright" not much later. His interest is "doing his own thing," leaving and assuming that others would take care of his needs.

Not only that, but his lifestyle was a "grief of mind" to Isaac and Rebekah (Genesis 26:35). Much of what was done during those years is left unsaid, but his lifestyle was so obviously out of sync with a family that was to be the epitome of God's "promise" that both of his parents struggled with Esau's obvious disdain for righteousness. When the inspired writer of the book of Hebrews commented on Esau, we are told that he was a "fornicator" and a "profane person" (Hebrews 12:16). The specific Greek word choices are important. *Pornos* is the word used for "fornicator." Its basic meaning is of a man who prostitutes his body to another's lust for hire. The modern English word "pornography" comes from that term. *Bebelos* is the word translated "profane person." Its basic meaning is unhallowed or common.

Esau was not nice!

As Esau grew into manhood, he became an open polygamist (Genesis 26:34). He also deliberately married into the Hittite population, even though he knew the great care that had been taken with the marriage of his father and mother to preserve the family lineage that had descended from Shem. And after the horrible incident at the formal blessing (Genesis 27), after Isaac had repented and sent Jacob away to find a wife from the proper family line, Esau ran down to Ishmael and married one of Ishmael's granddaughters (Genesis 28:9)—as if a *third* wife from the "son of the bondwoman" could appease his father's wishes. Gracious! How spiritually dense can one be?

Jacob

Contrasted with Esau is the very different lifestyle and character of Jacob. Rebekah, whose sacrificial attitude is often overlooked in this account, is a lady of godly demeanor and she loves Jacob, even though her husband loves Esau. Why this disparity?

The biblical translation of Genesis 25:27 reads, "Jacob was a mild man, dwelling in tents." The key word in that sentence is "mild" (or, as the KJV translates, "plain"). The Hebrew word is *tam*, which has the basic meaning of "perfect" or "complete." That Hebrew noun (here used as a descriptive adjective about Jacob) is used only 13 times in the Old Testament. Its primitive root, *tamam*, is used an additional 64 times. Both words mean "complete" or "finished." The places where they are used are always indicative of someone or something that is "the best" or the "most wholesome" or the one or thing that has the "most strength." Sometimes the root word *tamam* is used to describe something that is completely "destroyed" or absolutely "consumed."

The only time *tam* is used to imply "mild" or "plain" is in this unique verse about Jacob. Why? Most of the other uses of the Hebrew word *tam* are in the book of Job—and are about Job.

> There was a man in the land of Uz, whose name was Job; and that man was *blameless* and upright, and one who feared God and shunned evil. (Job 1:1)
>
> Then the LORD said to Satan, "Have you considered My servant Job, that there is none like him on the earth, a *blameless* and upright man, one who fears God and shuns evil?" (Job 1:8)
>
> Then the LORD said to Satan, "Have you considered My servant Job, that there is none like him on the earth, a

blameless and upright man, one who fears God and shuns evil? And still he holds fast to his integrity, although you incited Me against him, to destroy him without cause." (Job 2:3)

Then again in the Psalms, the word *tam* is used to describe a "perfect" (blameless) man.

Mark the *blameless* man, and observe the upright; For the future of that man is peace. (Psalm 37:37)

That they may shoot in secret at the *blameless*; Suddenly they shoot at him and do not fear. (Psalm 64:4)

It is worthy of note that the Lord Himself does not ever condemn Jacob or speak ill of him. In fact, it is Jacob who is most often *complimented* in Scripture. And of course, it is Jacob who has his name changed—by God Himself—to Israel, one who has "power with God" (Genesis 32:28). Even the use of the names of the patriarchs in Scripture is telling: Isaac appears only 123 times, Abraham 230 times, but Jacob 345 times. "Jacob" and "Israel" are used as equal terms for God's people in many places in Scripture (e.g., Micah 2:12; Romans 11:26; etc.).

Apparently, Jacob has an undeserved bad reputation.

The Birthright

There is some mystery surrounding the historical emphasis on the firstborn, as well as the "birthright." Nearly every culture across time has honored the firstborn (usually the male) and has connected some special rights to that birth order. However, there are obvious exceptions even in the Bible. God chose Abel over Cain, Jacob over Esau, Judah over Reuben, Ephraim over Manasseh, Moses over Aaron, and David over his brothers. The Lord told Samuel, "Do not look at his appearance or at his physical stature, because I have refused him. For the LORD does not see as man sees; for man looks at the outward appearance, but the LORD looks at the heart" (1 Samuel 16:7).

But there is an even more mysterious inference behind this custom. Throughout history, many non-firstborn children have exceeded their elder siblings, and yet almost all societies recognize the primogeniture as the "proper" way to transfer wealth, convey titles to properties, divide wills, and recognize the family name. Royal lineage and the right of the firstborn male to rule held sway for millennia across nations, tribes, and ethnic groups. What may have instilled this concept in nearly all human endeavors?

Certainly not evolutionary ascendancy or nature itself. That entire concept is one of randomness and struggle for survival. If anything, the philosophy of evolutionary development would give rise to the strongest taking over; the biggest animal would rule the herd, the strongest man would take over the tribe—or the most intelligent or most wealthy or...well, fill in the blanks. Evolution would not encourage a "firstborn birthright"—to anything!

So where does this concept come from?

Perhaps the concept is a "God thing."

The Firstborn

When Moses stood before Pharaoh, he was told to tell Pharaoh that "Israel is My son, My firstborn" (Exodus 4:22). Israel was not the first nation on Earth, not even close. Egypt was a nation long before Israel, and at the time the statement was made Israel was nothing more than a group of slaves with no government, no land, and certainly no birthright—except that God had "birthed" her through Abraham as His "firstborn" nation.

All of Scripture pointed toward the "firstborn" Son of God, the Redeemer, the Seed who would "take away the sins of the world." Over and over again, the prophetic utterances, the sacrificial dramas, and the open claims of the Lord Jesus Himself all point to the sovereign plan and triune nature of the Godhead as the basis for the emphasis on the firstborn.

The tithes of Israel involved people bringing the "firstfruits" of their agricultural work as an offering to the Creator. The Passover lamb must be a "firstling" of the flock, a male that was "without blemish and without spot." The "first man" bore the image of the Creator. The first human conception was designated by Eve as "a man from the LORD" (Genesis 4:1). Even firstborn daughters were given recognition and special provisions when there was no son in the family. In just about every conceivable way, the firstborn of humanity—in vivid contrast to the "natural" display of nature—is recognized as uniquely important in the affairs of men.

Thus in every culture—but especially emphasized throughout Scripture in the nation of Israel—the firstborn inherited the right of rank and privilege before his brothers and sisters. As this custom developed, it became enfolded in the laws of Israel under Moses. Although these laws were inaugurated well after the incident relating to Jacob and Esau, the transcendent God of Israel appears to have inculcated these practices into the life of humanity long before they were codified into Mosaic Law.

The Privileges

Essentially, the main privilege was the right of transfer of wealth. In the Mosaic Law, the firstborn was to be given a "double portion" of whatever was owned by the father whenever there were multiple children (Deuteronomy 21:17). Abraham did give sufficient gifts to his many sons to enable them to establish households for themselves, but he gave "all that he had" to Isaac (Genesis 25:5). That practice is easy to follow throughout Scripture and well-established in secular history.

The Responsibilities

The responsibilities are centered in the necessity to bear the family name and titles. In most families, that may well have been rather mundane. But in families of wealth and power, the eldest son was assumed to be the one to "take over" the family business or political authority that had been established in the past. Where there were ruling families, the dynasty would be extended through the lifetime of the heirs—unless and until there were no heirs or the family was deposed or destroyed through war or intrigue.

Since God had "birthed" Israel through the miraculous "seed" of Isaac, God intended for the transfer of His name (the name of God) to be prominent in that family. The reader will probably recall that Israel was initially structured as a theocracy—a nation that was ruled by God through delegated leaders. Initially that found focus in Abraham, Isaac, Jacob, and Joseph, but later through Moses and the Davidic line, consummating in the Lord Jesus Himself.

Under the Mosaic Law, every firstborn child was the "property" of God. That child would be "redeemed" by a tax paid to the Levitical priesthood—who themselves were to be dedicated to the service of God.

> Then the LORD spoke to Moses, saying, "Consecrate to Me all the firstborn, whatever opens the womb among the children of Israel, both of man and beast; it is Mine." (Exodus 13:1-2)

> Then the LORD spoke to Moses, saying: "Take the Levites instead of all the firstborn among the children of Israel, and the livestock of the Levites instead of their livestock. The Levites shall be Mine: I am the LORD." (Numbers 3:44-45)

> And Moses gave their redemption money to Aaron and his sons, according to the word of the LORD, as the LORD commanded Moses. (Numbers 3:51)

Much more could be said on the system that God specified to Moses during the codification of the Law at Mount Sinai. The purpose of recalling this to the reader at this juncture is merely to illustrate the unusual emphasis that had begun long before Moses and had been established so well at the time of Abraham and Isaac that both Jacob and Esau were completely aware of the privileges and responsibilities of the firstborn.

In the context of Jacob and Esau, the money aspect would have been muted. Their family's wealth was enormous and both brothers would have been rich. What was far more important was the grant of household rule and the spiritual authority and responsibility that went with that rule.

Selling the Birthright

> And Isaac loved Esau because he ate of his game, but Rebekah loved Jacob.
>
> Now Jacob cooked a stew; and Esau came in from the field, and he was weary. And Esau said to Jacob, "Please feed me with that same red stew, for I am weary." Therefore his name was called Edom. But Jacob said, "Sell me your birthright as of this day." And Esau said, "Look, I am about to die; so what is this birthright to me?" Then Jacob said, "Swear to me as of this day." So he swore to him, and sold his birthright to Jacob. And Jacob gave Esau bread and stew of lentils; then he ate and drank, arose, and went his way. Thus Esau despised his birthright. (Genesis 25:28-34)

This poignant passage forms the basis for our understanding of much that follows in the biblical record. With an amazing economy of words, the Holy Spirit pierces to the heart of the troubles that follow. The actual "sale" of the birthright is important because it records the specific incident wherein the identity of the nation of Israel passes from the elder son, Esau, to the younger son, Jacob.

Most likely, something much more than merely the two brothers' verbal exchange took place. Normally, an oath involved some legal action as well as the actual voicing of the agreement. The Hebrew word *sheba* (seven) is used here, and is the same term used when Abraham sealed an oath with Abimelech using seven lambs (Genesis 21:28-30). Jacob later serves Laban seven years for Rachel and another seven for Leah (Genesis 29:18, 29). This "seven" must have sealed the sale of the birthright in some way such that the entire family (and later posterity) would have been clearly satisfied that this important action was formally taken.

Making Stew

It is always intriguing to take notice of the special word choices designated by the Holy Spirit to describe an important event. Both the verb and the adjective are significant here. In this case, Jacob was said to be "cooking" a stew of "red" beans. The Hebrew verb is *zuwd*. The newer versions translate the term as "cooking," and the older versions (KJV, RSV, etc.) translate it "boil" or "sod." Actually, the verb and its derivatives are used some 40 times in the Old Testament, and all but this passage translate the terms with the basic idea of "proud" or "presumptive." The noun form (*nazyid*) often has a context where the term is applied to a "poison" or "unholy" mixture.

Interesting. Could it be that Jacob is planning this event? Is he presumptively preparing a mixture of food that he knows that Esau will "die" for? Why the emphasis on the "red" stew? This is evidently so significant that Esau will from this time forward be known as Red (*Edom*). The Hebrew adjective *'adom* (red) is modified into the proper noun *'edom* by which Esau and his descendants will be called.

The reader will recall that when Esau was born he emerged *'admoniy* (reddish) and was covered all over with hair as though he wore a coat. That unusual circumstance was duly recorded in the Scriptures and, apparently, followed Esau all through his life. Now, Jacob is preparing a food that he seems to know Esau will desperately want. That food is so well known that Esau is forever linked with its color—and forever links that color with power and passion, intent and impulse. Could it be that the sovereign Lord is behind this?

Reckless Decision

Esau has been out hunting for most of the day. He arrives at the compound worn out and famished. After unloading his gear and dismissing his servants, he smells the tantalizing and pungent whiff of Jacob's red lentil stew—maybe even the enticing smell of fresh-baked bread. Esau is drawn into the family kitchen where the stew is bubbling in the pot, the bread is still hot to the touch, and Jacob is ready and waiting.

"Feed me with that red, red" Esau demands, "I am worn out!" The Hebrew wording in this sentence does not give any hint of a "please, sir" attitude. The structure is imperative (a command) and not a request. Esau has not ever demonstrated any character other than the wild, boastful, lustful man that his family is well aware of. Nothing in the Scripture, Old or New Testament, gives the translators any leeway to insert a posture of manners or grace. Esau is demanding service from an insignificant (in his opinion) brother who doesn't share anything of Esau's manly traits. "I'm hungry! Feed me!" is the command.

Jacob, apparently, is ready for this. Quite probably Jacob (and maybe also Rebekah) has considered this very possibility within the recent past. Both Jacob and Rebekah (and Isaac) are well aware of the prophecy given at the birth of the twins that Jacob would rule the family and that Esau would be rejected. However, Isaac "loves Esau" and seems to be indifferent to his sinful behavior. Something must be done!

Jacob, prepared for his brother's impulsive behavior, says: "Sell your birthright to me today!" This is certainly a surprise. Jacob, the "upright" and "stay at home" guy, was demanding something of his elder brother! Obviously, Esau couldn't care less. "I'm dying. The birthright is worthless!" Jacob becomes bolder. "Swear (give me seven) now!" So, Esau executes (sells) whatever would have been necessary in that culture to "swear" (the sevens) that the birthright would henceforth belong to Jacob. Then Esau quietly eats the "red, red" and goes away.

Here's God's comment: "Thus Esau despised his birthright."

When the writer of the book of Hebrews later commented on this incident, he noted that "afterward, when he wanted to inherit the blessing, he was rejected, for he found no place for repentance, though he sought it diligently with tears" (Hebrews 12:17). At the time, arrogant and willful Esau "despised" anything to do with whatever the birthright entailed. He was a hunter. He had no time for this "heel grabber" of a brother—and besides that, he was absolutely worn out and famished. What good is a birthright?

Wandering and Instability

The biblical record changes abruptly after the sale of the birthright. It is not clear how many years have intervened, but it is likely that Isaac is at least in his 80s as chapter 26 of Genesis begins. We are told that Isaac is 60 at the birth of his two sons (Genesis 25:26). Jacob and Esau are young men with lifestyle reputations clearly established (Genesis 25:27), and enough time has elapsed for the family to know that Isaac favors Esau because he loves the taste of the wild game that Esau brings back from his hunting expeditions (Genesis 25:28).

Fleeing the Famine

Isaac and his family have been headquartered for some time at the well Beer Lahai Roi near the southern central region of Canaan "between Kadesh and Bered" (Genesis 16:14). This area had long been associated with Abraham and is near the northern borders of the land where Ishmael and his growing family live. A famine becomes severe in the area, and Isaac fears damage to his flocks and herds of livestock. He makes a move back westward toward the Mediterranean coastline, initially settling in the area around the Philistine city of Gerar.

Apparently, Isaac has it in his mind to move the business on to Egypt (as had Abraham nearly a century before), but suddenly the Lord appears! As far as Scripture reveals, this is the first time that Isaac has seen the Lord since his miraculous deliverance on Mount Moriah over 50 years before. The language and word choices quoting the message that God gives to Isaac indicate that this visit is a physical appearance, not merely a vision of some sort. Other than the stern warning not to go to Egypt, the instructions are almost verbatim to what God told Abram before he and Sarai went into Egypt—also because of a famine.

> "Do not go down to Egypt; live in the land of which I shall tell you. Dwell in this land, and I will be with you and bless you; for to you and your descendants I give all

these lands, and I will perform the oath which I swore to Abraham your father. And I will make your descendants multiply as the stars of heaven; I will give to your descendants all these lands; and in your seed all the nations of the earth shall be blessed; because Abraham obeyed My voice and kept My charge, My commandments, My statutes, and My laws." (Genesis 26:2-5)

The significant difference in this set of promises is that the blessings are *because* Abraham obeyed God—no mention is made of Isaac's obedience or faithfulness. Yes, Isaac had done well on Mount Moriah, but he has simply ignored the prophecy about Jacob, and thus far his adult life has only demonstrated that he "loves Esau"—a wild, reckless, pagan man who has shown no interest in the future promises of God. In fact, Esau "despised his birthright"!

Pandering to the Philistines

So Isaac dwelt in Gerar. And the men of the place asked about his wife. And he said, "She is my sister"; for he was afraid to say, "She is my wife," because he thought, "lest the men of the place kill me for Rebekah, because she is beautiful to behold." (Genesis 26:6-7)

Isaac had sense enough to heed the Lord's warning and settle down in Gerar. Yet even though he had no doubt had business dealings with these people, Isaac was fearful that Rebekah's beauty would become a source of danger for him. So, with much the same self-preservation worry that had caused Abram and Sarai so much embarrassment down in Egypt, Isaac adopts the half-lie of his father and spreads the word that Rebekah is his sister, not his wife.

Now it came to pass, when he had been there a long time, that Abimelech king of the Philistines looked through a window, and saw, and there was Isaac, showing endearment to Rebekah his wife. Then Abimelech called Isaac and said, "Quite obviously she is your wife; so how could you say, 'She is my sister'?" And Isaac said to him, "Because I said, 'Lest I die on account of her.'" And Abimelech said, "What is this you have done to us? One of the people might soon have lain with your wife, and you would have brought guilt on us." So Abimelech charged all his people, saying, "He who touches this man or his wife shall surely be put to death." (Genesis 26:8-11)

How long the deception continued is not clear, but one day the Philistine king Abimelech sees Isaac "enjoying" Rebekah and knows immediately that they are husband and wife. (This is probably not the same Abimelech who had dealt with Abraham.) The reaction of Abimelech is very different from that of the pharaoh who sent Abraham packing. This king rebukes Isaac, of course, but then issues an edict to protect him!

And for a while, things couldn't be better. "Then Isaac sowed in that land, and reaped in the same year a hundredfold; and the LORD blessed him" (Genesis 26:12). Faithful to His promise, the Lord makes sure that everything that Isaac does turns out well. This is the first time we have any hint that either Abraham or Isaac had developed crops. Heretofore, everything business-related seemed to be centered on their livestock. But now, the rancher tries farming, and the "man began to prosper, and continued prospering until he became very prosperous" (v. 13). So much so that "the Philistines envied him" (v. 14).

Running from the Philistines

Now the Philistines had stopped up all the wells which his father's servants had dug in the days of Abraham his father, and they had filled them with earth. And Abimelech said to Isaac, "Go away from us, for you are much mightier than we." (Genesis 26:15-16)

The tables turn for Isaac—Abimelech sends him away. Isaac is the stranger in the land. The land belongs to the Philistines, even though an earlier Abimelech had given Abraham the right to live anywhere in the land. Perhaps, since Isaac and his servants were "much mightier" than the Philistine foothold at Gerar, Isaac could have fought them—and probably won. The main force of the seafaring Philistine nation was still offshore on the island of Crete. But since it was obvious that the Philistines intended to establish a permanent presence in Canaan, Isaac turns eastward, following the course of the wells that his father had dug during the previous century.

> Then Isaac departed from there and pitched his tent in the Valley of Gerar, and dwelt there. And Isaac dug again the wells of water which they had dug in the days of Abraham his father, for the Philistines had stopped them up after the death of Abraham. He called them by the names which his father had called them.
>
> Also Isaac's servants dug in the valley, and found a well of running water there. But the herdsmen of Gerar quarreled with Isaac's herdsmen, saying, "The water is ours." So he called the name of the well Esek, because they quarreled with him. Then they dug another well, and they quarreled over that one also. So he called its name Sitnah. And he moved from there and dug another well, and they did not quarrel over it. So he called its name Rehoboth, because he said, "For now the LORD has made room for us, and we shall be fruitful in the land." (Genesis 26:17-22)

How long this nomadic existence continues is not clear, but it must have been several years. Isaac moves from Esek to Sitnah, each location fought over and moving them farther and farther away from the coastline and from the Philistines. Finally, at a newly re-opened well the attacks stop and Isaac recognizes that "the LORD has made room for us."

> Then he went up from there to Beersheba. (Genesis 26:23)

Up to this point there has been no mention of Esau and Jacob during the years that Isaac and Rebekah were living around Gerar.

The attempt to deceive Abimelech about Rebekah would have been utterly foolish with two grown sons hanging around, so it is likely that Esau and Jacob remained in the south caring for the large flocks that required the wide grazing lands available in the Negev. Since the well at Beersheba had been a major settlement for Abraham and Isaac for many years, it may well have been the place that the two sons held as their ranching headquarters. All of that may have figured into Isaac's thinking after he reached the strife-free well at Rehoboth. Thus, now unencumbered with relocation issues, Isaac finally returns to his boyhood home to reunite with his sons.

Calling on the Lord

Once again, the Lord appears to Isaac and renews His promise of blessing.

> And the LORD appeared to him the same night and said, "I am the God of your father Abraham; do not fear, for I am with you. I will bless you and multiply your descendants for My servant Abraham's sake." So he built an altar there and called on the name of the LORD, and he pitched his tent there; and there Isaac's servants dug a well. (Genesis 26:24-25)

Once again, the Lord makes it clear that the blessing and promises are *because* of the relationship that God had with Abraham. Although Isaac is certainly the "promised heir," he has yet to demonstrate his commitment to follow the Lord in his life—and there is still (most assuredly known to God) the future tragic episode with Jacob and Esau and "the blessing."

However, at this point Isaac is suitably subdued and begins to call "on the name of the LORD," building some form of permanent altar for worship and sacrifice. Prior to the Mosaic Law, the biblical data do not reveal much about the practice of animal sacrifice—except the hints from Adam on forward that there was a common knowledge among the descendants within the godly line of Seth, Enoch, Noah, Shem, Abraham, and now Isaac that an innocent animal was to be slain in the process of worshiping the Creator. All of that knowledge was codified under Moses, but in the lives of these early patriarchs the liturgy was either oral or traditional. Nonetheless, Isaac knew what was expected of him and "called" on God at the altar.

Peace with Others

Like Abraham before him, Isaac was strong enough and obviously under the blessing of *Elohim* (known but not worshiped by others) so that the growing encampment of the Philistines wanted peace with him.

> Then Abimelech came to him from Gerar with Ahuzzath, one of his friends, and Phichol the commander of his army. And Isaac said to them, "Why have you come to me, since you hate me and have sent me away from you?" But they said, "We have certainly seen that the LORD is with you. So we said, 'Let there now be an oath between us, between you and us; and let us make a covenant with you, that you will do us no harm, since we have not touched you, and since we have done nothing to you but good and have sent you away in peace. You are now the blessed of the LORD.'" (Genesis 26:26-29)

Enough had changed in the life of Isaac that even his former enemies now understood that Isaac had God's favor and that they needed to dwell together without conflict. This rather formal meeting took place over a feast and ended with an agreement that lasted for several decades. Just as the entourage of the Philistines was departing, Isaac's servants came with the happy news that the nearby well had been cleared and was now a sufficient source of water for their foreseeable future needs. Appropriately, Isaac rechristened the well "Beersheba"— the well of the oath.

Lingering Challenges

The closing verses of Genesis 26 are something of a sad commentary. Apparently the two sons are now living with their father and mother at Beersheba. Esau is now said to be 40 years old, indicating that the elapsed time from the sale of the birthright to the current situation is close to 20 years.

Nothing seems to have changed as far as Esau is concerned.

> When Esau was forty years old, he took as wives Judith the daughter of Beeri the Hittite, and Basemath the daughter of Elon the Hittite. And they were a grief of mind to Isaac and Rebekah. (Genesis 26:34-35)

In spite of what Esau surely knew about his grandfather's concern for the proper wife for Isaac, Esau not only marries a pagan Hittite, but marries *two* of them! It seems as though Esau is doing everything he can to flaunt his defiance of God's design for this special people, ignoring the obvious and living a flagrant life of polygamy and profligate foolishness in front of them all.

Yet Isaac "loves" Esau.

CHAPTER SEVEN
ON THE RUN

The family is finally back together after several difficult years. There is peace between the huge enterprise of Isaac and the Philistine holdings at Gerar. Isaac appears to have regained some of his early respect and worship of his father's God. The family altar has become a place of regular worship again, as it once was while Abraham was alive. The family business is enormously successful and everything seems OK—at least on the surface.

But, "Isaac loved Esau because he ate of his game, but Rebekah loved Jacob" (Genesis 25:28). That concise statement was recorded by Moses just prior to the time when Esau despised his birthright and sold it to Jacob for a bowl of red stew. That was a long time ago. However, the condition still simmered below the surface, occasionally stirred up into flame by Esau's flagrant disregard for the family's godly mission. Now Esau has added strain to the family by marrying two Hittite women whose polytheistic religion and practices would have indeed been "a grief of mind to Isaac and Rebekah" (Genesis 26:35).

Yet, Isaac *still* "loved Esau because he ate of his game."

Isaac Is Old

Now it came to pass, when Isaac was old and his eyes were

so dim that he could not see... (Genesis 27:1)

This short but significant notation sets the stage for one of the more momentous events in Scripture. Just how old is Isaac? The answer to that question may help us understand something of the subsequent actions that take place as Jacob tricks Isaac into blessing him instead of Esau. If Isaac is on his deathbed, one might tend to be a bit more tolerant of his anxious efforts to verify his son's identity. If Isaac is still relatively strong and sane, that would shade the way one might evaluate the activities surrounding the granting of the blessing.

The biblical data are always the place to focus. We can get some idea of Isaac's age at the time of the blessing from the chronology of the events that follow it. Jacob spends 20 years working for Laban in Haran (Genesis 31:41)—14 years in "payment" for his wives, and six years for a share of Laban's livestock. Joseph is the last son born to Jacob in Haran and may have been very young when the family left.

Jacob married Rachel at the start of the second seven-year service period (right after marrying Leah). The three other wives of Jacob all produced multiple children before Joseph's birth to Rachel, meaning that Rachel was barren for much if not most of that period. If Joseph arrived shortly before Jacob's final six years with Laban (which began after Joseph's birth—Genesis 30:25), it would make him no older than seven or so when the family leaves Haran to return to Canaan. Joseph then spends ten years with his family in Canaan before his brothers sell him into slavery at the age of 17 (Genesis 37:2).

At least 30 years are thus accounted for—the 20 years Jacob spent with Laban plus the ten years Joseph was in Canaan. Joseph is 17 when he is taken to Egypt (Genesis 37:2) and 30 when he begins to reign there (Genesis 41:46), accounting for 13 more years. There follow seven years of plenty (Genesis 41:29). Two years into the predicted seven years of famine, Joseph reveals himself to his brothers (Genesis 45:4-6). The move of Jacob and his family to Egypt and their settling in Goshen (Genesis 46:28-29) likely take another year. So, all told around 53 years have passed (30 + 13 + 7 + 2 + 1).

Jacob is 130 when he meets Pharaoh (Genesis 47:9). Isaac is 60 when the twin boys are born (Genesis 25:26), so that would make Jacob and Esau around 77 (130 – 53) and Isaac about 137 (77 + 60) at the time of the event at the bedside of Isaac recorded in Genesis 27. Perhaps these calculations are not terribly important, other than to establish this point: Isaac was not senile nor was he on his deathbed when the formal blessing was given. Both Esau and Jacob were fully grown adults, with their character and behavior patterns well established. Isaac and Rebekah were quite mature but still very active and intelligent. Isaac is still strong physically (he lives another 40 years or so). The only problem he had to deal with was failing eyesight.

Isaac knew what he was doing. He was both willing and determined to pass the family's leadership and responsibilities on to Esau—in spite of the prophecy from God Himself at the birth of the twins, in spite of Esau's ungodly life, in spite of Jacob's obvious legally acquired right to the birthright, in spite of his wife's own love for Jacob, in spite of the "grief" that Esau had caused in the family—and apparently *because* Isaac wanted to eat some wild game more than he wanted to follow God's instructions!

Obtaining the Blessing

> Isaac...called Esau his older son and said to him, "My son." And he answered him, "Here I am." Then he said, "Behold now, I am old. I do not know the day of my death. Now therefore, please take your weapons, your quiver and your bow, and go out to the field and hunt game for me. And make me savory food, such as I love, and bring it to me that I may eat, that my soul may bless you before I die." Now Rebekah was listening when Isaac spoke to Esau his son. And Esau went to the field to hunt game and to bring it. (Genesis 27:1-4)

This is the event that heaps undeserved scorn on Jacob and overlooks the terrible spiritual indifference of Isaac and the awful behavior of Esau when he found out he really had lost his birthright and his blessing. It has always been a mystery to this author why Jacob continues to be dissed by Bible scholars and preachers alike when God Himself records no word of condemnation, but to the contrary blesses Jacob more than any other of the patriarchs (except perhaps Abraham) and gives Jacob the new name by which the entire nation will forever be identified—Israel.

Instigated by Rebekah

> So Rebekah spoke to Jacob her son, saying, "Indeed I heard your father speak to Esau your brother, saying, 'Bring me game and make savory food for me, that I may eat it and bless you in the presence of the LORD before my death.' Now therefore, my son, obey my voice according to what I command you." (Genesis 27:6-8)

This deed had been a long time coming, but it is impossible that Rebekah and Isaac had not discussed the powerful prophecy that had been given to Rebekah during her pregnancy with the twins. These are the only children that they had together. The "boys" are now mature men with decades of lifestyle choices and reputation behind them. Esau has proven his ungodliness. Jacob has proven his commitment to follow God and to assume the role of family head and spiritual leader. Rebekah has ached over this for years and now hears her worst fears confirmed. Isaac is determined to bless Esau—even in the "presence of the LORD" (the Hebrew word is *paniym*, "face"). It is as though (at least in the mind of Rebekah) Isaac is standing up to the Lord—to His very face—and defying what God has prophesied must come to pass.

What is clear in the biblical text is that Rebekah "orders" Jacob to attempt this deception. He and Rebekah may well have thought and talked about what they might do if and when "the day" ever came, but it is Rebekah who sets the plan in motion.

> "Go now to the flock and bring me from there two choice kids of the goats, and I will make savory food from them for your father, such as he loves. Then you shall take it to your father, that he may eat it, and that he may bless you

before his death." And Jacob said to Rebekah his mother, "Look, Esau my brother is a hairy man, and I am a smooth-skinned man. Perhaps my father will feel me, and I shall seem to be a deceiver to him; and I shall bring a curse on myself and not a blessing." But his mother said to him, "Let your curse be on me, my son; only obey my voice, and go, get them for me."

And he went and got them and brought them to his mother, and his mother made savory food, such as his father loved. Then Rebekah took the choice clothes of her elder son Esau, which were with her in the house, and put them on Jacob her younger son. And she put the skins of the kids of the goats on his hands and on the smooth part of his neck. Then she gave the savory food and the bread, which she had prepared, into the hand of her son Jacob. (Genesis 27:9-17)

Rebekah hatches the plan. Jacob objects. Rebekah insists and sends Jacob to get the goats from the field. Rebekah prepares the meal and figures out a way to attach the goatskin patches to Jacob's arms and neck. The point is that Jacob certainly did the deed, but Rebekah is the motivator, coach, and human instigator of the plot.

There is no question that the intention of Jacob and Rebecca was to prevent horrible disobedience and catastrophe. Their action would give no immediate advantage and was taken at great personal risk. The deception is not rebuked by God, and Jacob is later honored by God far more than Isaac.

Sometimes God uses questionable human choices to work His will rather than supernaturally intervening in the affairs of men. The Hebrew midwives Shiphrah and Puah were brave enough to defy the edict of a later pharaoh to kill all the newborn male children of the captive Hebrews (Exodus 1:15-19). They refused and saved Moses, and then lied to Pharaoh about why they failed to obey his murderous command. God's evaluation? "Therefore God dealt well with the midwives, and the people multiplied and grew very mighty" (Exodus 1:20).

The prostitute Rahab hid Joshua's spies in her house and told the city leaders a lie that saved the spies and sent Jericho's killer squads on a wild goose chase. God honored her faith in the mission of *Elohim* for Israel (which she hardly knew anything about) and rescued her and her family (Joshua 2:3-6; 6:25). Later, Rahab would marry Salmon and would become the great-great-grandmother of King David (Matthew 1:5-6). Sometimes it is good for us to remember that even "the wrath of man shall praise" God when all is said and done (Psalm 76:10).

Determined by Isaac

> So he went to his father and said, "My father." And he said, "Here I am. Who are you, my son?" Jacob said to his father, "I am Esau your firstborn; I have done just as you told me; please arise, sit and eat of my game, that your soul may bless me." But Isaac said to his son, "How is it that you have found it so quickly, my son?" And he said, "Because the LORD your God brought it to me."
>
> Then Isaac said to Jacob, "Please come near, that I may feel you, my son, whether you are really my son Esau or not." So Jacob went near to Isaac his father, and he felt him and said, "The voice is Jacob's voice, but the hands are the hands of Esau." And he did not recognize him, because his hands were hairy like his brother Esau's hands; so he blessed him. Then he said, "Are you really my son Esau?" He said, "I am." He said, "Bring it near to me, and I will eat of my son's game, so that my soul may bless you." So he brought it near to him, and he ate; and he brought him wine, and he drank. (Genesis 27:18-25)

Please note how many times Isaac tries to make sure that he is dealing with Esau. First, he registers surprise that Esau has come back so quickly. (Isaac is not foolish, just partially blind.) Next, Isaac demands that he "feel" him to make sure that Jacob is "really my son Esau." Then, even though his touch has verified the hairy arms and neck of Esau, Isaac still wants to make sure because the voice sounds like Jacob. So after one final "are you really Esau" question, Isaac pronounces the blessing—on Jacob!

> Then his father Isaac said to him, "Come near now and kiss me, my son." And he came near and kissed him; and he smelled the smell of his clothing, and blessed him and said: "Surely, the smell of my son Is like the smell of a field Which the LORD has blessed. Therefore may God give you Of the dew of heaven, Of the fatness of the earth, And plenty of grain and wine. Let peoples serve you, And nations bow down to you. Be master over your brethren, And let your mother's sons bow down to you. Cursed be everyone who curses you, And blessed be those who bless you!" (Genesis 27:26-29)

Now the deed is done. Isaac still tries to convince himself that Jacob is Esau. He is still determined that he pass on both the birthright (which Isaac knew had been legally sold to Jacob) and the family blessing—to Esau! Esau, whom Isaac "loves" in spite of all the blatant evidence that Esau is a pagan rebel. Isaac has made up his mind to "bless" this awful son in contradiction and open disobedience to the stated will of the God of creation.

What arrogance! Please notice that Isaac uses almost the very words that God Himself used when blessing Abraham. This was no spur-of-the-moment forgetful splurge of emotional attachment. This was Isaac's conscious choice of an ungodly man to lead the future descendants of Abraham through whom the promised seed would come to bless "all the families of the earth." Satan must have been grinning!

Isaac Is Terrified

> Now it happened, as soon as Isaac had finished blessing Jacob, and Jacob had scarcely gone out from the presence of Isaac his father, that Esau his brother came in from his

hunting. He also had made savory food, and brought it to his father, and said to his father, "Let my father arise and eat of his son's game, that your soul may bless me." And his father Isaac said to him, "Who are you?" So he said, "I am your son, your firstborn, Esau." Then Isaac trembled exceedingly, and said, "Who? Where is the one who hunted game and brought it to me? I ate all of it before you came, and I have blessed him—and indeed he shall be blessed." (Genesis 27:30-33)

No sooner had Jacob gathered up the dishes and scurried out of the room to find Rebekah than in comes Esau, fresh from the field and bearing the "savory meat" that he knew Isaac loved. The reader can well imagine the scene. Isaac has convinced himself that he has gotten away with his long-held plan to put Esau in charge of the family's future. Then like a bolt of lightning, his disloyalty is uncovered. As he stumbles through the verbal exchange that verifies his worst nightmare, he "trembled exceedingly."

This is no mere shudder. The Hebrew words are about the strongest expression one might think of to describe a shaking that took over Isaac's entire body. Isaac knew what he had done—and he knew that God had overruled him. When Isaac could finally talk after the spasm of fear and dread had passed, he knew that God would indeed bless Jacob and nothing either he or Esau could do would ever change that. In something of a hoarse whisper, one would surmise, Isaac said: "I have blessed him—and indeed he shall be blessed."

Esau Seeks Repentance

When Esau heard the words of his father, he cried with an exceedingly great and bitter cry, and said to his father, "Bless me—me also, O my father!" But he said, "Your brother came with deceit and has taken away your blessing." And Esau said, "Is he not rightly named Jacob? For he has supplanted me these two times. He took away my birthright, and now look, he has taken away my blessing!"

And he said, "Have you not reserved a blessing for me?"
(Genesis 27:34-36)

This must have been quite an emotional outburst. The writer of
the book of Hebrews comments on this scene and observes, "For you
know that afterward, when he wanted to inherit the blessing, he was
rejected, for he found no place for repentance, though he sought it
diligently with tears" (Hebrews 12:17). Esau, you will note, blames
Jacob. No thought of the foolishness and indifference that caused him
to "despise" his birthright for a bowl of red stew and a slice of bread.
No mention of the flagrant lifestyle of ungodliness that had brought
him to this sorry state. No! Jacob was the "heel grabber" who had
"grabbed" him—twice! Esau was the victim here, what was "Dad"
going to do about it?

Even Isaac tries to blame Jacob. "Your brother [Isaac apparently
cannot yet bring himself to say Jacob's name] came with deceit and
has taken away your blessing." Please note: Isaac is still fixated on his
plan to bless Esau. He had done everything that he could to make sure
that Esau was the one getting the blessing.

When Isaac used the Hebrew *mirma* as an adjective to describe
Jacob's "deceit," he chose a term that is most often used to describe a
deed with intend to harm—even kill. "Treacherous" Jacob had ruined
everything. Even though the truth was slowly dawning on Isaac, he
still wanted somehow to justify himself and was having serious trouble coming to grips with what had happened.

Isaac Relents

Then Isaac answered and said to Esau, "Indeed I have
made him your master, and all his brethren I have given
to him as servants; with grain and wine I have sustained
him. What shall I do now for you, my son?" And Esau
said to his father, "Have you only one blessing, my father?
Bless me—me also, O my father!" And Esau lifted up his
voice and wept. Then Isaac his father answered and said
to him: "Behold, your dwelling shall be of the fatness of

the earth, And of the dew of heaven from above. By your sword you shall live, And you shall serve your brother; And it shall come to pass, when you become restless, That you shall break his yoke from your neck." (Genesis 27:37-40)

The flow of thoughts and emotions through Isaac must have torn him like a fierce storm. Over the space of an hour or so, he has gone from placid determination to commit an evil deed, to an awful realization that God knew what he was planning to do all along, to an intense fear that God might strike him dead on the spot. As his adrenalin stopped gushing and his heart rate began to bounce back toward normal, all he could summon was a weak defense to Esau that Jacob had pulled off a "treacherous" feat and robbed them both. Finally, some small speck of spiritual wisdom glowed out of the darkened recesses of Isaac's heart, and he consciously admitted that the blessing belonged to Jacob and that Esau would ultimately wind up outside the family and outside of the privileged nation.

There is no question that Isaac was "saved" (to use our New Testament terminology). In the Bible's own commentary on the great heroes of faith, Isaac is listed: "By faith Isaac blessed Jacob and Esau concerning things to come" (Hebrews 11:20). Yes, he had lost his close relationship with his Lord by focusing on a son whose life was ungodly, but even after his awful attempt to bless the one who God had said would not be blessed, he "came to himself" (as did the prodigal son—Luke 15:17) and carried out his responsibility.

There is some "Isaac" in each of us. We, like Isaac, should be most grateful for God's eternal longsuffering, sovereign grace, and marvelous mercy.

Jacob Driven Out

So Esau hated Jacob because of the blessing with which his father blessed him, and Esau said in his heart, "The days of mourning for my father are at hand; then I will kill my brother Jacob." (Genesis 27:41)

The gregarious "man of the field" who couldn't care less about his younger brother suddenly flies into an intense rage over the formal blessing that deprived him of his right of leadership and double portion of wealth. Completely ignoring the fact that the fault lay with him rather than Jacob, Esau's heart blackened into a tight focus of hatred and a vow to murder his brother as soon as Isaac is dead. As is the case with most sinful emotions, Esau is not content to keep the thoughts to himself, but either reveals his plans to close "hunting buddies" or mumbles them loud enough in his private quarters so that the household servants become aware.

> And the words of Esau her older son were told to Rebekah. So she sent and called Jacob her younger son, and said to him, "Surely your brother Esau comforts himself concerning you by intending to kill you. Now therefore, my son, obey my voice: arise, flee to my brother Laban in Haran. And stay with him a few days, until your brother's fury turns away, until your brother's anger turns away from you, and he forgets what you have done to him; then I will send and bring you from there. Why should I be bereaved also of you both in one day?" (Genesis 27:42-45)

Once again Rebekah is the source of the events that follow. She was a remarkable woman. The strength, energy, and ingenuity of her youth are still her greatest assets. Sharpened no doubt by her spiritual maturity and the insights granted her during her visit with the Lord while she was pregnant with the twin boys, she had remained true to God's plan for the family line. Once again she commands Jacob to follow her instructions and run away from the "fury" and "anger" of Esau.

This is where the personal risks that both Rebekah and Jacob understood were probable came to fruition. Their efforts had never been for personal gain but had been focused on preventing an awful human tragedy from unfolding should Isaac follow through with his intention to transfer the family leadership to Esau. They knew then, and were quick now to realize, that this would mean further sacrifice on their part. Jacob must flee and do so quickly. Esau's hostile passion was intense, but it was likely that his volatile personality would "forget" after a while and things could return to normal—or so they thought.

Contact had surely been maintained between the household of Isaac and the household of Bethuel back in eastern Syria. Rebekah was confident that her brother Laban would treat Jacob well "for a few days," and then he could return back home to Beersheba. She was mistaken (as we so often are when our emotions cloud our judgments). As far as the biblical record is concerned, neither Rebekah nor Jacob ever saw each other again. Sometimes doing the right thing the wrong way brings lifelong consequences that are hard to bear.

Would God have stepped in and prevented Isaac from blessing Esau? Possibly—or perhaps worked through others to bring about His will. Rebekah and Jacob brought serious consequences on themselves by "helping" God out. All of this is speculation, of course, but if they had spent more time praying rather than plotting, they may well have seen God work His will in a more marvelous way—and received a greater personal blessing instead of the very trouble they knew might happen.

But actions have consequences and the deed was done. Rebekah, as sharp and clever as she is, could think of no other solution than to go to Isaac (who ruled the roost) and "suggest" that he send Jacob away for a while. And what better way to manipulate Isaac than to remind him of those awful "daughters of Heth" married to Esau? Surely Isaac doesn't want his *other* son to wind up marrying one of those "daughters of the land." If that happens, Rebekah moaned, "I'll just die!"

> And Rebekah said to Isaac, "I am weary of my life because of the daughters of Heth; if Jacob takes a wife of the daughters of Heth, like these who are the daughters of the land, what good will my life be to me?" (Genesis 27:46)

Isaac Commissions Jacob

> Then Isaac called Jacob and blessed him, and charged him, and said to him: "You shall not take a wife from the daughters of Canaan. Arise, go to Padan Aram, to the house of Bethuel your mother's father; and take yourself a wife from there of the daughters of Laban your mother's brother. May God Almighty bless you, And make you fruitful and multiply you, That you may be an assembly of peoples; And give you the blessing of Abraham, To you and your descendants with you, That you may inherit the land In which you are a stranger, Which God gave to Abraham." So Isaac sent Jacob away, and he went to Padan Aram, to Laban the son of Bethuel the Syrian, the brother of Rebekah, the mother of Jacob and Esau. (Genesis 28:1-5)

However long it has been since the bedside blessing, Isaac has softened considerably. The language of the text would allow for some time to have elapsed (several days, perhaps), but that time had brought Isaac back to a keen recognition of God's purpose for him and his family. Now with no confusion in his mind, Isaac calls Jacob to him and charges him with the responsibility to find a wife from within the family line—just as Abraham had charged Eliezer to do so long ago for Isaac.

Isaac now endorses the blessing that he thought he had given to Esau, in full compliance and recognition that Jacob is the one to receive the blessing. Isaac emphasizes the necessity of the pure line through Abraham, insisting that Jacob is not to take a wife among the Canaanites but must go to his mother's relatives and take a wife from them. Now with full understanding that Jacob is the correct beneficiary, Isaac calls on God Almighty (*El Shaddai*) to bless Jacob with all of the components of the "blessing of Abraham."

At the bedside blessing (Genesis 27:28-29), Isaac had invoked the following:

- God's blessing of the earth and heaven.

- God's blessing of nations and authority over them.

- God's blessing of authority over the family of the Seed.

- God's blessing of worldwide blessing and protection.

At this second commission (Genesis 28:3-4), Isaac invoked the additional blessings:

- God's promise for many children.

- God's fulfillment of a large population for the nation.

- God's completion of the land transfer and possession.

Thus, Isaac appears to have come full circle and is back in sync with God's plan and in submission to his role in the sequence of patriarchs. As far as the biblical record provides, Isaac lives on at peace with the Lord for several decades and is finally buried by his two sons in the cave at Machpelah with his father and mother and his faithful wife, Rebekah.

Esau Attempts to Reconcile

Esau saw that Isaac had blessed Jacob and sent him away to Padan Aram to take himself a wife from there, and that as he blessed him he gave him a charge, saying, "You shall not take a wife from the daughters of Canaan," and that Jacob had obeyed his father and his mother and had gone to Padan Aram. Also Esau saw that the daughters of Canaan did not please his father Isaac. So Esau went to Ishmael and took Mahalath the daughter of Ishmael, Abraham's son, the sister of Nebajoth, to be his wife in addition to the wives he had. (Genesis 28:6-9)

Almost as a footnote, Moses records the pathetic attempt of Esau to regain the favor of his parents. After the traumatic and emotional event of the missed blessing, after being married to pagan women for over 20 years, after *finally* understanding that neither Isaac nor Rebekah like the Hittite women (or, for that matter, their pagan rituals), Esau decides that a close relative might please his parents.

And whom does he choose? A daughter of Ishmael, a descendant of the "bondwoman's son" who had been deliberately and specifically *excluded* from the family line! How dense could this man be? No wonder the Scriptures tell us that "the natural man does not receive the things of the Spirit of God, for they are foolishness to him; nor can he know them, because they are spiritually discerned" (1 Corinthians 2:14).

We hear nothing more about Esau for 20 years. The next time he comes into the picture he is on his way to meet Jacob with 400 men from Seir. With no thought for the genuine prophetic blessing that Isaac has pronounced on his behalf, Esau (apparently) moves out of the family compound to get as far away from Beersheba as he can. Genesis 36 lists the major sons of Esau who conquered the land that came to be known as Edom (the Red Land, south of the Dead Sea extending into the Sinai Peninsula) after the famous incident of the "red" stew.

The Flight of Jacob

> Now Jacob went out from Beersheba and went toward Haran. (Genesis 28:10)

The Bible seems to imply that Jacob was alone on this long journey. If so, that would have been very unusual. After all, Jacob is the son of a famous person and has been officially commissioned to go north and east to the land from which his grandfather, Abraham, had set out in response to God's promise. And although there were blossoming civilizations along the route, the roads (such as they were) would have been heavily traveled by trade caravans shuttling back and forth between Haran and Egypt. One such caravan of Midianites purchased Joseph less than 50 years later.

The biblical text here centers on Jacob and deals directly with God's affirmation and protection of him on the trail, but the reader should recall that Haran was a major trading center set near the center of what many history books call the Fertile Crescent. Trade goods from Babel and Nineveh would be received and prepared for sale and distribution all along the western route to Damascus (even then a growing city) and southward along the Mediterranean coastline to the empire of Egypt. Abraham and Isaac would have done business with these caravans. Jacob was traveling along a well-known commercial highway, with plenty of "traffic."

Yet, Jacob would have felt alone. He had essentially been kicked out of his family, his brother was threatening to kill him, and all of his plans had seemed to evaporate. No doubt he was sucking his spiritual thumb as well. After all, he had done all of this for God. Why was he abandoned in the middle of nowhere? All of the promises were centered in Canaan. Why was he running off to Haran? What was going to happen? Would he ever get back? Would he ever see his mother and father again? How was he going to make a living? What if he would be forced to marry some woman he didn't like? Why me?!

All of these questions and many more were no doubt running through Jacob's mind.

Jacob's Ladder

God doesn't leave him dangling for long. Now that Jacob was away from the tumult and turmoil of Beersheba, now that his heart was open and aching for direction and purpose, God began to speak and reaffirm the "big picture" to this very special servant.

> So he came to a certain place and stayed there all night, because the sun had set. And he took one of the stones of that place and put it at his head, and he lay down in that place to sleep. (Genesis 28:11)

This place Jacob later named Bethel—the "house of God." Abram had lived near there for a short time (Genesis 12:8) and then later came to stay where he'd earlier built an altar and "called on the name of the LORD" (Genesis 13:4). A small city had sprung up called

Luz (Genesis 28:19), probably as a way station for the caravan traffic that passed through. Jacob, not wanting to bring notice to himself, stopped on the outskirts of Luz, fashioned an encampment of sorts, and, using a rock for a pillow, fell asleep.

> Then he dreamed, and behold, a ladder was set up on the earth, and its top reached to heaven; and there the angels of God were ascending and descending on it. (Genesis 28:12)

What a vision! God pulled back the veil of the universe to reveal a "ladder" that provided a means of travel back and forth from the presence of God to Earth. Since the Hebrew word *cullam* is only used this one time in the Old Testament, it is difficult to get any clear picture of what Jacob actually saw. Some similar words have the meaning of "way up" or "to cast up," but whatever this "thing" was that Jacob saw, it was definitely not a ladder! Perhaps it was something like our science fiction ideas of a "wormhole"—a time warp in the fabric of space that permits nearly instantaneous movement from one spot in the universe to another.

Angels do "fly swiftly" (Daniel 9:21). They don't suddenly "pop" into existence. They have a finite condition and are not omnipresent. They are the messengers of God and were created to be "ministering spirits sent forth to minister for those who will inherit salvation" (Hebrews 1:14). We know very little about the place where God has his throne room. All the references imply it is somewhere "up" and "outside" what we consider the known universe. The Scriptures often speak of angels coming to Earth, and at least one reference speaks of Satan coming among other angels into the presence of God and nonchalantly telling God that he had been "going to and fro on the earth, and from walking back and forth on it" (Job 1:7).

The Creator of the universe would certainly be able to make some sort of a time-warp channel for His messengers to get back and forth to Earth quickly. There are likely many such channels—or at least one such *cullam* that obeys the Creator's command as needed. This *cullam* was "fastened" on the earth with its "source" in heaven. The angels of God were speeding up and down (through? on? in?) it. At the source, Jacob saw none other than the *Yahweh* (the I AM) of eternity standing in His "official" glory (compare Revelation 1:10-16).

Jacob's Personal Blessing

> And behold, the LORD stood above it and said: "I am the LORD God of Abraham your father and the God of Isaac; the land on which you lie I will give to you and your descendants. Also your descendants shall be as the dust of the earth; you shall spread abroad to the west and the east, to the north and the south; and in you and in your seed all the families of the earth shall be blessed. Behold, I am with you and will keep you wherever you go, and will bring you back to this land; for I will not leave you until I have done what I have spoken to you." (Genesis 28:13-15)

Jacob has heard of the Lord from his grandfather, his father, and his mother. Many nights, the stories have been told and retold of God's personal appearances to Abraham and of the miraculous calling and protection of his family over the decades. Surely Jacob has read some of the accounts of Noah and Shem that had been passed down to their family through the centuries and would have had a strong personal faith in the creation week, the disastrous rebellion of Adam and Eve, and the horrible Flood that ended the First Age. But up until this moment, Jacob had not personally met *Yahweh*.

Perhaps Jacob was aware that the place he had stopped for the night was the same area where Abraham had built an altar long ago. Maybe he had even used one of the discarded or fallen stones of that very altar for his pillow. Whatever may have been the case, God had surely led Jacob here—and now was granting a vision the like of which had never been seen before nor was ever to be repeated again. Jacob needed encouragement and affirmation. God responded in such a way that Jacob could endure the coming 20 years of discouragement and mistreatment and never look back.

As God speaks, Jacob no doubt was recognizing the very phrases that had been told to Abraham and Isaac. Time and again, he had heard them at the feet of others. Now God was speaking directly to him!

- God identifies Himself as the same Lord who appeared to Abraham and Isaac.

- God specifically repeats that "this ground" that Jacob is sleeping on will be his and will be passed on to his descendants.

- God reasserts that Jacob's descendants will "be as the dust of the earth" and that they will cover a vast territory in every direction.

- God also repeats the core of His plan for this new nation— that "all the families of the earth shall be blessed" through the seed of Jacob.

- God finally gives the personal promise that Jacob would be protected and would return back to the land of promise.

Jacob's Personal Vow

In response to this marvelous vision, Jacob cannot keep silent. All of his human fears had been washed away, his confidence renewed, and his heart steeled for whatever may lie ahead.

> Then Jacob awoke from his sleep and said, "Surely the LORD is in this place, and I did not know it." And he was afraid and said, "How awesome is this place! This is none other than the house of God, and this is the gate of heaven!" Then Jacob rose early in the morning, and took the stone that he had put at his head, set it up as a pillar, and poured oil on top of it. And he called the name of that place Bethel; but the name of that city had been Luz previously. (Genesis 28:16-19)

Probably trembling with the excitement and the awe of what has transpired, Jacob dedicates the rock that he has been sleeping on as a marker to commemorate the event and coins the name Bethel in recognition of the apparent connection that God has established with the *cullam* from heaven to Earth. Even though the little city there had been called Luz, the term Bethel stuck and became the permanent name for the place.

> Then Jacob made a vow, saying, "If God will be with me, and keep me in this way that I am going, and give me bread to eat and clothing to put on, so that I come back to my father's house in peace, then the LORD shall be my God. And this stone which I have set as a pillar shall be God's house, and of all that You give me I will surely give a tenth to You." (Genesis 28:20-22)

This is not a bargain with God. The phrase "if God will be with me" would better be translated "since God will be with me." This is a vow, not a conditional deal. It is an expression of confidence and thanks. It is also a voluntary promise to give a tenth back to God of everything that God will give him over the years to come.

This is the second time that a great man has given a "tithe" as an offering to God. When Abram came back from his victory over Chedorlaomer and the confederation of kings who came against Sodom and Gomorrah, he gave Melchizedek "a tithe of all" (Genesis 14:20). Jacob had surely heard of that event from his father, if not from Abraham himself. Now, with the magnificent picture of the Lord fresh in his mind, nothing else would suffice. Jacob could do no less than his grandfather did and promise a tenth of everything that he would come to possess.

Would to God more of the Lord's people would have the same reverence that Jacob and Abraham had. If all of God's people were to tithe their incomes, today's New Testament churches would not struggle to meet their budgets!

But for now, Jacob is an exiled outcast who has nothing. Maybe it appears easy to promise to tithe when you have little or nothing, but in truth it is much harder and of more consequence when first starting out than after one is rich to "put in offerings for God" (Luke 21:4). Jacob, though he doesn't know it yet, has 20 years of some of the most difficult and stressful days of his life ahead. It's some 500 miles from Beersheba to Haran, a long journey under the best of circumstances. Once there, he often wished he was back home.

CHAPTER EIGHT
ISRAEL IN THE MAKING

Jacob is in his late 50s or early 60s when he is exiled from the family at Beersheba. It would have taken him several weeks to cover the 500 miles from southern Canaan to Haran in northeastern Padan Aram (Syria). The miraculous dream on the outskirts of Bethel did strengthen and reconfirm Jacob's mission, but he was on the edge of the most intense 20 years of his life. God would meet him on the way back (as He had promised at Bethel) and give Jacob the new name that would stand as the future nation's identity for the rest of time. But before "Israel" could be named, Jacob must endure the constant deceit of his uncle, the internal jealousies and struggles of four wives, and a personal wrestling match with "the angel of the LORD."

Jacob Arrives in Haran

So Jacob went on his journey and came to the land of the people of the East. And he looked, and saw a well in the field; and behold, there were three flocks of sheep lying by it; for out of that well they watered the flocks. A large stone was on the well's mouth. Now all the flocks would be gathered there; and they would roll the stone from the well's mouth, water the sheep, and put the stone back in its place on the well's mouth. (Genesis 29:1-3)

Haran was the earlier home of Terah, the father of Abram and Nahor. Terah's third son, Haran, died in Ur of the Chaldees just before the family moved north and may have been the source for this trade city's name. Nahor remained behind when Abram took his family into Canaan and developed a major business around the trade routes that were moving along the Fertile Crescent from east to west. Nahor had eight sons, one of whom was Bethuel, the father of Rebekah and Laban. Abraham had sent Eliezer to Haran to find a wife for Isaac. Now Isaac's son Jacob had arrived looking for his mother Rebekah's brother, Laban.

Somewhere in the distance, Jacob spotted a well surrounded by three distinct flocks of sheep. This was probably the same well where Eliezer met Rebekah so long ago—and was probably the very one that Jacob was looking for, given the family history and the specific command from Rebekah and Isaac to find the family of Nahor. The description of the well given in this passage is very similar to that recorded by Eliezer (Genesis 24). The major difference seems to be that there was now a stone that covered the well's opening.

The territory around Haran was suitable for grazing animals. The Euphrates River was on the eastern edge of the area, and the rolling hills and valleys to its west were full of relatively high water tables ideal for regional wells. Most of the wells during that period were enhanced by the various family units and made into functional reservoirs, usually with protective walls and guarded or sealed entrances that would keep wild animals from fouling the water. Apparently, at the time of Abraham water was lifted from the well by hand and poured into troughs for the needs of the grazing flocks and the passing caravan animals.

> And Jacob said to them, "My brethren, where are you from?" And they said, "We are from Haran." Then he said to them, "Do you know Laban the son of Nahor?" And they said, "We know him." So he said to them, "Is he well?" And they said, "He is well. And look, his daughter Rachel is coming with the sheep." Then he said, "Look, it

is still high day; it is not time for the cattle to be gathered together. Water the sheep, and go and feed them." But they said, "We cannot until all the flocks are gathered together, and they have rolled the stone from the well's mouth; then we water the sheep." (Genesis 29:4-8)

Custom seemed to prevent the servants and sheepherders from opening the well without the authorization of the "owners." So when Jacob notices the assembled hired hands and the stone still on the well entrance, he opens the conversation with a polite greeting and inquiry about the territorial status. Confirmation! He has found the right place, and Laban's daughter is coming to authorize opening the well.

> Now while he was still speaking with them, Rachel came with her father's sheep, for she was a shepherdess. And it came to pass, when Jacob saw Rachel the daughter of Laban his mother's brother, and the sheep of Laban his mother's brother, that Jacob went near and rolled the stone from the well's mouth, and watered the flock of Laban his mother's brother. Then Jacob kissed Rachel, and lifted up his voice and wept. (Genesis 29:9-11)

All of the suspense and burden seemed to melt away when he saw Rachel. Years of serving in the shadow of Esau, the agony of the turmoil over the blessing, the fear of leaving his home—even the wonder of the great vision at Bethel—all welled up in a joyous cry of relief and confirmation. He had found it! The future was unknown, but he knew that he was in the place that the Lord wanted him to be for now, and he had the assurance that the Lord would see him through and bring him back to Canaan once again.

> And Jacob told Rachel that he was her father's relative and that he was Rebekah's son. So she ran and told her father. Then it came to pass, when Laban heard the report about Jacob his sister's son, that he ran to meet him, and embraced him and kissed him, and brought him to his house. So he told Laban all these things. And Laban said to him, "Surely you are my bone and my flesh." And he

stayed with him for a month. (Genesis 29:12-15)

Fourteen Years and Four Wives

The 30-day trial was over. Jacob was deemed "acceptable" and had become part of the family. During that time, he had come to love Rachel and was willing to strike a bargain with Laban for a proper dowry. Jacob had arrived virtually penniless and was still very unsure what his prospects would be back in Beersheba with Esau running things, so it looked like a "work-out" would be the best likelihood of gaining respect and a proper marriage.

> Then Laban said to Jacob, "Because you are my relative, should you therefore serve me for nothing? Tell me, what should your wages be?" Now Laban had two daughters: the name of the elder was Leah, and the name of the younger was Rachel. Leah's eyes were delicate, but Rachel was beautiful of form and appearance. Now Jacob loved Rachel; so he said, "I will serve you seven years for Rachel your younger daughter." And Laban said, "It is better that I give her to you than that I should give her to another man. Stay with me." So Jacob served seven years for Rachel, and they seemed only a few days to him because of the love he had for her. (Genesis 29:15-20)

Genuine love between a man and a woman is a powerful force. There is no doubt that Jacob loved Rachel in the proper sense of the term. Obviously, she was a beautiful woman, and that surely contributed to the initial infatuation. However, the intensity of that infatuation grew into a strong and enduring love for her—so much so that when he formally asked Laban for permission to marry, Jacob was willing to serve for "room and board" during the seven years that Laban had set as the "price" for Rachel.

The reader may recall that "sevens" were something of an established custom for formal vows, and seven years, while certainly significant and costly, would not have seemed out of place for Jacob. His grandfather and father had both made costly vows using the principle of "sevens," and since Jacob was a prosperous and experienced businessman (although broke currently), these seven years "seemed only a few days to him because of the love he had" for Rachel.

In the background was the other daughter, Leah. She was not quite as attractive as Rachel and had some feature that would have been considered a disadvantage to a prospective suitor. Leah's eyes were "weak." Several interpretations are possible for this observation. The Hebrew word *rak* is translated in a wide variety of ways, depending on the context. Most often, the English words "tender" or "delicate" are used. Occasionally, the context seems to imply an "inexperience" as the proper inference. The famous Keil and Delitzsch commentaries suggest that this is an idiom for "dull" eyes—eyes that lack the "fire" of intelligence. Their commentary included the observation that "bright eyes, with fire in them, are regarded as the height of beauty in Oriental women."[1]

Regardless of the social preferences of the day, or whether Leah was simply nearsighted and couldn't see well, Jacob fell in love with Rachel. Laban, on the other hand, was more concerned with the custom of marrying the eldest daughter before the younger and kept his thoughts to himself until the seven year "work-out" of the dowry was complete.

> Then Jacob said to Laban, "Give me my wife, for my days are fulfilled, that I may go in to her." And Laban gathered together all the men of the place and made a feast. Now it came to pass in the evening, that he took Leah his daughter and brought her to Jacob; and he went in to her. And Laban gave his maid Zilpah to his daughter Leah as a maid. So it came to pass in the morning, that behold, it was Leah. (Genesis 29:21-25)

Well, this was a surprise! Apparently Jacob was sufficiently satiated at the feast not to notice that Leah was in his bed rather than Rachel, but in the morning it was abundantly clear that Laban had

---

1.   C. F. Keil and Franz Delitzsch, 1951, *Biblical Commentary on the Old Testament,* Volume 1, Grand Rapids, MI: Eerdmans, 285.

pulled a fast one on him.

> And he said to Laban, "What is this you have done to me? Was it not for Rachel that I served you? Why then have you deceived me?" And Laban said, "It must not be done so in our country, to give the younger before the first-born. Fulfill her week, and we will give you this one also for the service which you will serve with me still another seven years." (Genesis 29:25-27)

Now that the deceitful character of Laban was revealed, Jacob nonetheless remained in an untenable position. He still didn't have any money, was still in the service of his uncle, and now he was stuck with Leah and still in love with Rachel. Although Jacob had to know that he was being used, because of his genuine love for Rachel, and now with some serious attachment to Leah as well, Jacob agreed to the new deal and committed himself for another seven years.

> Then Jacob did so and fulfilled her week. So he gave him his daughter Rachel as wife also. And Laban gave his maid Bilhah to his daughter Rachel as a maid. Then Jacob also went in to Rachel, and he also loved Rachel more than Leah. And he served with Laban still another seven years. (Genesis 28:28-30).

The biblical record leaves some room for discussion on when exactly the marriage with Rachel was consummated. On the surface it seems like Jacob's agreement was sufficient for Laban to allow the marriage to take place immediately. However, the seven-year dowry might lead some to suggest that Jacob did not marry Rachel until the completion of the time required. But when we look at the children who were born in quick succession and the fact that Rachel was unproductive for some time, it seems clear that Jacob married Rachel soon after the wedding night with Leah.

The ensuing seven years are very difficult for Jacob.

Leah Bears Four Sons

> When the Lord saw that Leah was unloved, He opened her womb; but Rachel was barren. So Leah conceived and bore a son, and she called his name Reuben; for she said, "The Lord has surely looked on my affliction. Now therefore, my husband will love me." Then she conceived again and bore a son, and said, "Because the Lord has heard that I am unloved, He has therefore given me this son also." And she called his name Simeon. She conceived again and bore a son, and said, "Now this time my husband will become attached to me, because I have borne him three sons." Therefore his name was called Levi. And she conceived again and bore a son, and said, "Now I will praise the Lord." Therefore she called his name Judah. Then she stopped bearing. (Genesis 29:31-35)

The open comment in this section of Scripture tells us that God saw into Jacob's heart about his attitude toward Leah. The Hebrew verb *sane* is an intense term most often translated "despise" or "hate." Jacob must have had a strong disgust for Leah, given how badly he had been fooled by Laban on his wedding night. No doubt Jacob moved in with Rachel immediately and left Leah alone for some time. But God had sovereign plans for the nation of Israel and did not approve of Jacob's "hatred" of Leah, so God closed Rachel's womb and it quickly became clear that no children would likely be born from that union.

So, Jacob moves over to Leah's bed and a quick succession of sons was born.

Reuben: the first born. The delight of Leah on the birth of her son must have created a scene in the birthing room—as Jacob came in to see his newborn child, Leah cried out, "Look, a son!" The exclamation stuck and Reuben became his name. This was the eldest son from the eldest daughter and would have made any family proud. God had begun the genealogical line of the nation of Israel.

Simeon: the second born. Within the subsequent year, Simeon was born. Word had obviously gotten around that Jacob loved Rachel and did not love Leah, but here she was with another son! "God has heard (Hebrew *shama'*) about my problem," Leah says, at least to herself, and suggests the name *Shim'own*—roughly "he heard."

Levi: the third son. By this time, Jacob appears to have lost his "disgust" or "hatred" for Leah. Within another year, the third son is conceived and brought to term. Leah is convinced that Jacob will permanently attach himself to her now and leave Rachel alone. Rachel is barren and Leah has produced three sons in quick succession. Jacob has really "joined" her now and, hopefully, will become "attached." Thus the name Levi.

Judah: the fourth son. Wow! Another son—and right after the last one. No other name would do but "Praise"! So Judah, who was later to become the father of the tribe from which the Messiah would come, is now considered the cause for praise to the Lord for His grace to Leah.

Trouble Begins

But then Leah stops being fertile and the trouble begins to brew.

> Now when Rachel saw that she bore Jacob no children, Rachel envied her sister, and said to Jacob, "Give me children, or else I die!" And Jacob's anger was aroused against Rachel, and he said, "Am I in the place of God, who has withheld from you the fruit of the womb?" So she said, "Here is my maid Bilhah; go in to her, and she will bear a child on my knees, that I also may have children by her." (Genesis 30:1-3)

Seems like this has happened before. In fact, as one reads the account of Abram and Sarai back in Genesis 16, it looks like Rachel is repeating the same mistake that Sarai did with Hagar, with Ishmael as the result. That impulsive action has wreaked enmity and wars that have lasted some 4,000 years!

Even the social mores of both situations were very similar. These maids were considered property of the family, and the social stigma of an inability to bear children was considered to be mitigated (or at least covered over) if the "owner" would "give" the maid to the husband to bear children *for* the barren wife. At the time of Jacob, that custom had endured for over a century and would continue in the customs of the land for many centuries to come. It was considered all right to bear children by proxy (this is still going on in the world today, by the way), so both Abram and Sarai and Jacob and Rachel capitulated.

There is one major difference, however. Hagar was an Egyptian and a slave in the household of Abram. God had given specific instructions to both Abram and Sarai that they would produce "the seed" from which the new nation would emerge. Sarai was driven by petulant impatience and in full knowledge that she was disobeying God's prophetic promise.

Not so with Jacob and Rachel. Yes, God's model for marriage has always been one man and one woman for the entirety of their lives—has been since the creation. And although God forbears with the foibles of human frailty as far as multiple wives are concerned (and even serial wives), there is absolutely not one instance in all of Scripture where there was a *happy* family in which multiple wives were involved. Jacob's family is certainly no exception.

Bilhah Has Two Sons

> Then she gave him Bilhah her maid as wife, and Jacob went in to her. (Genesis 30:4)

The "gift" of Bilhah to Jacob is out of desperation, not petulant impatience. "Give me children lest I die" is the plaintive cry of Rachel. Several emotions are wrapped up in this plea. Not only is Rachel barren (a social and familial stigma of great importance), but Jacob has apparently left her bed far too frequently since Leah has proven to be so fertile. Not only is she pining for the intimacy of their initial love passion, but the longer and more frequently Jacob stays away from her, the more likely it is she will never have any children, and that burden must have been a terrible pain for her.

Jacob's response is sharp and unfeeling: "It's not my fault! Do you think I can work miracles like God! Talk to Him about this problem. You are the one who is barren! Look at Leah if you think it is my fault!" Now, admittedly that paraphrase is a bit imaginative, but probably not far from what was implied. Jacob still loves Rachel and is no doubt frustrated at the dilemma, but he knows that God is planning to build a nation through him and is still slugging it out working for free to pay off his dowry to Laban. Rachel is barren, and now Leah has suddenly become unfertile.

"Behold my maid Bilhah," the King James Version translates. The Hebrew is a bit more forceful than most of the translations convey. "Command my handmaid" would be a more literal rendering. Rachel is demanding that Jacob use Bilhah as her surrogate and produce children through her. As was indicated above, this was not weird or strange in that time, even though it was unusual.

The reason that God does not intervene as He did with Hagar and Ishmael is that Bilhah is genetically related to the line of Shem (through whom Abraham, Isaac, and Jacob had come) and part of the "official" line of humanity through whom God has planned to raise up His nation. Not long after this, Jacob would have his name changed to Israel, and all of his sons would become heads of the tribes that would form the nation.

> And Bilhah conceived and bore Jacob a son. Then Rachel said, "God has judged my case; and He has also heard my voice and given me a son." Therefore she called his name Dan. (Genesis 30:5-6)

Dan: the fifth son. Notice that it is Rachel who names the son. Bilhah is a surrogate mother. Rachel is the "official" mother. She is the legal wife and the one whom Jacob still loves. And because Rachel thinks that God has "judged" her actions as either beneficial or correct, she names the son "Judge"—Dan.

Naphtali: the sixth son. Once again, Rachel names the son. This time she is a bit feisty as she gloats over the struggle that she has had with her sister Leah. She now feels vindicated with the birth of Naphtali, the son who represents her winning the "wrestling" match with her sister.

Zilpah Bears Two Sons

Now the kettle is at full boil. Leah finally figures out that she no longer is producing children and insists that Jacob take *her* maid and "give" Leah more children. Jacob seems to be a willing partner in all of this. The Scripture tells us that he *still* loves Rachel, but his affections are spread pretty thin. Four wives and six sons must have been the talk of the city. Laban must have been smirking behind his beard. What a deal he had made! Not only was he getting the business expertise of Jacob for free these many years, but all of the trouble of keeping a household of women was now dumped onto Jacob.

Gad ("a troop comes" or "fortunate") is quickly conceived and born as son number seven. Right after that, Asher ("happy"), the eighth son, is born. The family has grown to four wives and eight sons in fewer than seven years. Every man is proud to have sons to carry on his name. Jacob was probably bubbling over with enthusiasm (at least as far as the bedchamber was concerned) and was enjoying the compound full of young male children who all showed promise of health and strength. Things were beginning to look up.

Mandrakes

Legends by the score are associated with the root of the plant species *Mandragora officinarum*, which belongs to the broader family of hallucinogenic alkaloids called nightshades. Occasionally mandrake roots form protuberances (bifurcations) that can look like human figures; sometimes they even contain more bumps that look like male genitals. It's not hard to imagine how the rumors got started, especially when stews or soups containing the root produced euphoria or some sort of "high" that would bring on sexual urges.

Little Reuben (the firstborn), who was not much older than five or six, stumbled onto the plant while he was wandering around in the field. Curious about their weird shape, he brought them to his mother—no doubt proud of these "funny" plants and wondering what they could be used for. Leah, of course, knew about their supposed "magical" properties and bragged about what she was going to do with them.

> Rachel said to Leah, "Please give me some of your son's mandrakes." But she said to her, "Is it a small matter that you have taken away my husband? Would you take away my son's mandrakes also?" And Rachel said, "Therefore he will lie with you tonight for your son's mandrakes." (Genesis 30:14-15)

Rachel is still barren and sees a chance to work some "magic" for herself if she can get Jacob to take a potion made out of these mandrakes. She demands that Leah give her the roots, to which Leah rightly responds that Rachel has "taken away" Jacob from her—admitting that she knows that Jacob still loves Rachel. Rather than sell the mandrakes to someone else, Leah makes a bargain with Rachel for that night's bed rights. (Please note: There is no *happy* multiple marriage.)

Leah Bears Three More Children

> When Jacob came out of the field in the evening, Leah went out to meet him and said, "You must come in to me, for I have surely hired you with my son's mandrakes." And he lay with her that night. And God listened to Leah, and she conceived and bore Jacob a fifth son. Leah said, "God has given me my wages, because I have given my maid to my husband." So she called his name Issachar. Then Leah conceived again and bore Jacob a sixth son. And Leah said, "God has endowed me with a good endowment; now my husband will dwell with me, because I have borne him six sons." So she called his name Zebulun. Afterward she bore a daughter, and called her name Dinah. (Genesis 30:16-21)

Leah had evidently been praying to the Lord for other children. The tension between her and Rachel and between the two handmaids and the two sisters must have been palpable. Jacob seems to be the only one who is not troubled at home. He had enough to worry about in the field, all the while yearning for the day when he could leave his deceptive uncle and return to Beersheba.

Leah is impregnated quickly, and when the son is born in the normal time she names him Issachar in memory of the "wages" that God paid her for having given Zilpah to Jacob. Shortly after the birth of Issachar, Leah becomes pregnant again, and this sixth son of their union she names Zebulun, since she anticipates that she will become the "exalted" wife now that she has born Jacob six sons and all the other wives combined have only produced four.

Jacob now has ten sons, a bunch even for that time, and seems satisfied to remain with Leah. The result? Dinah—the only daughter recorded of these many wives and later to become a bitter disappointment to Jacob and the entire family.

Rachel Bears Joseph

Then God remembered Rachel, and God listened to her and opened her womb. And she conceived and bore a son, and said, "God has taken away my reproach." So she called his name Joseph, and said, "The LORD shall add to me another son." (Genesis 30:22-24)

Finally! Rachel gets pregnant as God allows her to bear the son who will one day provide shelter for the budding nation in Egypt. *Yowceph* is coined by Rachel as a reminder that she is now able to bear children and expects God to "add more" to their marriage. Joseph is son number 11. The fulfillment of Rachel's expectation for more children, Benjamin, is born many years later in Canaan (Genesis 35:16-18) and becomes son number 12.

Six Years for Wages

> And it came to pass, when Rachel had borne Joseph, that Jacob said to Laban, "Send me away, that I may go to my own place and to my country. Give me my wives and my children for whom I have served you, and let me go; for you know my service which I have done for you." And Laban said to him, "Please stay, if I have found favor in your eyes, for I have learned by experience that the LORD has blessed me for your sake." Then he said, "Name me your wages, and I will give it." (Genesis 30:25-28)

The 14 years are up! Jacob has fulfilled the deal with Laban for his wives and now is anxious to return to Beersheba. Although he has no "property" other than his wives and his children, Jacob does have the social expectation that Laban will provide sufficient capital and resources for him to take his family back to his homeland. When Jacob asks Laban to send him away, he has every right to expect that Laban will make that possible.

Laban Has an Experience

The response is something of a surprise to Jacob. Jacob has by now every reason to mistrust Laban and wants to get out from under his influence. Biblical data later reveal that Laban has begun to practice another religion, worshiping at least one other "god." Jacob surely knows about this and is all the more anxious to get away. But now, Laban insists that he has had a personal encounter with *Yahweh*.

The Hebrew word translated "experience" is *nachash* and is commonly used throughout the rest of the Old Testament to denote divination or fortune telling. The surprise was not that Laban was into divination but that he had "divined" from *Yahweh*. The structure of this specific text does not lend itself to a "Please stay" but rather to an imperative statement as Laban pronounces that he has learned from *Yahweh* that Jacob is to stay and work for him. "Tell me what you want," Laban says, "and I'll do it."

> So Jacob said to him, "You know how I have served you and how your livestock has been with me. For what you had before I came was little, and it has increased to a great amount; the LORD has blessed you since my coming. And now, when shall I also provide for my own house?" So he said, "What shall I give you?" (Genesis 30:29-31)

Jacob seems to abruptly change his mind about going home. This "experience" may have been God sending a message to Jacob, and after all he really is resource-poor. If Laban has been directed by God to give Jacob a real *paying* job, then here may be his chance to return home with something more than four wives and a batch of kids.

> And Jacob said, "You shall not give me anything. If you will do this thing for me, I will again feed and keep your flocks: Let me pass through all your flock today, removing from there all the speckled and spotted sheep, and all the brown ones among the lambs, and the spotted and speckled among the goats; and these shall be my wages. So my righteousness will answer for me in time to come, when the subject of my wages comes before you: every one that is not speckled and spotted among the goats, and brown among the lambs, will be considered stolen, if it is with me." (Genesis 30:31-33)

Now Jacob's commitment to God and his righteous character come to the forefront, and he sets a bargain that will clearly separate his future wealth from any connection with Laban. Jacob is fully aware that God has been working through and for him over the past 14 years, and he makes sure that Laban knows that he knows that all the prosperity Laban now has is because God has only blessed that scoundrel for Jacob's sake. Now is the proper time for Jacob to set a boundary between the family that God has made and the rest of the land of Padan Aram (Syria).

> And Laban said, "Oh, that it were according to your word!" (Genesis 30:34)

Speckled and Spotted

> So he removed that day the male goats that were speckled
> and spotted, all the female goats that were speckled and
> spotted, every one that had some white in it, and all the
> brown ones among the lambs, and gave them into the
> hand of his sons. Then he put three days' journey be-
> tween himself and Jacob, and Jacob fed the rest of Laban's
> flocks. (Genesis 30:35-36)

Please remember the purpose of this unusual event. Jacob had
agreed to stay on and continue to work for Laban on the premise that
nothing that belonged to Laban would ever be connected to Jacob.
Based on the agreement then struck, the speckled and spotted livestock were separated by a three-day journey from all of the pure-white
animals. Besides that, Jacob made sure that he would be in charge of
Laban's animals while others would be in charge of his family's yet-to-
be-developed herds.

Although several terms are used in this account for the livestock of
Jacob and Laban, it does appear that the animals were smaller sheep or
goats used mainly for their wool. If that is truly the case, then it would
make economic sense for Laban to keep the white animals and let
Jacob take all the multicolored livestock for his "wages." Just as today,
the lighter fleece was more valuable commercially, and Laban figured
he was getting away with a "steal" in this bargain.

Animal husbandry has discovered that sheep and goats, while
apparently the same type of animal, do not herd well together and
require different nutrients to grow strong. Both animals have their
commercial value, so it is likely that both Laban and Jacob kept the
herds apart but thriving. The interchange of the various terms in the
text seems to imply that Jacob was well aware of these issues, having
served with his father's very prosperous enterprise for several decades
prior to coming to Haran, and had put much of that practical knowledge to use during his 14 years with Laban. Now he was working for
himself and his family.

Selective Breeding

Modern breeding techniques have become more scientific over the centuries, but the observation of how things work would not have escaped those who worked the fields in the past. One does not have to be a Ph.D. geneticist to observe that "like begets like." Jacob did not have a university pedigree, but he had years of experience raising livestock and surely had known how to produce the favored kind of critter.

Besides that, the Creator was behind this, and *He* surely knows genetics.

Peeled Rods

> Now Jacob took for himself rods of green poplar and of the almond and chestnut trees, peeled white strips in them, and exposed the white which was in the rods. And the rods which he had peeled, he set before the flocks in the gutters, in the watering troughs where the flocks came to drink, so that they should conceive when they came to drink. So the flocks conceived before the rods, and the flocks brought forth streaked, speckled, and spotted. (Genesis 30:37-39)

Many a commentator has made fun of this passage. Jacob was not an ignoramus who was subject to the lore of the rural pub. He was an experienced rancher and astute businessman who knew how to increase his wealth. Jacob was not acting on his own with this "gimmick" of the peeled rods from specific trees; although he was using the practical experience of his life in the field, he was acting on instructions from God Himself.

Later, after six years of constant deception from Laban, and having had his wage-base changed ten times by his wicked uncle, Jacob revealed to his wives what God had shown to him from the beginning of his effort to establish the family's resources.

"And it happened, at the time when the flocks conceived,

that I lifted my eyes and saw in a dream, and behold, the rams which leaped upon the flocks were streaked, speckled, and gray-spotted. Then the Angel of God spoke to me in a dream, saying, 'Jacob.' And I said, 'Here I am.' And He said, 'Lift your eyes now and see, all the rams which leap on the flocks are streaked, speckled, and gray-spotted; for I have seen all that Laban is doing to you.'" (Genesis 31:10-12)

Laban's heart was deceitful, not Jacob's (Genesis 31:7). God is the One who took away the wealth of Laban (Genesis 31:8-9). Jacob's methodology with breeding is God-directed, not some fanciful, wishful experiment of an ignorant farmer. God had given Jacob prophetic insight. God knew which animals were heterozygous (possessing two different forms of a particular gene, one inherited from each parent) and not homozygous (possessing two identical forms of a particular gene)—Jacob did not.

The flocks were separated so that no "spotted" (etc.) cattle could breed into the "white" cattle, and Jacob carefully bred the stronger "brown" animals with the same kind and separated out the weaker "white" animals—as Laban had demanded. Jacob merely followed the techniques he had developed in the field. The manipulation was an obvious way to increase the breeding instinct and induce copulation and to "select" the stronger over the weaker. God controlled the "combinations" as promised.

Then Jacob separated the lambs, and made the flocks face toward the streaked and all the brown in the flock of Laban; but he put his own flocks by themselves and did not put them with Laban's flock. And it came to pass, whenever the stronger livestock conceived, that Jacob placed the rods before the eyes of the livestock in the gutters, that they might conceive among the rods. But when the flocks were feeble, he did not put them in; so the feebler were Laban's and the stronger Jacob's. Thus the man became exceedingly prosperous, and had large flocks, female and male servants, and camels and donkeys. (Genesis 30:40-43)

The last sentence of the text above tells us that the livestock were not limited to sheep and goats. Those animals might have been the "cash crop," but camels and donkeys were the beasts of burden and the means of transportation. Any prosperous agrarian organization would have had "large flocks" and known how to take care of and multiply those valuable animals as well. On top of that, such a working estate would require many "female and male servants." This was not a small business. Jacob was not a simple farmer. He was the Chief Operating Officer of a major enterprise. Laban was the titular owner, but Jacob made all the decisions.

Outta Here

Now!

After six years of effort on the part of Laban to ruin Jacob and six years of careful obedience to God's vision and hard work on the part of Jacob and his family, everything was in order for them to return to Beersheba.

The only trouble was Laban. He would never let them go. They had to slip quietly away in the night.

CHAPTER NINE
FAMILY TURMOIL

Twenty years! When Rebekah and Jacob had quickly reacted to Esau's threatened violence, neither one of them had any idea that the separation would last so long—nor that Jacob would never see his mother again. Sometimes the great God over our lives allows events to transpire that are well beyond our insight. But, as bad as the labor, family squabbles, and deceit were that Jacob and his family endured in Haran, the next 50 years would make the previous decades pale into dim memory.

Time to Go

> Now Jacob heard the words of Laban's sons, saying, "Jacob has taken away all that was our father's, and from what was our father's he has acquired all this wealth." And Jacob saw the countenance of Laban, and indeed it was not favorable toward him as before. Then the LORD said to Jacob, "Return to the land of your fathers and to your family, and I will be with you." (Genesis 31:1-3)

It was inevitable. God had seen to it that Jacob prospered even though Laban had done everything he could think of to thwart the bargain he had made with Jacob six years earlier. Even though Jacob's flocks were kept by his sons and their retainers "three days' journey" away (Genesis 30:36), the day finally came when the obvious was too obvious to ignore.

We haven't heard much about Laban after he married off his daughters to Jacob, dumped the "extra" maids on the girls, and extorted the decades of labor from Jacob. However, he had a much larger family than might have been gleaned from the biblical passages heretofore. Now we learn that Laban's sons were stirring up another effort to discredit Jacob by blaming him for the loss of the family wealth.

Surely more trouble with Laban lay ahead.

Once again, however, the Lord intervened with another set of instructions. It's not clear whether this was a personal visit as had happened to Abraham many times, once to Isaac, and at least once before to Jacob. That first visit to Jacob was to confirm him as the one through whom God would establish his seed and to encourage him for the long haul. Later, God sent a dream that had given him instructions on how to multiply his livestock, a vision Jacob kept secret all during the six years of God-directed prosperity. But now God's instructions were very clear: "Go home!"

Gathering the Family

So Jacob sent and called Rachel and Leah to the field, to his flock. (Genesis 31:4)

With his family back in the city and Jacob shuttling back and forth from his livestock to the various places where Laban's cattle were kept, assembling the family for a permanent departure was both difficult and perhaps divisive. So, after getting his wives to move out to the area where his flocks were grazing, Jacob begins to remind them of what they surely had observed over the past many years. The language of Scripture suggests that Jacob was not entirely sure how Rachel and Leah would react. There must have been some serious concern by everyone present. No doubt they all sensed that the time had come to settle affairs.

"I see your father's countenance, that it is not favorable

toward me as before; but the God of my father has been with me. And you know that with all my might I have served your father. Yet your father has deceived me and changed my wages ten times, but God did not allow him to hurt me. If he said thus: 'The speckled shall be your wages,' then all the flocks bore speckled. And if he said thus: 'The streaked shall be your wages,' then all the flocks bore streaked. So God has taken away the livestock of your father and given them to me." (Genesis 31:5-9)

Jacob recounts what they already knew. Then he reveals the vision that God gave him about the way to propagate the livestock so that the family would be enriched. That section of the text (Genesis 31:10-13) was discussed in the last chapter in connection with the peeled rods Jacob used to stimulate breeding of the preferred stock.

Rachel and Leah respond for the family.

Then Rachel and Leah answered and said to him, "Is there still any portion or inheritance for us in our father's house? Are we not considered strangers by him? For he has sold us, and also completely consumed our money. For all these riches which God has taken from our father are really ours and our children's; now then, whatever God has said to you, do it." (Genesis 31:14-16)

Although the biblical text records this answer as coming from both wives, Rachel, the younger, is listed first. This may indicate that Rachel has now assumed the role of First Wife. She and Leah have fought over Jacob's affections for a long time. With the birth of Joseph, all that appears to have reached a suitable conclusion. That was sufficient.

Then Jacob rose and set his sons and his wives on camels. And he carried away all his livestock and all his possessions which he had gained, his acquired livestock which he had gained in Padan Aram, to go to his father Isaac in the land of Canaan. (Genesis 31:17-18)

Confronting Laban

> Now Laban had gone to shear his sheep, and Rachel had
> stolen the household idols that were her father's. And Ja-
> cob stole away, unknown to Laban the Syrian, in that
> he did not tell him that he intended to flee. So he fled
> with all that he had. He arose and crossed the river, and
> headed toward the mountains of Gilead. And Laban was
> told on the third day that Jacob had fled. Then he took
> his brethren with him and pursued him for seven days'
> journey, and he overtook him in the mountains of Gilead.
> (Genesis 31:19-23)

The route that Jacob took with his family, servants, and flocks is
not easy to reconstruct from the short notations in the text. The area
around Haran (also called Padan Aram in the text) is north-central
to northeast Syria. Jacob had placed his herds at least "three days'
journey" from the encampment and grazing lands of Laban. If that
distance was west from where Laban was encamped, then Jacob's trek
to the land of Canaan would have been somewhat shortened. Laban
found out about Jacob's departure three days after he left and gathered
his "brethren" together, pursuing Jacob for another seven days and
finally catching up with him in the "mountains of Gilead" (Genesis
31:23).

Jacob has been moving his large herds and entourage as fast as
possible and has encamped somewhere near the border of modern
Jordan and Israel, south of Damascus, in the foothills of the mountainous area south of the Sea of Galilee. If "the river" he crossed is the
Jordan River, then the distance covered during the ten days that Jacob
has been on the trail is quite remarkable. If it is the Euphrates River,
that would indicate that Jacob had moved his flocks "three days' journey" eastward from Haran and would make the circular journey to the
east side of the Jordan River almost heroic.

Either way, Jacob and family would have been nearly exhausted,
and that might have contributed to the emotional scene that follows.

So Laban overtook Jacob. Now Jacob had pitched his tent in the mountains, and Laban with his brethren pitched in the mountains of Gilead. And Laban said to Jacob: "What have you done, that you have stolen away unknown to me, and carried away my daughters like captives taken with the sword? Why did you flee away secretly, and steal away from me, and not tell me; for I might have sent you away with joy and songs, with timbrel and harp? And you did not allow me to kiss my sons and my daughters. Now you have done foolishly in so doing. It is in my power to do you harm, but the God of your father spoke to me last night, saying, 'Be careful that you speak to Jacob neither good nor bad.' And now you have surely gone because you greatly long for your father's house, but why did you steal my gods?" (Genesis 31:25-20)

Jacob knew nothing of Rachel's theft and was ready to explode at the nerve of this awful man to pretend love for his daughters and offer foolish talk about a going-away feast. If it had not been for God's midnight visitation to warn Laban, Jacob would more likely have been fighting for his life—and he knew it. "Gods! What's this business about gods—that can't be!"

Then Jacob answered and said to Laban, "Because I was afraid, for I said, 'Perhaps you would take your daughters from me by force.' With whomever you find your gods, do not let him live. In the presence of our brethren, identify what I have of yours and take it with you." For Jacob did not know that Rachel had stolen them. (Genesis 31:31-32)

Here is one more indication that Laban had completely given his worship over to "other gods" and that long association with ungodly people will have a negative impact. Whatever may have been going through Rachel's mind when she snuck out with those idols may never be revealed, but it is certainly a warning that any of us can be tempted to do wrong—even when we know better. And, once we have sinned, the immediate reaction is to hide the deed from everybody. That, of course, is what Rachel did.

Laban made a thorough search of the main encampment, paying particular attention to the immediate family. Rachel had hidden the idols under the tack and supplies in the camel saddle and promptly sat down on it. When Laban burst into her tent, she sheepishly lied that she was unable to rise and honor his presence because "the manner of women is with me" (Genesis 31:35). Laban bought this lie—liars are often easily fooled because they think that they are smarter than everyone else.

Jacob's Rebuke of Laban

Jacob: "Put up or shut up!"

> Then Jacob was angry and rebuked Laban, and Jacob answered and said to Laban: "What is my trespass? What is my sin, that you have so hotly pursued me? Although you have searched all my things, what part of your household things have you found? Set it here before my brethren and your brethren, that they may judge between us both!" (Genesis 31:36-37)

That outburst seemed to uncork the bottle and Jacob spewed it all out.

> "These twenty years I have been with you; your ewes and your female goats have not miscarried their young, and I have not eaten the rams of your flock. That which was torn by beasts I did not bring to you; I bore the loss of it. You required it from my hand, whether stolen by day or stolen by night. There I was! In the day the drought consumed me, and the frost by night, and my sleep departed from my eyes. Thus I have been in your house twenty years; I served you fourteen years for your two daughters, and six years for your flock, and you have changed my wages ten times. Unless the God of my father, the God of

Abraham and the Fear of Isaac, had been with me, surely now you would have sent me away empty-handed. God has seen my affliction and the labor of my hands, and rebuked you last night." (Genesis 31:38-42)

This unleashing of the 20-year tension between Jacob and Laban gives a bit more insight into Jacob's internal struggles. Those whom the Lord chooses to work His will in history have often had to endure serious difficulties. We who are on the other side of the church reformation period can have little idea of the 1,500 years of conflict and turmoil that our brothers and sisters had to suffer. The "prosperity gospel" has lured many into believing that God "owes" us a life of happiness and ease. But Jesus said: "'A servant is not greater than his master.' If they persecuted Me, they will also persecute you. If they kept My word, they will keep yours also" (John 15:20).

Those 20 years, perhaps unbeknownst to Jacob, had prepared him for the hardships that were still ahead.

Covenant at Mizpah

And Laban answered and said to Jacob, "These daughters are my daughters, and these children are my children, and this flock is my flock; all that you see is mine. But what can I do this day to these my daughters or to their children whom they have borne? Now therefore, come, let us make a covenant, you and I, and let it be a witness between you and me."

So Jacob took a stone and set it up as a pillar. Then Jacob said to his brethren, "Gather stones." And they took stones and made a heap, and they ate there on the heap. Laban called it Jegar Sahadutha, but Jacob called it Galeed. And Laban said, "This heap is a witness between you and me this day." Therefore its name was called Galeed, also Mizpah. (Genesis 31:43-49)

The final parting is filled with innuendo and veiled threats. The

English translations do not quite reflect the intensity of the situation. Two peoples were separating for many centuries. Laban names the memorial "heap" in Arabic (*Jegar Sahadutha*) and Jacob in Hebrew (*Galeed* and *Mizpah*). If nothing else, those two native languages indicate the intended permanent separation between the two budding nations.

> "May the LORD watch between you and me when we are absent one from another." (Genesis 31:49)

This blunt statement by Laban is not meant as a pleasant wish of good will. Laban, who has just again repeated that he still thinks Jacob has robbed him of his wealth and family, is calling on *Yahweh* (Jacob's God) to be a "watchman" between them. This is not meant in the sense of "watch over" (as in protect and provide) but as a military sentry and warning station that would alert either party if and when the other should cross the borders.

> "If you afflict my daughters, or if you take other wives besides my daughters, although no man is with us—see, God is witness between you and me!" Then Laban said to Jacob, "Here is this heap and here is this pillar, which I have placed between you and me. This heap is a witness, and this pillar is a witness, that I will not pass beyond this heap to you, and you will not pass beyond this heap and this pillar to me, for harm. The God of Abraham, the God of Nahor, and the God of their father judge between us." (Genesis 31:50-53)

The border was set. Laban was threatening Jacob with warfare if he ever passed beyond the "heap" of stones that they had erected and on which they had eaten a solemn meal. The "witness" stands.

> And Jacob swore by the Fear of his father Isaac. Then Jacob offered a sacrifice on the mountain, and called his brethren to eat bread. And they ate bread and stayed all night on the mountain. And early in the morning Laban arose, and kissed his sons and daughters and blessed

them. Then Laban departed and returned to his place. (Genesis 31:53-55)

Anticipating Esau

A rather lengthy passage in Genesis 32 is given over to describing the meeting between the two brothers Esau and Jacob. Twenty years have separated them. Both are "middle-age" in terms of the lifespan of the day. They are approaching 80 at least and are well-established in their own right. The reader will recall that God had selected Jacob as the one that the future nation would build from. Esau had been rejected because of his ungodly choices (known by God before he was born) and had apparently moved to the "land of Seir" some time before.

The origin of this land is not identified in the Bible, and archaeologists and historians have not yet agreed on its original settlers. What is clear both in the Bible and in history is that the land of Seir became the land of Edom. That country encompassed territory south of the Dead Sea down toward the Red Sea and east across some of the Sinai Peninsula. Edom was the name given to Esau after the sale of his birthright for the "red" stew Jacob cooked in anticipation of the event (Genesis 25:30). The Edomites later became bitter enemies of Israel.

Jacob is understandably very nervous about the forthcoming meeting. As he and his entourage were traveling southward, Jacob saw a "host" (or "camp") of angels near the Jabbok River (Genesis 32:1-2, 22), roughly halfway between the Sea of Galilee and the Dead Sea on the east side of the Jordan River. Jacob gave the name Mahanaim to that spot to remember the "two hosts." Since Jacob had not yet learned of the 400-man army Esau was bringing to meet him, the "hosts" are a reference to the angels and his own large gathering of family, servants, and the thousands of animals that make up his flocks.

Servants were sent south to find Esau and tell him that Jacob was coming and that he was now self-sufficient, and to offer a gift of appeasement prior to their meeting. The servants soon returned with news that Esau was already on his way with an army of 400 men. Jacob, badly frightened by the news, divides his "host" into two groups, reasoning that if Esau attacked one band, the other would escape. So far, Jacob has no inkling of Esau's feelings.

It is worth noting that Jacob instructs the messengers to take a subservient position in their exchange with Esau (Genesis 32:3-5). Jacob is Esau's "servant" and Esau is to be addressed as Jacob's "lord." Jacob has plenty of wealth and there is no need for more. There is no attempt to claim "political" or property rights, although both were Jacob's by purchase of the birthright and the formal blessing given by Isaac. Since he is completely unaware of what Esau might do, he surrenders his life again into the hands of the God of Bethel who had spoken with him 20 years before.

> Then Jacob said, "O God of my father Abraham and God of my father Isaac, the LORD who said to me, 'Return to your country and to your family, and I will deal well with you': I am not worthy of the least of all the mercies and of all the truth which You have shown Your servant; for I crossed over this Jordan with my staff, and now I have become two companies. Deliver me, I pray, from the hand of my brother, from the hand of Esau; for I fear him, lest he come and attack me and the mother with the children. For You said, 'I will surely treat you well, and make your descendants as the sand of the sea, which cannot be numbered for multitude.'" (Genesis 32:9-12)

Wrestling with Elohim

As the afternoon waned and night was descending on the camps, Jacob assembled a fabulous gift of livestock to give to Esau. His servants were instructed to drive the 580 animals in sequential waves moving southward toward the coming army. The two "hosts" of Jacob were sent on their way as well, and he then took his immediate family over the ford at Jabbok, sent them on their way toward the Jordan, and remained alone in the dark of the night (Genesis 32:13-23).

The Bible teaches that "a man's heart plans his way, But the LORD directs his steps" (Proverbs 16:9). Jacob had done all that could be done.

There, in the pitch black of the river valley, "a Man wrestled with him until the breaking of day" (Genesis 32:24). Details of the struggle are not provided, but it is clear that this was a physical battle, not some spiritual prayer vigil as some might suggest. This was a man (*iysh*, the most common Hebrew term for a male human being). Jacob later recognizes that the "Man" who had battled him all night was none other than *Elohim*, whom he had seen face to face (Genesis 32:30).

All throughout Scripture, the Second Person of the Godhead is always presented as God in human form. He is "the Word" (John 1:1-4) and all that can be seen of the Trinity (John 14:9). Genesis records several pre-incarnate appearances of the Lord Jesus. This is one of the more unusual. Not only does Jacob fend off the human efforts of the Lord as He takes a temporary human form, but Jacob refuses to let go of his gripping embrace, bringing about an exercise of miraculous power to stop the fight.

One should remember that the Lord Jesus, while in His human body, felt the same hunger, tiredness, stress, and testing that all humans go through. Yes, "when the fullness of time had come" (Galatians 4:4), the Lord was "emptied" of the omnipotence and omniscience of the triune Godhead and entered—permanently—the human form that was "foreordained before the foundation of the world" (1 Peter 1:20). During the millennia before the Bethlehem manger, however, our Lord assumed the human form that was necessary to deliver God's personal messages that must be received prior to the "fullness of time."

The Name Change

The pronouns used during the verbal interchange between Jacob and the "Man" are a bit confusing unless one carefully follows the context and the use of the Hebrew. For clarity's sake, it is helpful to read Genesis 32:25-30 as though it were recorded as a script.

The Lord: Now when He saw that He did not prevail against him,

He touched the socket of his hip; and the socket of Jacob's hip was out of joint as He wrestled with him.

The Lord: "Let Me go, for the day breaks."

Jacob: "I will not let You go unless You bless me!"

The Lord: "What is your name?"

Jacob: "Jacob."

The Lord: "Your name shall no longer be called Jacob, but Israel; for you have struggled with God and with men, and have prevailed."

Jacob: "Tell me Your name, I pray."

The Lord: "Why is it that you ask about My name?"

> And He blessed him there. So Jacob called the name of the place Peniel: "For I have seen God face to face, and my life is preserved." (Genesis 32:29-30)

There is one note of emphasis that is easier to understand in Hebrew than in the English translations. When the Lord asks the final question before He blesses Jacob, the prominence of the rhetorical question is better rendered "Why do *you* ask about my name?" Jacob knows full well who this is. He has seen the Lord on at least three other occasions. Jacob's request was much more than a curious and passing thought. This time the meeting involved bodily contact. Jacob is seeking to understand something more profound. God has changed Jacob's name to "Power with God." How, Jacob wonders, should he address this Being who has commissioned and blessed him?

You may remember that the New Testament Christians were taught by the Lord Jesus to pray "Our Father in heaven, Hallowed be Your name" (Matthew 6:9)—but we are never given His name! In fact, when the Lord Jesus returns in glory in John's recorded vision, we are told that "He had a name written that no one knew except Himself" (Revelation 19:12). Many things are revealed to us in the Scriptures, but "the secret things belong to the LORD our God" (Deuteronomy 29:29).

The Lord: "Jacob, you know who I am. Now, I will bless you again."

Exit. Fade to black.

Meeting Esau

> Now Jacob lifted his eyes and looked, and there, Esau was coming, and with him were four hundred men. So he divided the children among Leah, Rachel, and the two maidservants. And he put the maidservants and their children in front, Leah and her children behind, and Rachel and Joseph last. Then he crossed over before them and bowed himself to the ground seven times, until he came near to his brother. But Esau ran to meet him, and embraced him, and fell on his neck and kissed him, and they wept. (Genesis 34:1-4)

Jacob, still in something of a daze because of his all-night bout with the Lord, dispersed the family as well as he could and, giving the most humble signs possible, began closing the distance between himself and Esau, bowing seven times in the process. (Remember the "sevens"?) Whatever may have been the angry passion that drove Jacob and Rebekah to decide on exile, all of that was gone in an instant. The brothers met, embraced, and wept on each other's shoulders. The meeting could not have been more different than what Jacob had feared.

Often our worries turn out to be just that—worries! If we are in the Lord's will, things will turn out as He has determined, and no amount of worry will change it. Yes, sometimes we are given the task to "suffer for His sake" (Philippians 1:29). But the worry is wasted. When we are in doubt, or in trouble, or need guidance, we are instructed:

> Be anxious for nothing, but in everything by prayer and supplication, with thanksgiving, let your requests be made known to God; and the peace of God, which surpasses all

understanding, will guard your hearts and minds through Christ Jesus. (Philippians 4:6-7)

Separate Ways

After being introduced to Jacob's wives and children, the two men enter into a typical gift exchange, with Esau finally agreeing to take the huge gift of livestock from Jacob. In the record of the dialogue, the word choices reveal more of the inner characters of the two men—and why God has chosen Jacob over Esau.

> Then Esau said, "What do you mean by all this company which I met?" And he said, "These are to find favor in the sight of my lord." But Esau said, "I have enough, my brother; keep what you have for yourself." And Jacob said, "No, please, if I have now found favor in your sight, then receive my present from my hand, inasmuch as I have seen your face as though I had seen the face of God, and you were pleased with me. Please, take my blessing that is brought to you, because God has dealt graciously with me, and because I have enough." So he urged him, and he took it. (Genesis 33:8-11)

After demurring according to custom, Esau accepts the gifts. Both say "I have enough" (referring to their wealth), but Esau uses the Hebrew *rab*, meaning "much," while Jacob uses the Hebrew *kol*, meaning "everything." The use of these terms provides insight into their opposite personalities. Esau is rich but will take more (see Proverbs 27:20). Jacob recognizes God's supply, is satisfied with what he has, and willingly gives away a significant portion without hesitation (see Psalm 37:21 and Proverbs 21:26).

After this transaction is finished, the dialogue over what they should do next further reveals the cautious duplicity of Esau and the diplomatic skills of Jacob. It seems that both brothers sense that this meeting will be one of their last. The Bible notes one final meeting when Isaac dies but no interchange during the interim.

> Then Esau said, "Let us take our journey; let us go, and I will go before you." But Jacob said to him, "My lord knows that the children are weak, and the flocks and herds which are nursing are with me. And if the men should drive them hard one day, all the flock will die. Please let my lord go on ahead before his servant. I will lead on slowly at a pace which the livestock that go before me, and the children, are able to endure, until I come to my lord in Seir." And Esau said, "Now let me leave with you some of the people who are with me." But he said, "What need is there? Let me find favor in the sight of my lord." (Genesis 33:12-15)

Esau initially suggests that Jacob follow him to Edom. This could be an expected exchange of pleasantries, but Jacob demurs, claiming "tender" flocks and children. It seems that Esau continues to try to get Jacob to come with him to Edom. Jacob appears to agree but asks to follow "softly" to accommodate his family. Esau suggests leaving some of his armed men for safety. Jacob assures Esau that it is not necessary. All of this subtle circling is an attempt on Esau's part to get Jacob under his power. Jacob, however, is gently letting Esau know that he has other plans.

> So Esau returned that day on his way to Seir. And Jacob journeyed to Succoth, built himself a house, and made booths for his livestock. Therefore the name of the place is called Succoth. (Genesis 33:16-17).

Shechem

The closing verses of Genesis 33 describe an undetermined period of time when Jacob stopped somewhere along the Jabbok River and built a solid structure for a home/headquarters and a more permanent series of corrals and stables for his livestock. The ancient sites are somewhat difficult to locate, but Succoth (as it came to be known) appears to be on the east side of the Jordan River, perhaps a day's hike from any ford across the Jordan (approximately 10-15 miles).

After resting there for some time, the entire enterprise was moved to the outskirts of Shechem, a city directly west from Succoth but well inside the land of Canaan. While encamped there, Jacob negotiated with the leading elders of the descendants of Hamor and purchased a plot of ground for 100 "pieces of money" (silver). To commemorate this new acreage, Jacob erected an altar and called it *El Elohe Israel*, meaning "God, the mighty God of Israel." Modern readers might infer that this focused on the nation of Israel. However, the recent personal encounter with God at Peniel would suggest Jacob is emphasizing his own new name (Israel)—that is, "My Mighty God."

The dominant tribe around Shechem was the Hivites, descendants of the sixth generation from Noah's son Ham. The name appears to mean "midlanders" or "villagers." The Hivites lasted well into the time of King David and primarily inhabited the northern portion of Israel from Mount Hermon to Gibeon. Esau had married the Hivite princess Aholibamah before Jacob left for exile in Syria.

Dinah

Chapter 34 of Genesis is given over in its entirety to an incident that takes place several years after the family left Succoth and settled near the city of Shechem, which was located near Mount Gerizim roughly 45 miles north of Jerusalem and 20 miles inland to the west from the Jordan River. Dinah, the last recorded child born to Leah, is now a young woman—at least in her mid- to late-teens. Benjamin, the last son of Jacob and Rachel, is not yet born.

> Now Dinah the daughter of Leah, whom she had borne to Jacob, went out to see the daughters of the land. And when Shechem the son of Hamor the Hivite, prince of the country, saw her, he took her and lay with her, and violated her. His soul was strongly attracted to Dinah the daughter of Jacob, and he loved the young woman and spoke kindly to the young woman. So Shechem spoke to his father Hamor, saying, "Get me this young woman as a wife." (Genesis 34:1-4)

The word choices in this chapter could be easily understood as indicating that Dinah was raped with force. However, the three verbs used would also support the conclusion that the main source of the ensuing conflict was that Dinah had been "humbled" (v. 2), rendered "unclean" (vv. 5 and 13), and made to look "foolish" (v. 7) in the eyes of Jacob's family. The emphasis seems to be more that the "honor" of the family has been violated than that the daughter has been raped.

The silence of Jacob at the subsequent meeting with Hamor and the young prince Shechem (vv. 5-17) may imply that he saw beyond the hot-headed impulses of his sons. The actions of the men of Shechem certainly did not seem to be violent, even if they saw an opportunity to slowly absorb this new family and its wealth into their city (vv. 21-23). Even the biblical text specifies that the young prince was "more honorable" than the rest of them (v. 19).

Forced Religion

> But the sons of Jacob answered Shechem and Hamor his father, and spoke deceitfully, because he had defiled Dinah their sister. And they said to them, "We cannot do this thing, to give our sister to one who is uncircumcised, for that would be a reproach to us. But on this condition we will consent to you: If you will become as we are, if every male of you is circumcised, then we will give our daughters to you, and we will take your daughters to us; and we will dwell with you, and we will become one people." (Genesis 34:13-16)

Jacob appears to be either overwhelmed by the passion of his sons or is sitting quietly in the background while they plot to "get even." Either way, this is not one of Jacob's more spiritual moments. The boys, however, are angry at this humiliation of their sister and are deceitful in their supposed "religious" offer of restoration and familial tolerance—if the men of Shechem agree to be circumcised, they can have Dinah.

Surely this incident is not recorded in Scripture just to give some nasty details about the life of Jacob's family. These events were record-ed "as examples" and "for our admonition," the New Testament insists (1 Corinthians 10:11). Perhaps the most obvious take-away lesson is that "forced" relationships never work, and any kind of "works"-based religion is a false religion (Ephesians 2:9). It is quite likely that the rite of circumcision had been known in Canaan well over a century, since Abraham, Isaac, and Jacob had all made that an open doctrine of their worship of *Yahweh*. And while the practice would not have been unknown, it would have been a serious physical debilitation for adult males—and Jacob's sons knew it.

> Hamor and Shechem his son came to the gate of their city, and spoke with the men of their city, saying: "These men are at peace with us. Therefore let them dwell in the land and trade in it. For indeed the land is large enough for them. Let us take their daughters to us as wives, and let us give them our daughters. Only on this condition will the men consent to dwell with us, to be one people: if every male among us is circumcised as they are circum-cised. Will not their livestock, their property, and every animal of theirs be ours? Only let us consent to them, and they will dwell with us." And all who went out of the gate of his city heeded Hamor and Shechem his son; every male was circumcised, all who went out of the gate of his city. (Genesis 34:20-24)

It worked! They fell for it. Led by Simeon and Levi, the "gang" of Jacob's sons descended on Shechem during the third day, when the healing process from the mass circumcision would have been at its most painful stage. All of the men of the city were essentially incapac-itated. Unsuspecting and unable to defend themselves, "all the males" were killed (v. 25)—murdered would be the more correct term.

Bloody Murder

> And they killed Hamor and Shechem his son with the edge of the sword, and took Dinah from Shechem's

house, and went out. The sons of Jacob came upon the slain, and plundered the city, because their sister had been defiled. They took their sheep, their oxen, and their donkeys, what was in the city and what was in the field, and all their wealth. All their little ones and their wives they took captive; and they plundered even all that was in the houses. (Genesis 34:26-29)

What a mess! The "godly" men of the newly named Israel murdered a city full of men, stole all the women and children to be slaves for their own use, and plundered anything of value from the homes of the murdered men. Yes, these were "pagans," and yes, they were themselves thinking of how they might absorb this new enterprise into their own city-state, but no amount of justification can excuse the supposed "honor killing" that *still* plagues much of the Near Eastern cultures. Jacob knew that what his sons had done was awful but seemed to be more concerned about his family's safety than about the horrible butchery of Simeon and Levi—who never did repent or admit that what they had done was wrong (Genesis 34:30-31)!

The Move to Bethel

Then God said to Jacob, "Arise, go up to Bethel and dwell there; and make an altar there to God, who appeared to you when you fled from the face of Esau your brother." (Genesis 35:1)

Bethel was a town about ten miles north of Jerusalem, some 35 miles south from where the family had been headquartered near Shechem. It had already played a major part in the history of the family. Abraham had built an altar there before he went down into Egypt and returned back there for a while before he settled in Hebron. Jacob had the vision of the "ladder" there while camping overnight on the way to his exile in Syria. So when God appears to him after this murderous incident at Shechem, it is not much of a surprise to be told to return there.

And Jacob said to his household and to all who were with

him, "Put away the foreign gods that are among you, pu-
rify yourselves, and change your garments. Then let us
arise and go up to Bethel; and I will make an altar there
to God, who answered me in the day of my distress and
has been with me in the way which I have gone." So they
gave Jacob all the foreign gods which were in their hands,
and the earrings which were in their ears; and Jacob hid
them under the terebinth tree which was by Shechem.
And they journeyed, and the terror of God was upon the
cities that were all around them, and they did not pursue
the sons of Jacob. (Genesis 35:2-5)

The tribes of Simeon and Levi would later suffer long-term judgment from God for their deeds on that awful day at Shechem, but for
now God withheld His anger and allowed the family to purge itself of
the pagan trappings of idols and earrings that had accumulated during
their years in Syria and, no doubt, had picked up from the Canaanites
living all around them. Jacob buries this pagan treasure under a sacred
tree near Shechem—perhaps as a token sacrifice for the damage his
family had caused.

As they travel to Bethel, the word is out among the local population that these strangers are not to be trifled with, and the "terror of
God" was sufficient to keep the family safe while they move the vast
herds and hundreds of servants some 30 miles southward. God was
building a nation, and He would not permit either the sinful behavior
of Simeon and Levi or the hostile intentions of the pagan neighbors
to deter His sovereign design for Israel. While this large group is ner-
vously watching for attack during their slow trek, God is keeping the
enemies behind their own walls in fear for their lives.

When they arrived at Bethel, they found that Rebekah, Jacob's
mother, had died some time before, and only her nurse, Deborah, remained with a remnant of the servants and entourage who had stayed
with Rebekah. But soon after they arrived, Deborah died. Then God
met with Jacob and reaffirmed the promises that had been given in
that very place decades ago.

Then God appeared to Jacob again, when he came from Padan Aram, and blessed him. And God said to him, "Your name is Jacob; your name shall not be called Jacob anymore, but Israel shall be your name." So He called his name Israel. Also God said to him: "I am God Almighty. Be fruitful and multiply; a nation and a company of nations shall proceed from you, and kings shall come from your body. The land which I gave Abraham and Isaac I give to you; and to your descendants after you I give this land." Then God went up from him in the place where He talked with him. (Genesis 35:9-13)

The Death of Rachel

For a while, Jacob and his family remain at Bethel, and he builds a more permanent altar to establish the site. But whatever ties that Jacob felt to the place eventually fade. After some time there, Jacob feels the need to travel on south to find his father and whatever is left of his family. Once again, the servants are told to pack up and move the herds toward Hebron, some 50 miles further south toward the southern end of the Dead Sea.

Rachel is pregnant again with the twelfth son, and the pregnancy has been very difficult for her. Somewhere on the way, near a little village that will later become known as Bethlehem, Rachel goes into labor and is in extreme pain.

> Then they journeyed from Bethel. And when there was but a little distance to go to Ephrath, Rachel labored in childbirth, and she had hard labor. Now it came to pass, when she was in hard labor, that the midwife said to her, "Do not fear; you will have this son also." And so it was, as her soul was departing (for she died), that she called his name Ben-Oni; but his father called him Benjamin. (Genesis 35:16-18)

This is one of the early insights that the Bible gives into the process of death. The popular thought is that death is somehow instantaneous when it finally comes. But as mysterious as the process is, medical science understands that the life force resides in the blood contained in the body (Leviticus 17:11), and there is some time (some medical sources suggest about four to six minutes) until the blood either drains out or solidifies after the heart stops pumping.[1] As her soul was departing, Rachel moaned out, "This is the son of my sorrow." Jacob, however, named him "Son of the Right Hand"—an indication of his love for Rachel and his expectations for the children that she had borne him.

> So Rachel died and was buried on the way to Ephrath (that is, Bethlehem). And Jacob set a pillar on her grave, which is the pillar of Rachel's grave to this day. (Genesis 35:19-20)

Reuben Sins

> Then Israel journeyed and pitched his tent beyond the tower of Eder. And it happened, when Israel dwelt in that land, that Reuben went and lay with Bilhah his father's concubine; and Israel heard about it. (Genesis 35:21-22)

The affair with Bilhah is not given much attention here other than to record the event. Whether or not there would have been any particular genetic problem for potential offspring is not at issue. There is, however, an obvious violation of a relationship of respect and dignity. Bilhah was not a "formal" wife of Jacob, but she was the mother of some of Reuben's half-brothers and, of course, was much older than he. Whatever may have led to the relationship, Jacob was bound to find out about it. At the time, he appeared to do little except put a stop to it.

At the end of his life, however, Jacob had retained the knowledge for many years and finally notes that because of his lustful behavior and violation of the covenant of family integrity, Reuben would never "excel" among the tribes and would lose his right of "primogeniture,"

---

1. Molly Edmonds, What happens during the dying process?, posted on science.howstuffworks.com, accessed November 23, 2013.

the double blessing and the right of leadership (Genesis 49:3-4). That tribe never did excel and finally was absorbed into the "lost ten tribes" who were taken captive into Assyria.

Isaac Dies

After erecting an appropriate tomb for his wife (which has been restored and is still a significant tourist site in Bethlehem), Jacob moves on to Hebron, where he meets Isaac before he dies at 180 years old. Then he and Esau take Isaac's body back to Mamre, to the cave at Machpelah where Abraham, Sarah, and Rebekah, Isaac's wife, were already buried (Genesis 35:27-29). We are not told when Leah died, but she probably died before Rachel, since she is also buried in the cave at Machpelah (Genesis 49:31).

The Nation of Esau

Genesis 36 is given over to the genealogical record of Esau and the nation of Edom. Although God has rejected Esau (as He did Ishmael), God still blesses his descendants (as He did Ishmael's) under the promise that He had given to Abraham when He called him from Ur of the Chaldees.

Esau's descendants are traced through one wife from the Hittites, one from the Hivites, and one from the Ishmaelites. Those three genetic lines were merged into the nation of Edom that settled a rather large territory south of the Dead Sea, including the famous site of Petra and much of southern Jordan. The list of these key leaders is translated as "dukes" by the King James Version of the Bible and as either "chiefs" or "kings" by other versions. Whatever their titles may have been in those days, the names of these men provide us with a very accurate record of the history of this nation that began around the time of Abraham and lasted well into the time of the divided kingdom of Israel—most often troubling the nation of Israel in one way or another.

It is significant that although God is no longer focused on these "many nations" as far as the Messianic line is concerned, He still cares for them "for my servant Abraham's sake" (Genesis 26:24). Indeed, "God so loved the world that He gave His only begotten Son, that whoever believes in Him should not perish but have everlasting life" (John 3:16).

The magnificent gospel came to its full revelation when the Lord Jesus was incarnated, lived in our world in a human body, died for all the sins of the whole world, and was resurrected the third day "according to the Scriptures" (1 Corinthians 15:3-4). But even in these ancient days we can find examples of God's love—even in the Edomites. May we never forget how much God has done to make it possible for you and me to be twice-born.

CHAPTER TEN
JOSEPH THE SLAVE

The final chapters of this magnificent book of beginnings mainly focus on the life of Joseph, the first child of Rachel and the last child born while Jacob was in exile working under the harsh hand of Laban the Syrian. Joseph is 17 when his story is picked up in Genesis 37:2 and 110 when he dies (Genesis 50:22). The intervening 93 years are recorded (probably by Joseph) and ultimately edited by Moses to show those signal events that set the stage for the next nearly two millennia until the promised Seed would be brought into the world.

Without these insights, we would be hard-pressed to make sense of what follows.

Two Prophetic Dreams

Now Jacob dwelt in the land where his father was a stranger, in the land of Canaan. This is the history of Jacob. Joseph, being seventeen years old, was feeding the flock with his brothers. And the lad was with the sons of Bilhah and the sons of Zilpah, his father's wives; and Joseph brought a bad report of them to his father. Now Israel loved Joseph more than all his children, because he was the son of his old age. Also he made him a tunic of many colors. But when his brothers saw that their father loved him more than all his brothers, they hated him and could not speak peaceably to him. (Genesis 37:1-4)

Much has been made of the "tunic of many colors." There are almost as many ideas about what that was as there are commentators. More than likely, it was an exquisite over-garment of some sort that was made from the finest fabrics available, woven with precious metals (gold and silver, for sure) and garnished with precious stones. Don't forget, Jacob was one of the richest men of his day and could well afford luxury if he desired it.

Sometime during these teenage years, Joseph was given two prophetic visions indicating that he would rule over his brothers—and even over his father and mother.

> Now Joseph had a dream, and he told it to his brothers; and they hated him even more. So he said to them, "Please hear this dream which I have dreamed: There we were, binding sheaves in the field. Then behold, my sheaf arose and also stood upright; and indeed your sheaves stood all around and bowed down to my sheaf." And his brothers said to him, "Shall you indeed reign over us? Or shall you indeed have dominion over us?" So they hated him even more for his dreams and for his words. (Genesis 37:5-8)

What made the brothers jealous and hostile, probably, was that Joseph flaunted his favored status and may well have been the epitome of a "spoiled brat" during these early years. God had some wonderful things in mind for Joseph, but he would have to learn some very hard lessons before he could be turned into a "vessel for honor, sanctified and useful for the Master, prepared for every good work" (2 Timothy 2:21).

> Then he dreamed still another dream and told it to his brothers, and said, "Look, I have dreamed another dream. And this time, the sun, the moon, and the eleven stars bowed down to me." So he told it to his father and his

brothers; and his father rebuked him and said to him, "What is this dream that you have dreamed? Shall your mother and I and your brothers indeed come to bow down to the earth before you?" And his brothers envied him, but his father kept the matter in mind. (Genesis 37:9-11)

This dream even disturbed Jacob! What was going on here? Jacob had repeatedly been given direct visits from the Lord and was as secure in his role as anyone could possibly be. But now, this teenage kid (even though he really liked him) was talking about the sun and the moon and the 11 stars all bowing down to him. Good heavens! What was God doing?

One of the apparent conflicts with the information provided here in the text is that a previous chapter recorded the death of Rachel, who died while they were on the road to Hebron to find Isaac (Genesis 35:19). The solution lies in the likelihood that Joseph had these dreams while they were still living in Shechem, prior to their relocation to Hebron. In fact, it may well be one of the main reasons why Jacob had this special tunic made for him in the first place. The text in chapter 37 can be easily understood in a "past perfect" tense (an event that took place in the past with effects continuing into the future).

By the time Joseph is sent from Hebron back to Shechem to give an account of the welfare of the flocks under the care of the older brothers, he is 17 and living at home with Jacob and Benjamin, who is still a young boy. The dreams are "guarded" by Jacob as "words" (Genesis 37:11). Apparently, Jacob could sense the truth of these visions and was watching closely to see what would unfold. He certainly did not expect what did happen!

Sold into Slavery

The ten older sons are basically independent now, most of them married with families of their own. Joseph has become *persona non grata* to them and has remained behind with Jacob in Hebron. The grazing land northward near Shechem is still favored, in spite of the awful earlier events led by Simeon and Levi, and most of the herds are being kept there by the older brothers. They have not reported back for some time, and Jacob is concerned for their welfare. Joseph is tasked to find them and bring information back to Jacob.

> And Israel said to Joseph…"Please go and see if it is well with your brothers and well with the flocks, and bring back word to me." So he sent him out of the Valley of Hebron, and he went to Shechem. Now a certain man found him, and there he was, wandering in the field. And the man asked him, saying, "What are you seeking?" So he said, "I am seeking my brothers. Please tell me where they are feeding their flocks." And the man said, "They have departed from here, for I heard them say, 'Let us go to Dothan.'" So Joseph went after his brothers and found them in Dothan. (Genesis 27:13-17)

Shechem is over 50 miles from Hebron. Joseph would have been on the road for at least two days (more, if he was traveling with others, as would have probably been the case). While he was wandering in the vast fields around Shechem, he is told by a man that Jacob's flocks have moved another ten miles to the northeast near Dothan. Tired and perhaps a bit peeved, Joseph finds the brothers late in the afternoon—but they spot him first.

> Now when they saw him afar off, even before he came near them, they conspired against him to kill him. Then they said to one another, "Look, this dreamer is coming! Come therefore, let us now kill him and cast him into some pit; and we shall say, 'Some wild beast has devoured him.' We shall see what will become of his dreams!" But Reuben heard it, and he delivered him out of their hands, and said, "Let us not kill him." And Reuben said to them, "Shed no blood, but cast him into this pit which is in the wilderness, and do not lay a hand on him"—that he might deliver him out of their hands, and bring him back to his father. (Genesis 37:18-22)

Of all people, Reuben tries to save him. This is the same Reuben who had the affair with his father's concubine, but he has sobered up enough to see the horror of what is about to happen and deflects the intense hatred of the other nine brothers with a compromise that might serve the same purpose without them actually having to kill Joseph. Everyone agrees, and Reuben secretly hopes to come back that night and rescue the lad.

But as God would have it (and indeed, God was planning this all along), a group of Ishmaelites from Midian is seen in the distance on their way to Egypt to sell the wares obtained in their trading. Dothan is inland somewhat from the coastal road, so this group of traders may have been coming from a side trip to some of the cities around the southern tip of the Sea of Galilee or perhaps have taken a "short cut" rather than travel through Damascus and down the coast.

From the brothers' perspective, this is too good a chance to pass up. They can sell their screaming, snotty brother to the Ishmaelites and be rid of him for good—and never have to deal with the guilt of murder (although they had done plenty of that at Shechem some years before). They struck a deal for 20 pieces of silver and Joseph was no longer their problem (Genesis 37:28).

Reuben, however, having been away making arrangements to get Joseph out of the dry well and back to Jacob, was absolutely horrified when he returned and found Joseph gone. "No big deal," the rest of the brothers said. "We'll just kill one of the goats and smear his pretty little coat with the blood and tell Dad that wild animals must have eaten him." Please pardon the literary license, but that's just about what happened (Genesis 37:29-33). Of course, when Jacob ultimately hears the story, it just about kills *him* instead.[1]

> Then Jacob tore his clothes, put sackcloth on his waist, and mourned for his son many days. And all his sons and

---

1. There is much, much more contained in the details of these chapters. The nature of this book does not permit the luxury of exploring all of the comparisons and parallels that are illuminated by these historical events. Detailed outlines of all of the lives of the patriarchs are provided freely on www.teachallthings.org for those who want to explore more or teach about these intriguing lives.

all his daughters arose to comfort him; but he refused to be comforted, and he said, "For I shall go down into the grave to my son in mourning." Thus his father wept for him. (Genesis 37:34-35)

Judah Marries

Sometime in the ensuing years, probably while Joseph was living in Potiphar's house in Egypt, Judah moved to Adullam, a Canaanite village roughly eight miles northwest of the family home in Hebron. Genesis 38 contains a rather detailed account of what took place.

Judah "departed from his brothers, and visited a certain Adulla-mite whose name was Hirah" (Genesis 38:1). The word choices give us some insight. Judah "breaks away" from his brothers (probably over the incident with Joseph) and begins to "lean on" his friendship with Hirah, a nobleman who lives in Adullam. Soon, Judah marries the daughter of Shua, a Canaanite, without giving it the consideration that should be given to any marriage. The language may even imply that Judah and Shua's daughter do not marry but merely "move in" together.

The marriage produces three sons (Genesis 38:3-5). Er, the first-born, is named "the watcher" by Judah. Onan, the middle son, is named "the strong one" by his mother. Shelah, the last son, is also named by his mother while Judah is in another city, implying that by this time the relationship is over and Judah is living by himself (Genesis 38:5).

Judah's wife is a Canaanite pagan and there is no indication that she ever embraced the God of Judah or cared anything about the work that God was doing with Israel. As his sons grow, Judah attempts to guide them to worship *Yahweh* by choosing a suitable wife for Er, the eldest son and the one who would inherit the mantle of responsibility from Judah. Er seems to rebel as soon as he can and becomes "wicked in the sight of the LORD, and the LORD killed him" (Genesis 38:7). God is carefully "watching" (just as the name Er implies).

Tamar was selected by Judah for Er, but Er apparently had no say in her selection, and it seems that he refused to consummate the marriage. Tamar is now widowed, rejected, and despised, and has little hope of any security or normal life apart from the family of Judah. With Er dead, Judah orders Onan to "raise up an heir" for Er (Genesis 38:8). Onan refuses his duty and "displeased the LORD" (Genesis 38:10). Onan's flagrant rebellion further humiliates and isolates Tamar.

Some scholars have established that there seems to have been a custom of male sibling responsibility to marry the wife of a deceased brother as early as the Code of Ur-Nammu, king of Ur in the century prior to Abraham's birth (around 2050 B.C.). The formal Israelite law was later established under Moses (Deuteronomy 25:5-10). Essentially, the younger brother was to produce an heir for the childless widow and ensure that the "name" of the dead brother (and any property legally his) would provide for the widow and perpetuate the family line. The most famous incident of this sort was with Ruth and Boaz, narrated in the book of Ruth.

Onan's act, however, was "despised" by the Lord. He "went in to" Tamar (the biblical idiom for the act of marriage) and "emitted on the ground," a flagrant and conscious refusal to impregnate her. Onan's behavior results in his "execution" by the Lord (Genesis 38:10). Although "onanism" is listed in many dictionaries as a formal term for masturbation and coitus interruptus and many Christian books teach that these behaviors are sinful, the Bible is silent on these issues—except by implication when mental "lust" is involved (Matthew 5:28). The Bible certainly condemns sexual deviation (adultery, homosexuality, fornication, etc.) in the strongest terms, but Onan is condemned for his willful disobedience to Judah and humiliation of Tamar, not for distorted sexual behavior.

Judah and Tamar

Tamar, now twice widowed, was told by Judah:

"Remain a widow in your father's house till my son Shelah

is grown." For he said, "Lest he also die like his brothers."
And Tamar went and dwelt in her father's house. (Genesis 38:11)

There is no record of the city from which Tamar came. The implication is that she left Adullam and was essentially "put away" and left to fend for herself. She would have been considered "damaged goods," and the prospects of her ever finding another husband were nil. Formally, she was still under the control of Judah and expected to marry the youngest son, Shelah. But time passed and he was now grown—and she sensed that Judah had no intention of marrying her to his last son.

After Judah's wife, the unnamed daughter of Shua, died, he decided to go to Timnah to be with the workmen who were shearing his sheep. Timnah was a good day's journey northeast from Adullam. Judah was trying to run away from all his problems and expected to find companionship and distractions among his field hands. Tamar heard about the "vacation" and decided to take matters into her own hands.

> So she took off her widow's garments, covered herself with a veil and wrapped herself, and sat in an open place which was on the way to Timnah; for she saw that Shelah was grown, and she was not given to him as a wife. When Judah saw her, he thought she was a harlot, because she had covered her face. (Genesis 38:14-15)

The rather terse description of Tamar's actions may seem a bit strange to our modern way of thinking. The Canaanite religions (and there were several of them) all involved some form of fertility cult behavior. Some practiced public sexual orgies in a "temple" or around a sacred grove of trees—even in open-air festivities within earth or stone constructions designed in a pattern that had some meaning to the worshipers. Others, and this appears to be the case with Tamar, set up little tents alongside the road and offered their "worship" for hire.

Judah would not have thought twice about the presence of a temple prostitute by the roadside, and since Tamar had clothed herself in a way that disguised her identity, Judah impulsively decided he needed to be "comforted."

> Then he turned to her by the way, and said, "Please let me come in to you"; for he did not know that she was his daughter-in-law. So she said, "What will you give me, that you may come in to me?" And he said, "I will send a young goat from the flock." So she said, "Will you give me a pledge till you send it?" Then he said, "What pledge shall I give you?" So she said, "Your signet and cord, and your staff that is in your hand." Then he gave them to her, and went in to her, and she conceived by him. (Genesis 38:16-18)

Although buying sex from a roadside prostitute would not have been that big of a deal in that culture, the leaving of his family signet ring as a guarantee of payment was! Tamar had this all figured out. Judah was not thinking at all. Perhaps he might be given some slack because of the death of his wife. It is quite possible that he had not shared her bed for some time. But being so driven or so drunk that he would leave his family's crest and personal identification with an unknown harlot on the roadside? He must have been both desperate and foolish. Tamar, however, has a plan.

> So she arose and went away, and laid aside her veil and put on the garments of her widowhood. And Judah sent the young goat by the hand of his friend the Adullamite, to receive his pledge from the woman's hand, but he did not find her. Then he asked the men of that place, saying, "Where is the harlot who was openly by the roadside?" And they said, "There was no harlot in this place." So he returned to Judah and said, "I cannot find her. Also, the men of the place said there was no harlot in this place." Then Judah said, "Let her take them for herself, lest we be shamed; for I sent this young goat and you have not found her." (Genesis 38:19-23).

As always, the word choices inspired by the Holy Spirit are very specific. As Judah is telling his friend Hirah about the episode, he uses the common Hebrew word *zanah* for the "harlot" who was on the side of the road. Hirah, Judah's more streetwise Canaanite friend, uses the Hebrew word *cedesha*, "one who is set apart." Hirah attempts to locate the woman. None of the locals know anything about a woman who frequented that spot, and Hirah returns with the news that the "one set apart" is not to be found.

Judah passes off the incident as unimportant—which is the main point of recording it. Tamar has been greatly wronged by Judah, who sent her away into oblivion and who now demonstrates further disdain for his responsibilities by ignoring the value of his family reputation and leaving the signet ring, the cord that held the signet to his person, and the tribal "staff" that identified his family. The pledge of the price is worth much more than the price of the sex. Apparently neither one means much to Judah.

> And it came to pass, about three months after, that Judah was told, saying, "Tamar your daughter-in-law has played the harlot; furthermore she is with child by harlotry." So Judah said, "Bring her out and let her be burned!" (Genesis 38:24)

His own behavior and the loss of his family insignia evidently mean little to Judah, but the fact that his daughter-in-law has become pregnant working as a temple harlot does mean a great deal! "Burn this wretch!" is the command. This is an unusually harsh death sentence—even to the callous Canaanites. Later in the Mosaic Law, such a burning would become the sentence for a priest's daughter who becomes a temple prostitute of a Canaanite deity (Leviticus 21:9). It is likely that Judah understood something of the plans for Israel and the promise of a Messiah, and that may be why he reacted so strongly.

However, Judah is publicly exposed as the father and the guilty party.

> When she was brought out, she sent to her father-in-law, saying, "By the man to whom these belong, I am with

child." And she said, "Please determine whose these are—the signet and cord, and staff." So Judah acknowledged them and said, "She has been more righteous than I, because I did not give her to Shelah my son." And he never knew her again. (Genesis 38:25-26).

Tamar becomes a single mother under Judah's protection. The birth of her twins was startlingly similar to the birth of Jacob and Esau—Esau came out first but Jacob grabbed his heel and was chosen by God to be the heir and father of the 12 sons of Israel. In Tamar's case, Zerah emerges first but is "breached" by Perez, who becomes the ancestor of King David as God continues to work His promise through the genetic line of Judah (Genesis 38:27-30).

Joseph in Potiphar's House

Now Joseph had been taken down to Egypt. And Potiphar, an officer of Pharaoh, captain of the guard, an Egyptian, bought him from the Ishmaelites who had taken him down there. (Genesis 39:1)

Part of the information that will help us understand later incidents in this home is the specific description of Potiphar. The Hebrew word *cariyc* is translated "officer" in this passage but is the official word for "eunuch"—a process that was performed as a man entered the court service of the pharaoh. Usually, the medical procedure was done to prevent "accidental" impregnation of any of the various wives of Pharaoh and to insure that the royal bloodline would remain pure. The eunuch, in most cases, could still perform sexually, but both the desire and ability to produce children were curtailed.

The LORD was with Joseph, and he was a successful man; and he was in the house of his master the Egyptian. And his master saw that the LORD was with him and that the LORD made all he did to prosper in his hand. So Joseph found favor in his sight, and served him. Then he made him overseer of his house, and all that he had he put under his authority. (Genesis 39:2-4)

With his background as a favored son of a very prosperous household back in Canaan, Joseph quickly became a favorite of Potiphar, whose role as "Slaughter" (something of a chief of military command) kept him away for significant lengths of time. Potiphar was a wealthy man and his house would have been more like an estate, with grounds and outbuildings, and servants and vendors who would need constant care and intervention. Potiphar quickly recognized the talents of young Joseph and put him in charge.

> So it was, from the time that he had made him overseer of his house and all that he had, that the LORD blessed the Egyptian's house for Joseph's sake; and the blessing of the LORD was on all that he had in the house and in the field. Thus he left all that he had in Joseph's hand, and he did not know what he had except for the bread which he ate. (Genesis 39:5-6)

Potiphar saw that "the LORD was with" Joseph, a thought that appears five times during Joseph's captivity, and as the next several verses unfold, Potiphar seems to be aware that the source of the problem with his wife...is his wife, not Joseph. Joseph has proven himself to be both capable and faithful, and has built a reputation as a religious young man, openly confessing his worship of *Yahweh*. Potiphar may have equated *Yahweh* with Ra, the all-powerful sun god of the Egyptians, but nonetheless had developed a respect for Joseph.

> And it came to pass after these things that his master's wife cast longing eyes on Joseph, and she said, "Lie with me." (Genesis 39:7)

Adultery, although not sanctioned, was not uncommon among the wealthy—and tacitly accommodated among the courtiers. Joseph's rise to power in Potiphar's household makes him more attractive, and the repeated attempts by Potiphar's wife indicate that she was no stranger to daytime dalliances.

> But he refused and said to his master's wife, "Look, my master...has committed all that he has to my hand. There

is no one greater in this house than I, nor has he kept back anything from me but you, because you are his wife. How then can I do this great wickedness, and sin against God?" (Genesis 39:8-9)

Joseph's refusal was based on his commitment to integrity and righteousness. He could easily have rationalized the affair. The invitation must have flattered and tempted him, and the household staff likely would not have cared. He knew that those kind of affairs were common—even in his own family!

Joseph, gentle and diplomatic, tried to defuse the situation. He did not attempt to berate or ridicule her but merely reminded her of the trust that Potiphar had placed in him and of her position as Potiphar's wife. But in spite of his gracious efforts, the wife badgers Joseph "day by day," determined to have her way by force, if necessary. So, she arranges for all of the servants to be gone on some trumped-up errand, leaving an empty house. Then grabbing Joseph's "garment," she begins dragging him toward the bed. Joseph wiggled out of whatever he was wearing and "fled and ran outside."

The cost of obedience sometimes involves an unjust punishment. "For it is better, if it is the will of God, to suffer for doing good than for doing evil" (1 Peter 3:17). After being rejected, humiliated, exasperated, and (in her mind) insulted, Potiphar's wife shouts "rape" again and again all around the house to establish her alibi, then invents a plausible lie and publicly confronts Potiphar.

Joseph in Prison

When Potiphar's wife attempts to seduce Joseph, the reaction of this powerful eunuch of Pharaoh's court would indicate that the marriage is probably political and not romantic. And even though Joseph is "handsome in form and appearance" (Genesis 39:6), Potiphar seems to understand that his wife is at the bottom of the problem. His imprisonment of Joseph is mild under the circumstances, since he had the power and the right to execute him. Essentially, Potiphar gave Joseph the "best" punishment possible.

> Then Joseph's master took him and put him into the pris-
> on, a place where the king's prisoners were confined. And
> he was there in the prison. But the LORD was with Joseph
> and showed him mercy, and He gave him favor in the
> sight of the keeper of the prison. And the keeper of the
> prison committed to Joseph's hand all the prisoners who
> were in the prison; whatever they did there, it was his do-
> ing. The keeper of the prison did not look into anything
> that was under Joseph's authority, because the LORD was
> with him; and whatever he did, the LORD made it pros-
> per. (Genesis 39:20-23)

The king's prison was a political prison rather than a dungeon and
may well have been on the estates of Potiphar. It was most likely under Potiphar's control as a place for the ruling class, not for common
criminals. And once again, the "LORD was with Joseph" and he was
given "favor" by the warden, who probably knew Potiphar personally
and no doubt knew of Joseph's reputation. Again, Joseph was given
total freedom and responsibility, this time in the prison, where he was
in charge of everything that transpired—because "the LORD was with
him."

> It came to pass after these things that the butler and the
> baker of the king of Egypt offended their lord, the king of
> Egypt. And Pharaoh was angry with his two officers, the
> chief butler and the chief baker. So he put them in custo-
> dy in the house of the captain of the guard, in the prison,
> the place where Joseph was confined. And the captain of
> the guard charged Joseph with them, and he served them;
> so they were in custody for a while. (Genesis 40:1-4)

The timing of these two episodes is not clear in Scripture. Joseph
is 17 when he is captured and sold into Egypt (Genesis 37:2) and 30
when he is elevated by Pharaoh to the second rank in the kingdom
(Genesis 41:46). Thus, some 13 years transpire during the intervening
period, with only two years accounted for (Genesis 41:1) when Pharaoh's butler finally remembered that Joseph had correctly interpreted

his dream while he was in prison. It is likely that Joseph had spent several years in Potiphar's home as well as his prison. Certainly, some time had elapsed prior to the butler and the baker being sent over to "the house of the captain of the guard" (Potiphar's estate) where Joseph was in prison.

> Then the butler and the baker of the king of Egypt, who were confined in the prison, had a dream, both of them, each man's dream in one night and each man's dream with its own interpretation. And Joseph came in to them in the morning and looked at them, and saw that they were sad. So he asked Pharaoh's officers who were with him in the custody of his lord's house, saying, "Why do you look so sad today?" And they said to him, "We each have had a dream, and there is no interpreter of it." So Joseph said to them, "Do not interpretations belong to God? Tell them to me, please." (Genesis 40:5-8)

What follows is a detailed account of dreams with features that were related to the responsibilities that these senior court "princes" held when they were in charge of major functions in the palace. The "butler" was a close confidant of rulers and was in charge of protecting the ruler from being killed. He would have been a close friend or perhaps even a family member. The "baker" was a "prince" over the food service in the palace and would have been in charge of many people overseeing the food preparation for hundreds. He would have had opportunity to do great damage to the court.

Whatever may have happened, these two came under the anger of Pharaoh. More than likely, a plot to overthrow or kill Pharaoh was uncovered and their imprisonment was an expedient precaution until the true culprits could be determined. During the rather short intervening time, both of them dreamed "in one night" and were "sad" ("fretting").

Joseph offers to interpret the dreams, immediately letting them know that his understanding would come from *Elohim*. The butler, probably because he knew in his own heart that he was not guilty of any crime, told his dream first. He had seen a vine with three branches that budded and produced beautiful fruit. He personally prepared the grapes for the pharaoh's use and gave the cup into the hand of Pharaoh. It is likely that the butler could have interpreted his own dream, except for the meaning of those "three branches."

Joseph understands that the three branches represent three days, and tells the butler that he will be restored to his office in Pharaoh's court. Overjoyed, the butler promises to remember Joseph when he is restored to court and to plead for Joseph's release. It will be a full two years before the butler remembers (Genesis 41:1)

The baker, of course, seeing the good interpretation of the butler's dream, is hoping for some "God thing" to happen on his behalf as well. It is likely that the baker was part of whatever plot landed them both in prison and has been stewing over his duplicity since he was implicated. Now, with the favorable interpretation for the butler ringing in his ears, the baker blurts out what he had dreamt during the night.

There were three white baskets on his head. The top basket was full of "all kinds of baked goods," and while he was watching, birds came and started eating those delectable desserts and breads right out of the basket! Apparently interrupting the baker's narrative, Joseph tells the baker that he has only three more days to live, and that he will be found guilty, his head chopped off, and his body hung out for everybody to see while the birds peck on his body for their food.

> Now it came to pass on the third day, which was Pharaoh's birthday, that he made a feast for all his servants; and he lifted up the head of the chief butler and of the chief baker among his servants. Then he restored the chief butler to his butlership again, and he placed the cup in Pharaoh's hand. But he hanged the chief baker, as Joseph had interpreted to them. Yet the chief butler did not remember Joseph, but forgot him. (Genesis 40:20-23)

Joseph Before Pharaoh

Two years later, the butler remembers the prison incident! Joseph is still in prison, wondering what has happened. Twice Joseph has been given supernatural insight when the dreams of the butler and baker were made known to him. All during his service with Potiphar and while he was in prison, it was clear that the Lord blessed him. But he has been stuck in slavery or prison for 13 years! That's a long time to wait when you are young and anxious to "do something" for the Lord. Spiritual leadership is not for the immature (1 Timothy 3:6). Many of the key leaders in the Bible were at least 30 before they were put into positions of responsibility—even though their hearts were right and they wanted to serve. John the Baptist and our Lord Jesus Christ are two important servants who come to mind.

In Genesis 41:1-7, Pharaoh has two back-to-back dreams that leave him agitated and unable to resolve their meanings. He senses that the interpretation is critical for the kingdom that he rules. The first dream centers around seven cows that are fat and healthy, followed by seven small and ugly cows that eat up the fat and healthy ones. Both sets of cattle come up out of the river, which is obviously the Nile, the source of Egypt's prosperity. The second dream shows seven "heads of grain" that are full and sweet blossoming out of one stalk (this probably references a type of corn). Then an east wind begins to blow (coming from the desert), and up pops "seven thin heads, blighted by the east wind" that "devoured the seven plump and full heads" (Genesis 41:6-7).

> Now it came to pass in the morning that his spirit was troubled, and he sent and called for all the magicians of Egypt and all its wise men. And Pharaoh told them his dreams, but there was no one who could interpret them for Pharaoh. (Genesis 41:8)

The magicians and the wise men are astrologers and/or diviners and compose the "cabinet" or counselors of Pharaoh's court. None of them are able to interpret the dreams. (This should remind the reader of a very similar event with Daniel and Nebuchadnezzar in Daniel 2.) Finally, the butler "remembers his faults" (that he forgot Joseph) and recounts the incident that restored him to favor.

> Then Pharaoh sent and called Joseph, and they brought him quickly out of the dungeon; and he shaved, changed his clothing, and came to Pharaoh. And Pharaoh said to Joseph, "I have had a dream, and there is no one who can interpret it. But I have heard it said of you that you can understand a dream, to interpret it." So Joseph answered Pharaoh, saying, "It is not in me; God will give Pharaoh an answer of peace." (Genesis 41:14-16)

Pharaoh retells the two dreams in their entirety, emphasizing the frightening aspects. Pharaoh had "never seen" such "ugliness" in cattle. "When they had eaten them up, no one would have known that they had eaten them, for they were just as ugly as at the beginning" (Genesis 40:21). Then as Pharaoh recounts the second dream, he adds the adjective "withered" (small) to the memory of the dream about the "heads of grain." Finally, Pharaoh mentions the failure of the magicians and wise men to understand the meaning of the dreams. (With the court all listening—and probably with their knees knocking. Pharaoh can have them all executed! And they know it.)

As Joseph prepares to interpret the dreams for Pharaoh, he makes sure that God gets the credit for what is going to be revealed. Quite probably, Joseph has already been given the interpretations from God and knows that the two dreams are but one revelation. Without any fanfare or request for personal favor, Joseph gives a clear account of what is ahead for Egypt.

There will be seven years of great plenty followed by seven years of famine throughout all the land of Egypt, and "all the plenty will be forgotten in the land of Egypt; and the famine will deplete the land. So the plenty will not be known in the land because of the famine following, for it will be very severe" (Genesis 41:30-31). Emboldened by the confidence that this prophecy is the work of the Creator and that He has given Joseph (and Pharaoh) insight into the next 14 years, Joseph makes sure that Pharaoh knows that *Elohim* has ordered this and that it will start "shortly" (Genesis 41:32).

All of the previous 13 years' experience now blossom into a strategic plan for the nation. Joseph has learned a great deal about Egypt during his time in Potiphar's household and has had the time to reflect on the reasons for his captivity.

Joseph "The" Man

Now, when he could have taken advantage of the generosity of Pharaoh, Joseph does nothing more than give priceless advice to the court. A man of sound wisdom and administrative skills should be found who can be set over the coming task. Pharaoh is to appoint "officers" under him to carry out the plan and to tax 20 percent on all produce of the land. Furthermore, Pharaoh is to store the surplus to prevent starvation in the future, thereby insuring the strength of the nation and the likelihood that the rest of the civilized world would pour their wealth into Egypt as they sought supplies for their own survival.

> So the advice was good in the eyes of Pharaoh and in the eyes of all his servants. And Pharaoh said to his servants, "Can we find such a one as this, a man in whom is the Spirit of God?" (Genesis 41:37-38)

Joseph is recognized by Pharaoh and his court as "the" man who could do everything needed in light of what has been revealed. No one could better administrate the plan that *Elohim* had revealed than "the" man to whom God had made the matter clear. Therefore, Joseph is promoted to second-in-command of all Egypt.

CHAPTER ELEVEN
JOSEPH THE GOVERNOR

And Pharaoh said to his servants, "Can we find such a one as this, a man in whom is the Spirit of God?" Then Pharaoh said to Joseph, "Inasmuch as God has shown you all this, there is no one as discerning and wise as you. You shall be over my house, and all my people shall be ruled according to your word; only in regard to the throne will I be greater than you." And Pharaoh said to Joseph, "See, I have set you over all the land of Egypt." Then Pharaoh took his signet ring off his hand and put it on Joseph's hand; and he clothed him in garments of fine linen and put a gold chain around his neck. And he had him ride in the second chariot which he had; and they cried out before him, "Bow the knee!" So he set him over all the land of Egypt. (Genesis 41:38-43)

What a turnaround! Thirteen years as a household slave and a prison trusty, now suddenly riding in a capital city parade behind the pharaoh of the greatest nation on Earth. The closest picture that the reader may be able to recall might be scenes from *Cleopatra* or *Ben Hur*. This is a public investiture of power and authority to rule every facet of all the lives in Egypt, including the rich and powerful. Only Pharaoh can overrule Joseph.

Along with Pharaoh's signet ring and royal clothing, Joseph has his name changed to *Zaphnath-Paaneah* (Genesis 41:45). Although scholars are not certain of the precise meaning of this Egyptian title, there are several possible interpretations, any one of which would fit the role that is assigned to this young man: Abundance of Life, Savior of the World, Revealer of Secrets, God's Word Speaking Life, Furnisher of Sustenance.

Joseph became a very busy and very visible governor.

> Joseph was thirty years old when he stood before Pharaoh
> king of Egypt. And Joseph went out from the presence
> of Pharaoh, and went throughout all the land of Egypt.
> (Genesis 41:46)

Since most of us are familiar with Western civilization and the European and United States' forms of government, it is difficult for us to relate to the total powers afforded the kings and rulers of the ancient world. Probably, the most similar format known to some of us might be the British structure of a monarch who holds the right to rule and the prime minister who is "elected" (in Joseph's case, appointed) to execute the will of the monarch throughout the land.

Years of Plenty

> Now in the seven plentiful years the ground brought
> forth abundantly. So he gathered up all the food of the
> seven years which were in the land of Egypt, and laid up
> the food in the cities; he laid up in every city the food
> of the fields which surrounded them. Joseph gathered
> very much grain, as the sand of the sea, until he stopped
> counting, for it was immeasurable. (Genesis 41:47-49)

The Egypt of that era (2000 B.C.) was more fertile and rich than it is today, stretching from what we visualize as the Nile Delta in the north (Lower Egypt) to beyond the fifth cataract nearly 1,000 miles to the south (Upper Egypt). Effectively bordered on the west and the east by deserts, the kingdom was a "strip" with its head the Nile Delta and its long body an agricultural paradise dotted with major cities and temples that served both as a political and a religious unifier for hundreds of years.

During the seven years of plenty, Joseph is given Asenath, a daughter of "Poti-Pherah priest of On." On is the Egyptian name for the city of Heliopolis, one of the oldest cities of ancient Egypt, whose ruins can be found in the northeast quadrant of Cairo. Asenath means "Dedicated to Neith," an Egyptian deity equivalent to the Greek goddess Athena. Although Joseph remains faithful to his worship of *Elohim*, he has learned to live within the culture, speak the language, and adapt to the requirements of a national Egyptian leader.

A very similar situation happens centuries later with Daniel. Both are called on to serve God in a foreign and pagan nation. Both rise to the apex of political power. Both are faithful to their worship of God and do not ruin or compromise their testimony. It can be done. It needs to be done! Every nation needs godly leaders. When the nations are ruled by good and godly men, "the people rejoice; But when a wicked man rules, the people groan" (Proverbs 29:2).

Joseph marries Asenath and the union produces two sons (Genesis 41:50-52). Manasseh, the firstborn, is named for Joseph's new life. The name means "Forgetting," not reflecting a loss of memory but a loss of the pain and anguish he had felt at the betrayals he experienced—and probably a reference to the distance he feels from his former life in Canaan. Ephraim, the second son, is named for the blessings of God. The name means "Doubly Fruitful," stressing Joseph's thankfulness for God's blessings and the wonder of his advancement and success as his service to Pharaoh unfolds.

Years of Famine

> So when all the land of Egypt was famished, the people cried to Pharaoh for bread. Then Pharaoh said to all the Egyptians, "Go to Joseph; whatever he says to you, do." The famine was over all the face of the earth, and Joseph opened all the storehouses and sold to the Egyptians.

> And the famine became severe in the land of Egypt. So all countries came to Joseph in Egypt to buy grain, because the famine was severe in all lands. (Genesis 41:55-57)

As among all people, when things are going great no one tends to anticipate or be concerned about coming problems. Joseph and Pharaoh and his court are all aware of the looming disaster, but the rest of the population seems to be oblivious. And whatever had caused the famine in Egypt had also spread to "all the face of the earth." God had foretold this and was surely behind the execution of this particular series of events to work "all things according to the counsel of His will" (Ephesians 1:11).

Almost 200 years before, God had told Abraham that "your descendants will be strangers in a land that is not theirs, and will serve them, and they will afflict them four hundred years" (Genesis 15:13). Joseph was now the one chosen to oversee the transfer of this budding nation to the land of Egypt and settle them in a farming and ranching territory that would preserve them until they were ready to become the nation that God had in mind.

Model Government

The distribution of food was a masterpiece of governmental authority. Strategic stockpiles were developed throughout the entire nation during the years of plenty. All of the supplies were obtained by lawful and fair means. No one was taken advantage of during the time of prosperity, but when the economy fell the government was in the position to help the entire population with the surplus gained previously. If anything, this excerpt demonstrates governmental responsibility at its best.

- Supply was withheld until the need was real.

- Nothing was given away but was sold at a fair price.

- Industry was encouraged, not indolence.

- Strict control was maintained over supplies to prevent looting and waste.

- Those in genuine poverty were likely used in distribution work.

- Income from the sale was used to provide for necessary national functions.

- The population was able to get by on less than in the years of "plenty."

- The tax of 20 percent each year during the prosperous years was sufficient to feed the nation and supply the needs of other lands for many years.

Since the words of Scripture are never incidental, it is of some interest to note that Genesis 47:13-26 contains a rather detailed record of Joseph's plan for the government of Egypt during one of the worst "depressions" in world history. It is a testimony to the amount of surplus that was available during the prosperous years, as well as the adjustment that was necessary to accommodate the time of famine. That model is a textbook case for governmental management—even as Joseph managed the sale of goods that ultimately transferred the wealth of several countries to the nation of Egypt.

- "Bread" (grain for food and feed) was purchased for money.

- When the money was gone, cattle were bartered.

- When the cattle were gone, land was sold.

- When the land was sold, employment was granted.

- Taxation was still at 20 percent of all GNP for the nation.

Genesis 50:19-20 is the summary verse of this period and of all the events that preserved the nation of Egypt as well as set in motion the care of the nation of Israel for the next 400 years.

> Joseph said to [his brothers], "Do not be afraid, for am I in the place of God? But as for you, you meant evil against me; but God meant it for good, in order to bring

it about as it is this day, to save many people alive."

Joseph and the Brothers

Twenty-plus years have gone by since Joseph was sold to the Midianite traders. You may recall that Joseph was 17 when he started work in Potiphar's house and 30 when he was lifted up by Pharaoh to become the second-highest ruler in the land. Those 13 years were then followed by seven years of bounty as the land exploded in prosperity and Joseph began his amazing stewardship of the nation's resources.

When Jacob calls a family meeting to discuss going down into Egypt, perhaps as much as a year had elapsed in which the "famine was severe in all lands" (Genesis 41:57). The agricultural resources of Jacob's family were vast and required feed and seed stock storage in various locations across the grazing lands of their herds. Local vendors would have been contracted to deliver basic supplies as needed, and supplemental food grain would have been accumulated from the surrounding farmers to maximize the efficiency of the operation.

As the famine increased, supplies would have been more difficult and more expensive to obtain, along with an ever-decreasing harvest as the drought, winds, depleted soils, and vanishing reservoirs brought growth to a trickle. The foreign caravans became less frequent, and larger enterprises like that of Jacob's family would have begun to experience severe shortages even more quickly than smaller, local tribesmen, since their business spanned many miles north and south and they would have felt the choking pinch tightening around their ability to fulfill their own contracts.

No doubt they had developed many contacts in Egypt as they supplied some of the large meat requirements of that great nation, but they may not have spent any time there, since trade fulfillment would have been handled primarily through caravan businesses and the wholesale factors in the major cities of Egypt. Now, however, it was time to develop a personal relationship with the government of Egypt, since word had come north that sufficient feed and seed grain had been developed for the surrounding nations through the stunning success of the "bread basket" of the Nile.

So, when Jacob brought his sons together from their widespread field duties, he was really perplexed when he saw them "look at one another" at the mention of a trip to Egypt.

> When Jacob saw that there was grain in Egypt, Jacob said unto his sons, "Why do you look at one another?" And he said, "Indeed I have heard that there is grain in Egypt; go down to that place and buy for us there, that we may live and not die." (Genesis 42:1-2)

Obviously, Jacob did not know that the ten brothers had for years been concealing the awful secret of their duplicity in the attempted murder and ultimate sale of their little brother to a band of Midianite trader-slavers. Although they may have heard scraps of "did you know" gossip over the 20-plus years, as far as they *knew*, Joseph was probably dead—or more likely grubbing it out under a blazing hot son as a field hand or struggling for life in the desert mines of Upper Egypt.

The brothers have lived with this guilt for all this time. No doubt they have relived the awful "anguish of [Joseph's] soul" (Genesis 42:21-22) many times as they spent time in the dark around campfires. Surely you have noticed how the "tales" of memories grow more somber as the night wears on. Maybe a recent rumor had surfaced that mentioned a young Hebrew lad on the dock in one slave market or another. Still, they had hardened their hearts against any repentance, having told and retold the story of finding Joseph's bloody coat all ripped and torn by "wild beasts."

Jacob and Benjamin (probably still just a young man at this point) were totally ignorant of those events. The word "Egypt" was hardly out of Jacob's mouth when he noticed all their heads jerk quickly to look at each other. Interpreting that look (correctly) as a fear of going to Egypt, Jacob wasted no time discussing the reason. Their business was approaching a state of emergency, and it would have been utterly foolish to wait any longer to secure the permission of Egypt's Minister of Commerce, or whatever they were calling this "Golden Boy" of Pharaoh's court. This was no time for dialogue. This was time for action—and since Jacob was the patriarch and the owner of the business, he issued the order: "Go to it! Get packing! Get down there and do what you are paid to do!" (Or something to that effect.)

The First Trip to Egypt

Jacob was quite elderly, nearing the time when he would meet Pharaoh himself at age 130 (Genesis 47:9). Benjamin was thought to be the only remaining son of Rachel, Jacob's first love who had died on the trip to Hebron. Benjamin was far too precious in Jacob's sight to make the trek, so the ten adult brothers made the necessary preparations to travel the three to four weeks down to the city of On (Heliopolis), where the seat of Egypt's government was at that time, and return with sufficient grain and supplies to conduct their affairs in Canaan.

Jacob's agricultural wealth was vast (Genesis 30:43), so a caravan to secure critical feed and seed would have been enormous. Each of the ten brothers assembled the equipage and necessary servants for the round trip, choosing "asses" for the pack animals (Genesis 42:26 KJV). Although these beasts were smaller than camels, they were larger than donkeys and more mild-tempered. And since their journey would be along well-traveled trade highways, there would be no need for the camel's fabled endurance.

Meeting Joseph

> Now Joseph was governor over the land; and it was he who sold to all the people of the land. And Joseph's brothers came and bowed down before him with their faces to the earth. (Genesis 42:6)

Knowing that they must gain what would today be considered a governmental contract for "foreign aid," the brothers arrived at the palace of the governor. Joseph would have been dressed as an Egyptian royal, speaking the court language, looking nothing like what they might remember about their "long lost" brother. They would have met with him in an open public courtyard or business forum of the palace among many other delegates from other nations who would have been seeking an official contract. Political protocol would have required that they show proper obeisance, presenting themselves before Joseph's "throne" by bowing prostrate "with their faces to the earth."

The situation evokes echoes of an earlier scene between Joseph and his brothers.

> "There we were, binding sheaves in the field. Then behold, my sheaf arose and also stood upright; and indeed your sheaves stood all around and bowed down to my sheaf." And his brothers said to him, "Shall you indeed reign over us? Or shall you indeed have dominion over us?" So they hated him even more for his dreams and for his words. (Genesis 37:7-8).

There, right in front of Joseph, was the fulfillment of his dream of 20-plus years before. Not only did the dream foretell that the older brothers would yield to Joseph's rule over them, but even the reason for the submission was clear—grain! Back then, they made mockery of Joseph and harassed him unmercifully. Now they were plagued by the guilt of their deeds and trembling before the very one whom they would have murdered. God's justice may often seem delayed, but it is very certain. "The LORD is slow to anger and great in power, And will not at all acquit the wicked" (Nahum 1:3).

> Joseph saw his brothers and recognized them, but he acted as a stranger to them and spoke roughly to them. (Genesis 42:7)

The first impression when we read that Joseph spoke roughly to them is that he might be getting ready to "get even." But this is really not at all what is in Joseph's mind. You may recall that he had named his first child Manasseh to express his "forgetting" about the old life, and the second son was named Ephraim to recognize the joy of his new life and the "doubly fruitful" blessings that God had allowed him to appreciate. No, there is little thought of vengeance, but he does want reconciliation—and that means that his brothers must genuinely repent. But Joseph does not know their current spiritual or mental state, so he must devise a way to test their character.

> Joseph...said to them, "You are spies! You have come to see the nakedness of the land!" And they said to him, "No, my lord, but your servants have come to buy food. We are all one man's sons; we are honest men; your servants are not spies." But he said to them, "No, but you have come to see the nakedness of the land." (Genesis 42:9-12)

Their being spies would have been a real possibility in that political and economic situation, and accusing them of it would have been the quickest way for Joseph to verify if they had any awareness of who he was. They are immediately on the defensive and try to assure this "Prince of Egypt" that they are ten of 12 sons of one man, with the youngest son back with his father in Canaan and "one [who] is no more" (Genesis 42:13). Interesting! Even now they are reluctant to admit their guilt to anyone but themselves, although—as will become clear in a few moments—they are well aware of the just punishment for their attempted murder.

> But Joseph said to them, "It is as I spoke to you, saying, 'You are spies!' In this manner you shall be tested: By the life of Pharaoh, you shall not leave this place unless your youngest brother comes here. Send one of you, and let him bring your brother; and you shall be kept in prison, that your words may be tested to see whether there is any truth in you; or else, by the life of Pharaoh, surely you are spies!" So he put them all together in prison three days. (Genesis 42:14-17)

If true repentance and reconciliation to take place with his brothers, Joseph must know the truth of what they are saying and bring about their genuine confession and willingness to rectify the wrongs that have been done. He would have had no word of them at all for more than 20 years, and the brothers would know that the *Zaphnath-Paaneah* of Egypt had the right to demand proof of their credentials. It wouldn't have been too much of a surprise, then, when Joseph repeated his accusation and demanded that they prove their truthfulness. What would have stunned them, however, would have been his insistence that they be sent to prison until one of them could go back to Canaan and bring Benjamin to Egypt.

The brothers are summarily tossed into confinement for foreign dignitaries (probably attached to Joseph's palace). Being isolated with fellow co-conspirators is a sure way to bring out the details of crimes committed—especially if it seems like no one can overhear or understand the conversations. Of course, Joseph has made arrangements to do just that. At the end of three days, he calls the brothers back into his presence. Since he has been using an interpreter, the brothers don't know he understands their Canaanite speech, so he hears their confession to each other of the earlier evil inflicted on him so long ago. Most importantly, Joseph hears them acknowledge the justice of their troubles.

Joseph repeats his demand that the brothers bring Benjamin to him.

> Then Joseph said to them the third day, "Do this and live, for I fear God: If you are honest men, let one of your brothers be confined to your prison house; but you, go and carry grain for the famine of your houses. And bring your youngest brother to me; so your words will be verified, and you shall not die." And they did so. Then they said to one another, "We are truly guilty concerning our brother, for we saw the anguish of his soul when he pleaded with us, and we would not hear; therefore this distress has come upon us." (Genesis 42:18-21)

Reuben reminds the brothers of his attempt to intervene and rescue Joseph from the murder they had plotted, only to find they had bundled the wailing Joseph into the hands of Midianite slavers.

> And Reuben answered them, saying, "Did I not speak to you, saying, 'Do not sin against the boy'; and you would not listen? Therefore behold, his blood is now required of us." (Genesis 42:22)

Simeon is selected by Joseph to remain behind as hostage. He had long manifested a cruel nature, evidenced by the murder and pillage of the people of Shechem after the seduction of Dinah, and he needed time to reflect and repent more than any of them. And now that Joseph had said that he "fears God" (*Elohim*), the brothers don't seem to be bothered by the thought of leaving Simeon in Egypt for a rather lengthy time—in fact, they don't seem to be in any hurry at all (except to get home)!

Prophecy in Motion

Having heard enough to assure himself that the brothers have not yet hardened their hearts, Joseph sets in motion a plan to bring about reconciliation and perhaps to bring the entire family to Egypt under his protection. It is likely that Joseph is now aware of the reason God had brought him through the challenges of slavery and imprisonment and placed him at the pinnacle of prestige and power. He is surely aware of God's foundational promises to Abraham and would have heard the testimony of his own earthly father. No doubt he was aware that *Elohim* had told Abraham that his descendants would be "strangers in a land that is not theirs, and will serve them, and they will afflict them four hundred years" (Genesis 15:13).

> Then Joseph gave a command to fill their sacks with grain, to restore every man's money to his sack, and to give them provisions for the journey. Thus he did for them. So they loaded their donkeys with the grain and departed from there. But as one of them opened his sack to give his donkey feed at the encampment, he saw his money; and there it was, in the mouth of his sack. So he said to his brothers, "My money has been restored, and there it is, in my

sack!" Then their hearts failed them and they were afraid, saying to one another, "What is this that God has done to us?" (Genesis 42:25-28)

Please notice the contrast of the generosity and grace of Joseph and the instant reaction of the brothers to blame God for their growing problems! Joseph is focused on bringing about restoration. The brothers are focused on getting out of trouble. Obviously, the discovery of the money in the food sack of one of them was a surprise, but rather than seeking to understand what God had done *for* them, they were afraid and could only wonder what God had done *to* them.

Yes, God was behind all of this, but His plan was to bring about an awakening of their consciences that would bring about full confession, which would make "cleansing" possible. Guilt is a horrible burden to bear, and a slowly awakening conscience is almost like the awful tingling and prickling of a leg or arm after it has been "deadened" while blood flow has been restricted.

The month-long journey back to Bethel must have been really strained. What a mess! They had only partially fulfilled their duties. They did not have an open-ended contract with Egypt. The supplies were only a one-time purchase. They need to tell Jacob that if the famine lasts much longer they cannot return to Egypt unless they take Benjamin with them, and Simeon was left behind as a hostage. And to top all of that off, somehow one of their money pouches had been left in their grain packs.

> Then they went to Jacob their father in the land of Canaan and told him all that had happened to them, saying: "The man who is lord of the land spoke roughly to us, and took us for spies of the country. But we said to him, 'We are honest men; we are not spies. We are twelve brothers, sons of our father; one is no more, and the youngest is with our father this day in the land of Canaan.' Then the man, the lord of the country, said to us, 'By this I will know that you are honest men: Leave one of your broth-

ers here with me, take food for the famine of your households, and be gone. And bring your youngest brother to
me; so I shall know that you are not spies, but that you
are honest men. I will grant your brother to you, and you
may trade in the land.'"

Then it happened as they emptied their sacks, that sur-
prisingly each man's bundle of money was in his sack;
and when they and their father saw the bundles of money,
they were afraid. (Genesis 42:29-35)

What couldn't get any worse, did! After "spinning" the story to
Jacob in their favor as well as could be done under the circumstances,
the brothers discovered *all* the money in *each* of their grain packs!
None of them had an explanation, and none of them knew what to
do. Jacob was having none of this, either. There was no way he would
let them take Benjamin away from him.

And Jacob their father said to them, "You have bereaved
me: Joseph is no more, Simeon is no more, and you want
to take Benjamin. All these things are against me." Then
Reuben spoke to his father, saying, "Kill my two sons if I
do not bring him back to you; put him in my hands, and
I will bring him back to you." But he said, "My son shall
not go down with you, for his brother is dead, and he is
left alone. If any calamity should befall him along the way
in which you go, then you would bring down my gray
hair with sorrow to the grave." (Genesis 42:36-38)

Jacob's observation that "all these things are against me" seems to
define the attitude of the entire family. Jacob can only think about the
possibility that his family might be taken from him, seems to crawl
into self-pitying depression, and becomes unwilling to deal with the
problem. He bemoans his bereavement and hardens his heart against
the obvious need and solution.

The brothers are simply self-defensive and shift the blame to Joseph. They have relied on the absolutely futile argument that Joseph

was "not fair" and unreasonable. They had been truthful to Joseph, but he was cruel and unjust. They only see Joseph as "the man" of the country, calling him "Lord" several times. God is definitely at work in their hearts, but there is no genuine repentance yet—only remorse and fear of retribution.

Reuben bursts out with an emotional (and impossible) vow that he would bring Benjamin back, and if not, then Jacob could kill his two sons in retribution (two for one, so to speak). Maybe there was some self-pity for his not having been able to save Joseph. It is unlikely that either Jacob or the other brothers took Reuben seriously. He loses whatever leadership role he may have had in the past from this point onward.

The family is still in disarray with no plan or recourse to prevent further disaster. The famine is still ongoing and has years to run. The purchased supplies will last only a matter of months, and the requirements for a return to Egypt are still in force. The imminent pall of starvation and bereavement still stands.

The Second Trip to Egypt

> Now the famine was severe in the land. And it came to pass, when they had eaten up the grain which they had brought from Egypt, that their father said to them, "Go back, buy us a little food." (Genesis 43:1-2)

The biblical record helps us gain some perspective on the time involved for the initial trip to Egypt and the arrival of the second caravan from Bethel. Joseph himself comments when he reveals himself to his brothers that the famine had only lasted two years thus far and that there were still five years to run (Genesis 45:6). Apparently, Jacob had anticipated setting up some sort of ongoing contract with Egypt since his purchase would be too large for one trip—even for a well-equipped caravan. But the regular "runs" were not authorized. The initial supplies were fast running out and they needed "a little food."

It is risky to assume too much when the biblical record is sparse, but it is well within the context to recognize Jacob's meek request for a "little food" when contrasted with the initial order: "I have heard that there is grain in Egypt; go down to that place and buy for us there" (Genesis 42:2). It seems that Jacob is still depressed and has lost focus on the business needs, merely wanting a "little food" to keep the family alive.

Judah Steps Up

Fortunately, although Reuben has lost any influence among the brothers and the rest of them seem to be indifferent, Judah assumes his future role of leadership among them.

> But Judah spoke to him, saying, "The man solemnly warned us, saying, 'You shall not see my face unless your brother is with you.' If you send our brother with us, we will go down and buy you food. But if you will not send him, we will not go down; for the man said to us, 'You shall not see my face unless your brother is with you.'" (Genesis 43:3-5)

Perhaps the most significant point to recognize in this short interchange is that Judah (along with all of the brothers) has come to acknowledge that Joseph is "the man" to deal with—twice in these two verses and once again in the quick response from the brothers. Joseph's earlier dream of having authority over them is part of their reality now, and they will never again see him in any other role than that of ruler, provider, and protector. Many times God will use difficult pressures to turn around the lives of the children whom He truly loves. Our response is usually worry, remorse, or self-pity—just like Jacob and the brothers.

> And Israel said, "Why did you deal so wrongfully with me as to tell the man whether you had still another brother?" But they said, "The man asked us pointedly about ourselves and our family, saying, 'Is your father still alive? Have you another brother?' And we told him according to these words. Could we possibly have known that he

would say, 'Bring your brother down'?" (Genesis 43:6-7)

Talk about a blame game! Jacob blames the brothers, and the brothers blame Joseph. Just like Adam and Eve—Adam blamed God; Eve blamed the serpent (Genesis 3:12-13). All of humanity has been doing the same thing ever since. Unconfessed sin is a demanding boss! "Do you not know that to whom you present yourselves slaves to obey, you are that one's slaves whom you obey, whether of sin leading to death, or of obedience leading to righteousness?" (Romans 6:16). That Jacob could fall prey to this easy-to-spot behavior should be a warning to all of us. No one is immune. Check your attitude! Frequently!

> Then Judah said to Israel his father, "Send the lad with me, and we will arise and go, that we may live and not die, both we and you and also our little ones. I myself will be surety for him; from my hand you shall require him. If I do not bring him back to you and set him before you, then let me bear the blame forever. For if we had not lingered, surely by now we would have returned this second time." (Genesis 42:8-10)

Judah senses that he must take charge, reminding his father that "the man" was very serious about the need to bring Benjamin back with them. Reuben has faded into the background with his previous emotional outburst, and Simeon is in prison. Both Simeon and Levi have been mistrusted by the family ever since the Shechem incident, and Benjamin is too young to take leadership over his much-older brothers. Most of the remaining brothers seem to be content to "go with the flow" and are either incapable or unwilling to assume responsibility. Judah, however, uses command language: "Send the lad with me! We will get up and go. We must live!" Judah has the courage to say what all of them know: The delay is Jacob's fault.

That seems to have been enough to jolt Jacob out of his lethargy, since he is called Israel for the first time in 22 years. The last recorded time was in Genesis 37:13, when Jacob sent Joseph to check on the brothers who were wandering off north near Shechem. Now Jacob considers sending Benjamin to Egypt and appears to begin trusting God again.

> And their father Israel said to them, "If it must be so, then do this: Take some of the best fruits of the land in your vessels and carry down a present for the man—a little balm and a little honey, spices and myrrh, pistachio nuts and almonds. Take double money in your hand, and take back in your hand the money that was returned in the mouth of your sacks; perhaps it was an oversight. Take your brother also, and arise, go back to the man. And may God Almighty give you mercy before the man, that he may release your other brother and Benjamin. If I am bereaved, I am bereaved!" (Genesis 43:11-14)

Joseph's second dream now comes into focus. Jacob, the patriarch and the thrice-visited and God-appointed descendant of Abraham, prepares to honor "the man" in Egypt whom he has either ignored or distrusted heretofore. He recognized that he has been acting selfishly and prepares a lavish present of all the delectable fruits of Canaan to give to Joseph. He also authorizes "double money" to be taken on the return trip, assuming the best possible scenario of an oversight by the Egyptians on that first trip rather than thievery or entrapment. This change of heart is both sudden and cleansing. Israel is back in his rightful place as leader of the nation.

Once again, Jacob calls on God Almighty to protect them and fulfill the promises. This is the name that Isaac used in his blessing of Jacob when Jacob was sent from his family to Laban in Syria (Genesis 28:3). Later on that same journey, when Jacob was alone at night under the stars sleeping on a rock for a pillow, heaven was opened and a "ladder" was revealed that permitted the angels to run up and down bearing messages for "the LORD God of Abraham" (Genesis 28:13). There, at Bethel, Jacob received his personal calling and assurance of protection, provision, and future promises. Now, with these decades-old memories rekindled in his heart, Jacob sends his sons off to Egypt.

Joseph Receives His Brothers

> So the men took that present and Benjamin, and they took double money in their hand, and arose and went down to Egypt; and they stood before Joseph. When Joseph saw Benjamin with them, he said to the steward of his house, "Take these men to my home, and slaughter an animal and make ready; for these men will dine with me at noon." Then the man did as Joseph ordered, and the man brought the men into Joseph's house. (Genesis 43:15-17)

As soon as they arrive at Joseph's palace, they are ushered into the audience room and totally surprised by a formal invitation to dine with Joseph that very noontime! There is no indication that any words passed between them, but a command was issued from Joseph's steward after he had been told to prepare a separate "formal" meal—apparently already a practice for the Egyptians who were part of Joseph's entourage and staff (Genesis 43:32).

> Now the men were afraid because they were brought into Joseph's house; and they said, "It is because of the money, which was returned in our sacks the first time, that we are brought in, so that he may make a case against us and fall upon us, to take us as slaves with our donkeys." (Genesis 43:18)

The brothers are brought into Joseph's home by the steward, still ignorant of the reason for this sudden hospitality, and they can only imagine that they will be captured and harmed. Their guilt is still clouding their thinking, and their communication with Joseph has always been through an interpreter. They still do not suspect that this is "their" Joseph and can only see the trappings of a close confidant of Pharaoh with all the pomp and lavish surroundings of the house-royal. Canaan, their vast holdings, and personal wealth are microscopic in comparison to the wealth of Egypt. They are the penitent and the petitioners here, not the other way around.

When they drew near to the steward of Joseph's house, they talked with him at the door of the house, and said, "O sir, we indeed came down the first time to buy food; but it happened, when we came to the encampment, that we opened our sacks, and there, each man's money was in the mouth of his sack, our money in full weight; so we have brought it back in our hand. And we have brought down other money in our hands to buy food. We do not know who put our money in our sacks." But he said, "Peace be with you, do not be afraid. Your God and the God of your father has given you treasure in your sacks; I had your money." Then he brought Simeon out to them. So the man brought the men into Joseph's house and gave them water, and they washed their feet; and he gave their donkeys feed. (Genesis 43:19-24)

Immediately, they attempt to explain their innocence to the steward, hardly pausing for breath. The steward insists that he "had their money" but that "your God" (*Elohim*) had made the "treasure" possible for them. There is absolutely no indication that the steward is fabricating the story, so it may be concluded that Joseph had brought about a household worship of the "LORD God" whom Joseph served. All of those assumptions seem to fit the context of a pharaoh who recognized that the Creator God had revealed his dreams to Joseph and that Joseph was guided in his political and administrative acumen by that same all-powerful God.

The Final Test

The next few hours must have been filled with mystery. The servants of Joseph are still not privy to the private concerns of their master. The brothers are bewildered by their apparent release from potential confinement now that Simeon has been returned. Joseph treats the brothers as honored guests and provides for their personal refreshment prior to the formal luncheon. When they finally are ushered into his presence, Joseph receives the gifts sent by Jacob with graciousness and inquires again after their family's welfare—just as though they were regular business associates.

The details are recorded in the text of Genesis 43:26-34. During the protocol of the lavish presentation of the food, Joseph personally sends portions from his table to the Hebrew guests, with an extra portion to Benjamin. No doubt the regular Egyptian guests are perplexed by all of this special treatment. The story has surely gotten out about these men from Canaan who had their money restored. Just as might happen in any similar situation, the rumors would have flown thick and fast, some absolutely sure that the men from Canaan had somehow finagled a slick deal with Joseph and others just as sure that Joseph had lost his fabled wisdom and forgotten to charge them for the grain.

Finally, Joseph is overwhelmed by personal emotion and runs off to his private quarters to weep and restore his decorum. During that lull, the brothers are becoming a bit more bold and sure of their "good luck"—especially since Benjamin seems to be a "hit" with this lord of the Egyptians. Although the many guests have been segregated according to ethnicity and rank, the brothers feel safe and happy. But Joseph is not yet sure of the brothers' attitude. How would they react if they must sacrifice Benjamin? How would they respond if suddenly required to protect their own personal welfare at the cost of their youngest brother's? So, Joseph arranges for a final test to be given.

The steward is instructed to prepare for the brothers' return home by placing all of their money back in their baggage. (He might have thought this odd, but he had been asked to do it before.) But then Joseph's "silver cup" is placed in Benjamin's baggage. This will have the effect of making Benjamin appear greedy and would test the brothers' loyalty toward Benjamin and their father. Furthermore, this opens up the brothers to accusations of ingratitude, theft, and apostasy.

Egypt was both a polytheistic and a mystical society. Egyptians were known to use such cups to predict the future. Diviners could "see" tokens in reflections or in arrangements of gold or silver in the cup. (Later, pagan societies turned to entrails and cast bones.) The reputation of Joseph strongly reinforced his "divination" capabilities. His interpretation of Pharaoh's dream was widely known, and his success in managing the country was spectacular. Joseph's wisdom would have been attributed by many Egyptians as coming from such a "divining cup."

> As soon as the morning dawned, the men were sent away, they and their donkeys. When they had gone out of the city, and were not yet far off, Joseph said to his steward, "Get up, follow the men; and when you overtake them, say to them, 'Why have you repaid evil for good? Is not this the one from which my lord drinks, and with which he indeed practices divination? You have done evil in so doing.'" So he overtook them, and he spoke to them these same words. (Genesis 44:3-6)

The steward catches the brothers just outside the city soon after their departure and confronts them. He hears their expected denial and relates the sentence for the guilty one. They are escorted back to the city and to Joseph's house, where Judah and his brothers once again bow before him and are formally accused of criminal activity. Joseph castigates their foolish attempt to defraud him and implies his "divine insight" gave him the knowledge of their supposed theft (done to test whether they will attempt to placate the Egyptian culture by acquiescing to "other gods").

Judah intercedes and pleads for the family, indicating a great change in the brother's character. His plea does not attempt to deny the apparent guilt of Benjamin but emphasizes the family history and their attempt to comply with Joseph's demands. Judah's willingness to become a substitute for Benjamin's punishment is enough to satisfy Joseph judicially and emotionally—and is a clear parallel to our Lord's substitutionary atonement.

> Then Joseph could not restrain himself before all those who stood by him, and he cried out, "Make everyone go out from me!" So no one stood with him while Joseph made himself known to his brothers. And he wept aloud,

and the Egyptians and the house of Pharaoh heard it. (Genesis 45:1-2)

Ordering everyone out of the room, the emotion that Joseph has been holding in for nearly two years now totally overwhelms him and he begins to sob uncontrollably. You may not have yet had a sorrow or joy that probed your heart that strongly, but should it ever come, you will understand the wracking spasms that seem to come from the innermost core of your body. Few human experiences come near that kind of emotion—and the brothers (and the Egyptian household who were hearing it) were stunned!

Before the men could collect themselves to react, Joseph said: "I am Joseph; does my father still live?"

> But his brothers could not answer him, for they were dismayed in his presence. And Joseph said to his brothers, "Please come near to me." So they came near. Then he said: "I am Joseph your brother, whom you sold into Egypt." (Genesis 45:3-4)

Can you picture the scene? All of these are well-grown men except Benjamin. Men with families of their own and business responsibilities that any of us would be pleased with. Can you picture the CEO of a large corporation sobbing? Can you visualize how the collective officers of the company would react—what their faces would look like as they tried to make sense of what was happening? The ten brothers (all except Benjamin, who was clueless) were trying to grasp the monumental event that was unfolding before them. This was Joseph! This was the teenager they had planned to murder who now stood in front of them as the prime minister of all of Egypt—telling them that he had known about them for two years and had planned all of this!

Joseph must have sensed their bewilderment. How would they react? Would they erupt in hostility and try to finish the murder, or would they collapse in grief and humility at being found out?

> "But now, do not therefore be grieved or angry with yourselves because you sold me here; for God sent me before

you to preserve life. For these two years the famine has been in the land, and there are still five years in which there will be neither plowing nor harvesting. And God sent me before you to preserve a posterity for you in the earth, and to save your lives by a great deliverance. So now it was not you who sent me here, but God; and He has made me a father to Pharaoh, and lord of all his house, and a ruler throughout all the land of Egypt." (Genesis 45:5-8)

Slowly, the men realize what God has done for them. Slowly, the background sound of Joseph's words starts filtering through to them. God was in charge all these 22 years! Trouble was still in the offing—the famine would still run for five more awful years—but Joseph had been given this lofty position to protect and provide for them and their families!

"Hurry and go up to my father, and say to him, 'Thus says your son Joseph: "God has made me lord of all Egypt; come down to me, do not tarry. You shall dwell in the land of Goshen, and you shall be near to me, you and your children, your children's children, your flocks and your herds, and all that you have. There I will provide for you, lest you and your household, and all that you have, come to poverty; for there are still five years of famine."' And behold, your eyes and the eyes of my brother Benjamin see that it is my mouth that speaks to you. So you shall tell my father of all my glory in Egypt, and of all that you have seen; and you shall hurry and bring my father down here." Then he fell on his brother Benjamin's neck and wept, and Benjamin wept on his neck. Moreover he kissed all his brothers and wept over them, and after that his brothers talked with him. (Genesis 45:9-15)

Pharaoh Told of the Reunion

The rest of Genesis 45 records how the news of the reunion traveled to the throne room through Pharaoh's servants. Pharaoh and his key advisors are thrilled that the father and family of the "savior of Egypt" are still alive, and they quickly reiterate and affirm Joseph's offer of permanent residence in Egypt for the family.

The "official" offer from the king could not have been more generous. Not only are the brothers to be given supplies to take home, but in conveying the offer of Pharaoh to Jacob the brothers are to make sure that Jacob knows that Egypt will provide everything that the family could need when they move. Egypt will supply land and grain for the family's enterprise, as well as transportation for all of the people. A storybook ending!

> And Joseph gave them carts, according to the command of Pharaoh, and he gave them provisions for the journey. He gave to all of them, to each man, changes of garments; but to Benjamin he gave three hundred pieces of silver and five changes of garments. And he sent to his father these things: ten donkeys loaded with the good things of Egypt, and ten female donkeys loaded with grain, bread, and food for his father for the journey. So he sent his brothers away, and they departed; and he said to them, "See that you do not become troubled along the way." (Genesis 45:21-24)

CHAPTER TWELVE
JOSEPH THE PROTECTOR

Jacob Hears the News

> And they told him, saying, "Joseph is still alive, and he is governor over all the land of Egypt." And Jacob's heart stood still, because he did not believe them. But when they told him all the words which Joseph had said to them, and when he saw the carts which Joseph had sent to carry him, the spirit of Jacob their father revived. Then Israel said, "It is enough. Joseph my son is still alive. I will go and see him before I die." (Genesis 45:26-28)

After 22 years of living with the agony of Joseph's presumed tragic death, the news finally comes to Jacob that Joseph is alive, well, and virtually in charge of all of Egypt. It is probably not possible for you or me to comprehend the rush of joy and excitement that flooded Jacob at that moment. The most-loved son from the wife of his first love who had been thought horribly killed as a teenager is alive. The Hebrew words are that Jacob's *ruwach* (spirit) *chayah* "came to life." It is as though he had been living a "dead" life, merely going through the motions for two decades, and has now suddenly "come alive"!

> So Israel took his journey with all that he had, and came to Beersheba, and offered sacrifices to the God of his fa-

ther Isaac. Then God spoke to Israel in the visions of the night, and said, "Jacob, Jacob!" And he said, "Here I am." So He said, "I am God, the God of your father; do not fear to go down to Egypt, for I will make of you a great nation there. I will go down with you to Egypt, and I will also surely bring you up again; and Joseph will put his hand on your eyes." (Geneses 46:1-4)

Jacob had maintained a headquarters in Hebron for several years. The family, through the oversight of the brothers, had scattered their herds up and down the central Canaan grazing lands and was now required to assemble them from all points toward the familiar grounds of Beersheba, the "well of the sevens." There, over a century before, Abraham had made peace with the Philistines and Isaac had spent many years.

Now the family is winding its circuitous route from the various grazing fields and scattered homesteads southward toward Beersheba, near the northern headlands of the Dead Sea and bordering on the southeast side of the coastal trade route that led into Egypt. And while Jacob is at Beersheba, *Elohim* once again meets with him in a night vision to reaffirm the promises that had been given to him and his fathers and to reiterate that God would oversee the development of the nation in Egypt as He had promised Abraham (Genesis 15:13).

Then Jacob arose from Beersheba; and the sons of Israel carried their father Jacob, their little ones, and their wives, in the carts which Pharaoh had sent to carry him. So they took their livestock and their goods, which they had acquired in the land of Canaan, and went to Egypt, Jacob and all his descendants with him. (Geneses 46:5-6)

Jacob's decision to leave Canaan is immediate and confident. He is once again "Israel" and recognizes the hand of God, yields in obedience to this major change to his life, and assembles his family for the pilgrimage to Egypt. Joseph had sent word that they were to meet him in Goshen, the lush Nile River Delta region with the major cities of

Zoan and Ramses. Goshen was some 50 miles north of Lower Egypt's capital of On, the likely residence of Joseph and the pharaoh.

The logistics of relocation are enormous. Not only must the family pack and cart the possessions of their many and widespread households, but moving the herds, field equipment, and associated field hands would require both time and resources. Joseph had gained the use of some of Egypt's transport vehicles for their journey, which was most assuredly a significant asset and help. But the work involved and travel labors were all up to the family.

It is always interesting to note whom the Lord finds worthy of listing in one of the several tables of important folks who have been used by God over the centuries. Each of them has played a significant part in the work of the nation-building that the Creator has been involved in. Here is a convenient table for reference of the names of the key family heads who were part of the move into Egypt during the time of Joseph, as recorded in Genesis 46:8-27.

The children of the four wives of the patriarch Jacob			
Leah	**Zilpah**	**Rachel**	**Bilhah**
Reuben	Gad	Joseph	Dan
Simeon	Asher	Benjamin	Naphtali
Levi			
Judah			
Issachar			
Zebulun			
Dinah			

Descendants of Leah					
Reuben	**Simeon**	**Levi**	**Judah**	**Issachar**	**Zebulun**
Hanoch	Jemuel	Gershon	Er	Tola	Sered
Pallu	Jamin	Kohath	Onan	Puvah	Elon
Hezron	Ohad	Merari	Shelah	Job	Jahleel
Carmi	Jachin		Perez	Shimron	
	Zohar		Zerah		
	Shaul		Hezron		
			Hamul		

Descendants of Zilpah		Descendants of Rachel		Descendants of Bilhah	
Gad	**Asher**	**Joseph**	**Benjamin**	**Dan**	**Naphtali**
Ziphion	Jimnah	Manasseh	Belah	Hushim	Jahzeel
Haggi	Ishuah	Ephraim	Becher		Guni
Shuni	Isui		Ashbel		Jezer
Ezbon	Beriah		Gera		Shillem
Eri	Serah		Naaman		
Arodi	Heber		Ehi		
Areli	Malchiel		Rosh		
			Muppim		
			Huppim		
			Ard		

The family had grown to 70 "souls," including Joseph and his two sons already down in Egypt (Genesis 46:27).

The Number Seventy

These 70 original Israelites are the founders of the nation:

- Jacob and his 12 sons

- 51 grandsons (Judah's sons Er and Onan died in Canaan)

- 4 great-grandsons

- 1 daughter (Dinah) and 1 granddaughter (Serah)

The number 70 seems to have significance with Israel. It is tied to the 70 original nations first established by God (Genesis 10; Deuteronomy 32:8). There are 70 elders who were chosen to lead Israel (Numbers 11:16, 24). Seventy years of captivity were used to punish Israel (2 Chronicles 36:21). Seventy "weeks" were determined to finish the transgression on Israel (Daniel 9:24). Seventy members of the Sanhedrin (identified as "the council" in the New Testament) ruled Israel, and 70 "witnesses" were sent out by the Lord Jesus in the days of His earthly ministry (Luke 10:1).

Jacob Before Pharaoh

Judah has been sent ahead to bring Joseph to meet Jacob in Goshen. When at last the father and the son meet, there is a time of joyous weeping and preparation for the formal meeting that must take place before Pharaoh. The family has the "visa" permission to enter the land, but must be formally "nationalized" if they are to become part of the country's permanent economy.

> Then he sent Judah before him to Joseph, to point out before him the way to Goshen. And they came to the land of Goshen. So Joseph made ready his chariot and went up to Goshen to meet his father Israel; and he presented himself to him, and fell on his neck and wept on his neck a good while. And Israel said to Joseph, "Now let me die,

since I have seen your face, because you are still alive."

Then Joseph said to his brothers and to his father's household, "I will go up and tell Pharaoh, and say to him, 'My brothers and those of my father's house, who were in the land of Canaan, have come to me. And the men are shepherds, for their occupation has been to feed livestock; and they have brought their flocks, their herds, and all that they have.' So it shall be, when Pharaoh calls you and says, 'What is your occupation?' that you shall say, 'Your servants' occupation has been with livestock from our youth even till now, both we and also our fathers,' that you may dwell in the land of Goshen; for every shepherd is an abomination to the Egyptians." (Genesis 46:28-34)

The land has not yet been "officially" given to Israel. This requires some politicking. Jacob and the brothers are to stress their occupation as shepherds. Although there is not much information about the Hyksos dynasty that ruled Egypt for several hundred years from the time of Abraham, many scholars believe that these non-Egyptian conquerors were the rulers during the time of Joseph. That dynasty was known as the "shepherd kings" and seems to have its genetic origins through Shem rather than Ham. If so, that would explain some of the apparently incidental notations.

Shepherding (cattle raising) was considered a lowly occupation. Though it was necessary for feeding the country, it was beneath the dignity of the "pure" Egyptians because such occupations subjected the workers to the dirt and dust of the field and the necessary association with less-than-sanitary conditions. Most Egyptians were fastidious about their personal hygiene, and several of the religious cult requirements stressed cleanliness. Joseph therefore knew exactly what his family needed to say in order to be placed in the area where he wanted them.

When Jacob is later brought before Pharaoh, the interchange between them is both cordial and gracious. After the formal greetings are exchanged, Pharaoh allows permission for Israel to settle in Goshen, where "the best of the land" is granted to the family. And as has been previously suggested to Pharaoh by Joseph, he asks for any "men of activity" among the family who might be suitable to manage his own herds (Genesis 47:6).

Thus, while keeping his own hands free of the lowly occupation, Pharaoh grants an official recognition to the family as "keepers" of the royal food and breeding stock, thereby resolving some negative political nuances that might have otherwise lingered.

Joseph Rules Egypt and Goshen

> And Joseph situated his father and his brothers, and gave them a possession in the land of Egypt, in the best of the land, in the land of Rameses, as Pharaoh had command-ed. Then Joseph provided his father, his brothers, and all his father's household with bread, according to the num-ber in their families.
>
> Now there was no bread in all the land; for the famine was very severe, so that the land of Egypt and the land of Canaan languished because of the famine. And Joseph gathered up all the money that was found in the land of Egypt and in the land of Canaan, for the grain which they bought; and Joseph brought the money into Pharaoh's house. So when the money failed in the land of Egypt and in the land of Canaan, all the Egyptians came to Joseph and said, "Give us bread, for why should we die in your presence? For the money has failed." (Genesis 47:11-15)

Goshen has now become something of a separate province, pro-vided for and overseen by Joseph himself. If indeed these events took place during the times of the Hyksos dynasty, as many historians be-lieve, then the Egyptians' unique dislike of the cattle-raising profes-sion would have segregated and sheltered the descendants of Jacob both geographically and politically. Joseph, although respected and honored throughout Egypt, was still part of the royal entourage and would have been expected to reign and rule from On, not Ramses.

As the ruling arm of Pharaoh and the agent through which Pharaoh exercised his financial policies, Joseph kept a strong hand on the economy during the remaining five years of famine. The grain that had been so plentiful during the time of prosperity now became a scarce commodity. Joseph could have jacked up the prices and demanded far more than was just, but he kept the currency stable (did not "invent" money or lower rates) and maintained a fair price for all goods. When the money began to run out, rather than inflate the prices or lower the currency rate, Joseph began to grant loans of currency value against the livestock.

> Then Joseph said, "Give your livestock, and I will give you bread for your livestock, if the money is gone." So they brought their livestock to Joseph, and Joseph gave them bread in exchange for the horses, the flocks, the cattle of the herds, and for the donkeys. Thus he fed them with bread in exchange for all their livestock that year. (Genesis 47:16-17)

After ownership of the livestock was transferred to the government, Joseph granted liens against the land property of the citizens. As the land became the property of the king, he began to indenture the service of the population. None of this was done foreseeably. Everything was done as the need arose and dictated.

> When that year had ended, they came to him the next year and said to him, "We will not hide from my lord that our money is gone; my lord also has our herds of livestock. There is nothing left in the sight of my lord but our bodies and our lands. Why should we die before your eyes, both we and our land? Buy us and our land for bread, and we and our land will be servants of Pharaoh; give us seed, that we may live and not die, that the land may not be desolate." Then Joseph bought all the land of Egypt for Pharaoh; for every man of the Egyptians sold his field, because the famine was severe upon them. So

the land became Pharaoh's. (Genesis 46:18-20)

Please notice—no one complained! And as the population became indentured to the royal family, even the religious systems began to respond to the generosity of the pharaoh. This was a masterpiece of political service and ingenuity.

> And as for the people, he moved them into the cities, from one end of the borders of Egypt to the other end. Only the land of the priests he did not buy; for the priests had rations allotted to them by Pharaoh, and they ate their rations which Pharaoh gave them; therefore they did not sell their lands. (Genesis 47:21-22)

Ultimately, of course, all the rest of the land and all the families were "owned" by the royal household. If ever there were a time and cause for common revolution, this would have been it. However, as the people had been treated fairly under Joseph's administration, they looked to him to plan a future that would reward their service properly and still honor the debt that they had incurred (for certain values—not a "forever" debt). So, having moved the population up and down the Nile Valley in a wonderful foresight of labor distribution, Joseph began to dole out the seed stock so that the fields that were now returning to potential fruitfulness might be developed accordingly.

> Then Joseph said to the people, "Indeed I have bought you and your land this day for Pharaoh. Look, here is seed for you, and you shall sow the land. And it shall come to pass in the harvest that you shall give one-fifth to Pharaoh. Four-fifths shall be your own, as seed for the field and for your food, for those of your households and as food for your little ones."
>
> So they said, "You have saved our lives; let us find favor in the sight of my lord, and we will be Pharaoh's servants." And Joseph made it a law over the land of Egypt to this day, that Pharaoh should have one-fifth, except for the land of the priests only, which did not become Pharaoh's. (Genesis 47:23-26)

Even now, with total control over the land and over the people, Joseph began to return the seed stock to the people to work the land where they were located, with only a 20 percent tax on the gain to be returned to Pharaoh. Don't miss this. He had full opportunity to do evil, full opportunity to hold the nation in slavery for generations to come, but rather than respond in power and greed, Joseph (and Pharaoh) set a flat tax of just 20 percent that would be sufficient to run the government, keep the military, secure the transportation systems, and pay the wages of those who maintained services that were not profitable from a business perspective—and the people were happy!

> So Israel dwelt in the land of Egypt, in the country of Goshen; and they had possessions there and grew and multiplied exceedingly. And Jacob lived in the land of Egypt seventeen years. So the length of Jacob's life was one hundred and forty-seven years. When the time drew near that Israel must die, he called his son Joseph and said to him, "Now if I have found favor in your sight, please put your hand under my thigh, and deal kindly and truly with me. Please do not bury me in Egypt, but let me lie with my fathers; you shall carry me out of Egypt and bury me in their burial place." And he said, "I will do as you have said." Then he said, "Swear to me." And he swore to him. So Israel bowed himself on the head of the bed. (Genesis 47:27-31)

And so, 17 years pass. With the famine now forgotten, Jacob asks his dear son to promise him that he would not remain in Egypt when the prophecy of their ultimate release would come about. Jacob (and later Joseph) wanted to be buried in the land that God promised Abraham would become their inheritance forever.

Israel Blesses Joseph

> Now it came to pass after these things that Joseph was told, "Indeed your father is sick"; and he took with him his two sons, Manasseh and Ephraim. And Jacob was

told, "Look, your son Joseph is coming to you"; and Israel strengthened himself and sat up on the bed. Then Jacob said to Joseph: "God Almighty appeared to me at Luz in the land of Canaan and blessed me, and said to me, 'Behold, I will make you fruitful and multiply you, and I will make of you a multitude of people, and give this land to your descendants after you as an everlasting possession.'" (Genesis 48:1-4)

Joseph had gone back to his palace in On, and Jacob had grown older and more feeble. Finally, Joseph learns that his father is failing, and he wants to have Jacob bless Manasseh and Ephraim, the two sons born to him and his Egyptian wife. With his sons at his side, Joseph brings them to Jacob's bedside, anticipating the traditional "primogeniture" blessing for the firstborn (Manasseh).

Jacob, who seems to consider his life to have begun at his meeting with God at Bethel on his way to Laban in Syria, begins to chant some of the blessings that he received from *Elohim* as he had heard them from his grandfather, Abraham, and his father, Isaac.

"And now your two sons, Ephraim and Manasseh, who were born to you in the land of Egypt before I came to you in Egypt, are mine; as Reuben and Simeon, they shall be mine. Your offspring whom you beget after them shall be yours; they will be called by the name of their brothers in their inheritance. But as for me, when I came from Padan, Rachel died beside me in the land of Canaan on the way, when there was but a little distance to go to Ephrath; and I buried her there on the way to Ephrath (that is, Bethlehem)." (Genesis 48:5-8)

Perhaps Joseph feels something of a surprise when Jacob equates Manasseh and Ephraim with his two oldest sons, Reuben and Simeon. Those men had proven themselves not worthy of leadership. Jacob, however, seems intent on insuring that the sons of Joseph share in some special way with the other sons in the new nation that God has promised to build in the centuries ahead.

> Then Israel saw Joseph's sons, and said, "Who are these?"
> And Joseph said to his father, "They are my sons, whom
> God has given me in this place." And he said, "Please
> bring them to me, and I will bless them." Now the eyes of
> Israel were dim with age, so that he could not see. Then
> Joseph brought them near him, and he kissed them and
> embraced them. And Israel said to Joseph, "I had not
> thought to see your face; but in fact, God has also shown
> me your offspring!"
>
> So Joseph brought them from beside his knees, and he
> bowed down with his face to the earth. And Joseph took
> them both, Ephraim with his right hand toward Israel's
> left hand, and Manasseh with his left hand toward Isra-
> el's right hand, and brought them near him. Then Israel
> stretched out his right hand and laid it on Ephraim's head,
> who was the younger, and his left hand on Manasseh's
> head, guiding his hands knowingly, for Manasseh was the
> firstborn. (Genesis 48:8-14)

Now this *was* a surprise! Jacob had laid his right hand (the hand of official blessing) on the head of Ephraim instead of Manasseh. Joseph knew that his father could not see well, so he had made every effort to place the sons in the proper order for the blessing, but Jacob had crossed his hands—on purpose! This must not be!

It may well be that Joseph had heard the story from his father how Jacob had "tricked" Isaac into blessing him instead of Esau. Perhaps he was afraid that something would go terribly wrong if such a mistake were made again. But whatever may have been going through Joseph's mind, Jacob was most assuredly doing what God had told him to do.

> And he blessed Joseph, and said: "God, before whom my
> fathers Abraham and Isaac walked, The God who has fed
> me all my life long to this day, The Angel who has re-
> deemed me from all evil, Bless the lads; Let my name be

named upon them, And the name of my fathers Abraham and Isaac; And let them grow into a multitude in the midst of the earth."

Now when Joseph saw that his father laid his right hand on the head of Ephraim, it displeased him; so he took hold of his father's hand to remove it from Ephraim's head to Manasseh's head. And Joseph said to his father, "Not so, my father, for this one is the firstborn; put your right hand on his head." But his father refused and said, "I know, my son, I know. He also shall become a people, and he also shall be great; but truly his younger brother shall be greater than he, and his descendants shall become a multitude of nations." So he blessed them that day, saying, "By you Israel will bless, saying, 'May God make you as Ephraim and as Manasseh!'" And thus he set Ephraim before Manasseh. (Genesis 48:15-20)

We who are at a distance from those early days when God was far more active with His key people than He appears to be today, sometimes have trouble understanding how specifically God speaks or inspires the words that will become reality over the following centuries. As Jacob consciously sets his crossed hands of blessing on the two sons of Joseph—over the objections of Joseph—God sets in motion a condition that will be a common observance among the tribes of Israel: Ephraim is more blessed than Manasseh.

Then Israel said to Joseph, "Behold, I am dying, but God will be with you and bring you back to the land of your fathers. Moreover I have given to you one portion above your brothers, which I took from the hand of the Amorite with my sword and my bow." (Genesis 48:21-22)

Israel's Final Blessings

Joseph bows down before Jacob in recognition of his father's position as Jacob expresses God's sovereign plan for the nation. All that has transpired to this point has brought complete fulfillment of the dreams that young Joseph had as a teenager so long ago. Now Jacob is near his death at age 147. Joseph had been in the land of Egypt for nearly 60 years. Most of his brothers were older men with grandchildren and great-grandchildren.

It is certainly worthy of note that God has often bypassed the oldest in favor of a younger son. Here is just a partial list:

- Isaac instead of Ishmael.

- Jacob instead of Esau.

- Joseph instead of Reuben.

- Judah instead of Reuben.

- Ephraim instead of Manasseh.

- David instead of Eliab, the firstborn.

- Gideon was the "least" in his father's house.

The rule is: "The LORD looks on the heart" (1 Samuel 16:7).

In his final moments, Jacob calls all of his sons to his bedside and delivers a prophetic overview of what he knows will become of the descendants of his sons. It is spoken in poetry (Hebrew rhyme and meter), symbol, and prophecy—not in a "normal" conversational style. All who are there are fully aware that God is speaking through Jacob to them as the heads of the tribes of Israel. They are commanded to "gather together, that I may tell you what shall befall you in the last days" (Genesis 49:1).

Each prophecy is given in mostly birth-order sequence.

Reuben the Firstborn (Genesis 49:3-4)

"Reuben, you are my firstborn, My might and the beginning of my strength, The excellency of dignity and the excellency of power. Unstable as water, you shall not excel, Because you went up to your father's bed; Then you defiled it —He went up to my couch."

Even though Reuben was Jacob's "might," "strength," "dignity," and "power," he became "unstable as water" and lost respect and leadership. Some have suggested that this unusual string of adjectives is indicative of the genetic transfer of the "best" of the father to the firstborn. That may or may not be true physically, but it is certainly not true spiritually. The previous list of God's choices of other sons is proof enough for that.

Reuben, however, never furnished a leader in Israel or excelled in anything. The tribe of Reuben was the first tribe to request an inheritance in the land and never crossed the Jordan (Numbers 32). Leaders of Reuben erected an unauthorized place of worship (Joshua 22) and failed to answer the call to war under Deborah (Judges 5).

Simeon and Levi (Genesis 49:5-7)

> "Simeon and Levi are brothers; Instruments of cruelty are in their dwelling place. Let not my soul enter their council; Let not my honor be united to their assembly; For in their anger they slew a man, And in their self-will they hamstrung an ox. Cursed be their anger, for it is fierce; And their wrath, for it is cruel! I will divide them in Jacob And scatter them in Israel."

These brothers are connected together because of their joint action of murder at Shechem. Since they are common "instruments of cruelty," their anger is "cursed" and they would be "divided" and "scattered" in Israel. Simeon's descendants were given an inheritance in Judah, but many were captured and lived with the Edomites and Amalekites (1 Chronicles 4:39-43) and were later totally assimilated by Assyria.

Aaron, from the tribe of Levi, later stood with his brother Moses against idolatry (Exodus 32). Levi was chosen to become the priestly tribe in Israel, however, they were not given an inheritance of their own land, but granted houses in various "cities of refuge" scattered throughout the nation (Joshua 21).

Judah Would Rule Israel (Genesis 49:8-12)

"Judah, you are he whom your brothers shall praise; Your hand shall be on the neck of your enemies; Your father's children shall bow down before you. Judah is a lion's whelp; From the prey, my son, you have gone up. He bows down, he lies down as a lion; And as a lion, who shall rouse him? The scepter shall not depart from Judah, Nor a lawgiver from between his feet, Until Shiloh comes; And to Him shall be the obedience of the people. Binding his donkey to the vine, And his donkey's colt to the choice vine, He washed his garments in wine, And his clothes in the blood of grapes. His eyes are darker than wine, And his teeth whiter than milk."

Judah's name means "praise," and he would be praised by his brethren. He would also be strong and courageous, and the land that he controlled would be fruitful. Although he was designated to become the ruling tribe in Israel, the "scepter" did not come to Judah until 640 years later. But once the authority was recognized, there would always be a "lawgiver from between his feet."

Obviously, this is much more than a prophecy about earthly rule. "One who decrees" would be continuous until "Shiloh" would come—a male (Genesis 49:10) who would draw the people together. Although the Roman general Titus destroyed Jerusalem in 70 A.D. and all Jewish records (mostly of the tribe of Judah) were destroyed by that time, the Messiah—the true "Prince of Peace" (Shiloh)—had already come. One day, the tribes of Israel will be reformed by the only One who could possibly keep genealogical records straight (Revelation 7), and the eternal Son of David, the Lion of the Tribe of Judah, will sit on Jerusalem's throne forevermore.

Zebulun (Genesis 49:13)

"Zebulun shall dwell by the haven of the sea; He shall become a haven for ships, And his border shall adjoin Sidon."

These several tribes that follow are not given much coverage, either in the Scriptures or in history. All but Judah and Benjamin are taken captive by Assyria and become the "lost ten tribes" of legend. Warriors of Zebulun are cited in some passages.

Issachar (Genesis 49:14-15)

"Issachar is a strong donkey, Lying down between two burdens; He saw that rest was good, And that the land was pleasant; He bowed his shoulder to bear a burden, And became a band of slaves."

There is some confusion about this prophecy. Does it recognize their strength or prophesy their doom? Probably both. The men of Issachar were said to have "had understanding of the times" (1 Chronicles 12:32), but did not seem to excel in spite of their wisdom.

Dan (Genesis 49:16-18)

"Dan shall judge his people As one of the tribes of Israel. Dan shall be a serpent by the way, A viper by the path, That bites the horse's heels So that its rider shall fall backward. I have waited for your salvation, O LORD!"

Dan becomes the tribe of great wickedness and is truly "lost." They are not part of the tribes that are reformed in the Millennium or enter into the record of the "new heaven and new earth" (Revelation 7; 21:1). The Danites introduced idolatry to Israel officially (Judges 18), and under Jeroboam set up two golden calves for the Northern Tribes to worship (1 Kings 12).

Gad (Genesis 49:19)

"Gad, a troop shall tramp upon him, But he shall triumph at last."

This small tribe (whose name means "troop") would settle in a land east of the Jordan on the edge of the kingdom of the Ammonites and other desert peoples. They, therefore, would be most susceptible to attack—but would be able to defend themselves. Assimilated by the Assyrian armies, they merged with the polyglot peoples of the Near East as part of the "lost ten tribes."

Asher (Genesis 49:20)

"Bread from Asher shall be rich, And he shall yield royal dainties."

Asher would enjoy rich food and royal delicacies, but would fail to take the Tyre-Sidon region (Judges 1:31) and fall into insignificance.

Naphtali (Genesis 49:21)

"Naphtali is a deer let loose; He uses beautiful words."

The tribe of Naphtali, the brother of Dan, would be known as swift warriors and composers of eloquent speech and beautiful literature. Barak (Judges 4:6, 15) is the best-known of the descendants of Naphtali; his "song" (with Deborah) is recorded in Judges 5.

Joseph (Ephraim and Manasseh)—Genesis 49:22-26

"Joseph is a fruitful bough, A fruitful bough by a well; His branches run over the wall. The archers have bitterly grieved him, Shot at him and hated him. But his bow remained in strength, And the arms of his hands were made strong By the hands of the Mighty God of Jacob (From there is the Shepherd, the Stone of Israel), By the God of your father who will help you, And by the Almighty who will bless you With blessings of heaven above, Blessings of the deep that lies beneath, Blessings of the breasts and of the womb. The blessings of your father Have excelled the blessings of my ancestors, Up to the utmost bound of the everlasting hills. They shall be on the head of Joseph, And on the crown of the head of him who was separate from his brothers."

Joseph is to be the "fruitful bough" in Israel through the twofold tribe (Ephraim and Manasseh) that would be strong and numerous. And, although beset by enemies from every side, they would prevail.

Ephraim would later become synonymous with the northern ten tribes.

The picture of God as "the Shepherd" and "the Stone" is first mentioned in connection with Joseph in light of His unique protection of the son who would be "separate" from his brothers. Later when the tribes are restored, a tribe of Joseph replaces the tribe of Dan (Revelation 7:8), even as the tribe of Manasseh is retained.

Benjamin (Genesis 49:27)

> "Benjamin is a ravenous wolf; In the morning he shall devour the prey, And at night he shall divide the spoil."

Benjamin would be strong and successful in warfare, but would have a tendency to be cruel and voracious. Judges 20 records the near-extinction of Benjamin in an awful display of hostility toward the tribe that was set in motion when a group of Benjamite homosexuals raped and killed a concubine of a lecherous Levite. Israel's first King was Saul, a Benjamite, whose character exemplifies the prophecy of Jacob.

Epilogue

The last chapter of this great book of beginnings ends with Joseph leading his family back to Canaan to bury Jacob in the cave at Machpelah. All that can be done to honor the memory of Jacob is done. He is embalmed by the royal embalmers, the entire nation mourns for Jacob for 70 days, and then a royal entourage is sent to convey his coffin into Canaan for final interment.

> So Joseph went up to bury his father; and with him went up all the servants of Pharaoh, the elders of his house, and all the elders of the land of Egypt, as well as all the house of Joseph, his brothers, and his father's house. Only their little ones, their flocks, and their herds they left in the land of Goshen. And there went up with him both chariots and horsemen, and it was a very great gathering. Then they came to the threshing floor of Atad, which is

beyond the Jordan, and they mourned there with a great and very solemn lamentation. He observed seven days of mourning for his father.

And when the inhabitants of the land, the Canaanites, saw the mourning at the threshing floor of Atad, they said, "This is a deep mourning of the Egyptians." Therefore its name was called Abel Mizraim, which is beyond the Jordan. So his sons did for him just as he had commanded them. For his sons carried him to the land of Canaan, and buried him in the cave of the field of Machpelah, before Mamre, which Abraham bought with the field from Ephron the Hittite as property for a burial place. (Genesis 50:7-13)

This must have been some sight. Not only was the crowd large, but even the whole countryside understood that "a deep mourning of the Egyptians" was taking place. Nothing had been seen like it before or was ever seen again.

Many have suggested or hinted that Jacob was a "scoundrel" of some sort because of his trickery of Isaac. But the Scriptures do not portray him so. Nothing is ever said negatively about Jacob—in fact, quite to the contrary. He is "Israel" for the rest of Scripture, the man who "prevailed with God." Jacob is honored—even by the greatest nation on Earth at the time.

So Joseph dwelt in Egypt, he and his father's household. And Joseph lived one hundred and ten years. Joseph saw Ephraim's children to the third generation. The children of Machir, the son of Manasseh, were also brought up on Joseph's knees. And Joseph said to his brethren, "I am dying; but God will surely visit you, and bring you out of this land to the land of which He swore to Abraham, to Isaac, and to Jacob." Then Joseph took an oath from the children of Israel, saying, "God will surely visit you, and you shall carry up my bones from here." So Joseph died, being one hundred and ten years old; and they embalmed him, and he was put in a coffin in Egypt. (Genesis 50:22-26)

If ever there were to be a "happily ever after" ending in the Old Testament, this is the one that would qualify. After Jacob's death, Joseph's brothers again fear Joseph will seek retribution for their past misdeeds. Joseph, however, reassures them that there is no ill will toward them or their children. As they repeat their sorrow for their sin against Joseph, he reiterates the role of protector that had been granted to him by God.

Joseph spoke "kindly to them" and insisted that they carry his bones back to Canaan when God releases the nation in the coming centuries. Joseph finally dies at 110 and was placed in a "coffin in Egypt."

It would be generations later that the Hyksos dynasty was broken and another Pharaoh who did not know Joseph would take over. But for a long time, the "beginnings" were complete and the Second Age was underway.

ABOUT THE AUTHOR

 Dr. Henry M. Morris III holds four earned degrees, including a D.Min. from Luther Rice Seminary and the Presidents and Key Executives MBA from Pepperdine University. A former college professor, administrator, business executive, and senior pastor, Dr. Morris is an articulate and passionate speaker frequently invited to address church congregations, college assemblies, and national conferences. The eldest son of ICR's founder, Dr. Morris has served for many years in conference and writing ministry. His love for the Word of God and passion for Christian maturity, coupled with God's gift of teaching, have given Dr. Morris a broad and effective ministry over the years. He has authored numerous articles and books, including *The Big Three: Major Events that Changed History Forever; Exploring the Evidence for Creation; 5 Reasons to Believe in Recent Creation; The Book of Beginnings, Vol. 1: Creation, Fall, and the First Age; The Book of Beginnings, Vol. 2: Noah, the Flood, and the New World; Pulling Down Strongholds: Achieving Spiritual Victory through Strategic Offense; A Firm Foundation: Devotional Insights to Help You Know, Believe, and Defend Truth; Six Days of Creation;* and *Your Origins Matter.*

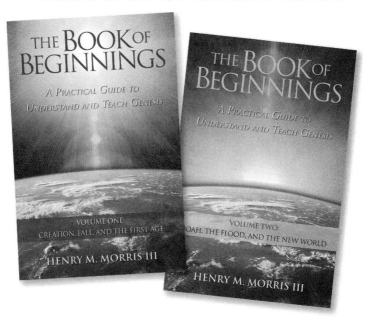

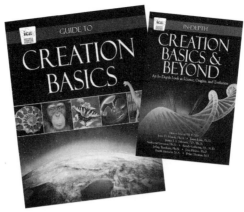

NEW FROM ICR

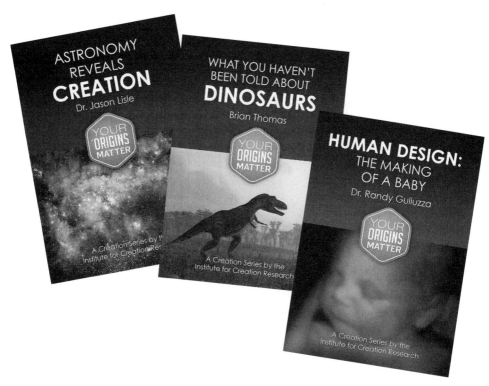

Explore creation science with these exciting new DVD presentations from ICR.

Science Writer Brian Thomas reveals *What You Haven't Been Told about Dinosaurs,* examining clues from science, history, and Scripture as he presents answers to the biggest dinosaur questions. In *Astronomy Reveals Creation*, Director of Research Dr. Jason Lisle confirms that when we really understand the Bible and the universe, we find that the scientific evidence lines up with Scripture. And ICR National Representative Dr. Randy Guliuzza demonstrates that life's fully integrated biological systems couldn't possibly have evolved in *Human Design: The Making of a Baby.*

To order, call **800.628.7640** or visit **www.icr.org/store**.

FOR MORE INFORMATION

Sign up for ICR's FREE publications!

Our monthly *Acts & Facts* magazine offers fascinating articles and current information on creation, evolution, and more. Our quarterly *Days of Praise* booklet provides daily devotionals—real biblical "meat"—to strengthen and encourage the Christian witness.

To subscribe, call 800.337.0375 or mail your address information to the address below. Or sign up online at www.icr.org.

Visit ICR online

ICR.org offers a wealth of resources and information on scientific creationism and biblical worldview issues.

- ✓ Read our news postings on today's hottest science topics
- ✓ Explore the evidence for creation
- ✓ Investigate our graduate and professional education programs
- ✓ Dive into our archive of 40 years of scientific articles
- ✓ Listen to current and past radio programs
- ✓ Watch our *That's a Fact* video show
- ✓ Order creation science materials online
- ✓ And more!

Visit our online store at www.icr.org/store for more great resources.

INSTITUTE FOR **CREATION RESEARCH**

P. O. Box 59029
Dallas, TX 75229
800.337.0375

Notes

Notes

Notes

Notes

Notes

Notes

Notes

Notes